A Fellowship of Baptism

Princeton Theological Monograph Series

K. C. Hanson, Charles M. Collier, and D. Christopher Spinks,
Series Editors

Recent volumes in the series:

Nikolaus Ludwig von Zinzendorf
Christian Life and Witness: Count Zinzendorf's 1738 Berlin Speeches

Randall W. Reed
*A Clash of Ideologies: Marxism, Liberation Theology,
and Apocalypticism in New Testament Studies*

Myk Habets
The Anointed Son: A Trinitarian Spirit Christology

Christopher L. Fisher
*Human Significance in Theology and the Natural Sciences:
An Ecumenical Perspective with Reference to Pannenberg,
Rahner, and Zizioulas*

William A. Tooman
*Transforming Visions: Transformations of Text, Tradition,
and Theology in Ezekiel*

William J. Meyer
*Metaphysics and the Future of Theology:
The Voice of Theology in Public Life*

David H. Nikkel
Radical Embodiment

Joel Burnell
*Poetry, Providence, and Patriotism: Polish Messianism
in Dialogue with Dietrich Bonhoeffer*

Roger A. Johnson
*Peacemaking and Religious Violence:
From Thomas Aquinas to Thomas Jefferson*

A Fellowship of Baptism

Karl Barth's Ecclesiology in Light of His Understanding of Baptism

Tracey Mark Stout

☙PICKWICK *Publications* · Eugene, Oregon

A FELLOWSHIP OF BAPTISM
Karl Barth's Ecclesiology in Light of His Understanding of Baptism

Princeton Theological Monograph Series 139

Copyright © 2010 Tracey Mark Stout. All rights reserved. Except for brief quotations in critical publications or reviews, no part of this book may be reproduced in any manner without prior written permission from the publisher. Write: Permissions, Wipf and Stock Publishers, 199 W. 8th Ave., Suite 3, Eugene, OR 97401.

Pickwick Publications
An Imprint of Wipf and Stock Publishers
199 W. 8th Ave., Suite 3
Eugene, OR 97401

www.wipfandstock.com

ISBN 13: 978-1-60608-995-8

Cataloging-in-Publication data

Stout, Tracey Mark.

    A fellowship of baptism : Karl Barth's ecclesiology in light of his understanding of baptism / Tracey Mark Stout.

    Princeton Theological Monograph Series 139

    viii + 200 p. ; 23 cm. —Includes bibliographical references.

    ISBN 13: 978-1-60608-995-8

    1. Barth, Karl, 1886–1968. 2. Church — History of doctrine. 3. Barth, Karl, 1886–1968 — Contributions in doctrine of the sacraments. 4. Barth, Karl, 1886–1968 — Contributions in ecclesiology. I. Title. II. Series.

BV600.2 .S76 2010

Manufactured in the U.S.A.

Contents

Acknowledgments / vii

Introduction / 1
1. Karl Barth's Doctrine of Baptism / 15
2. Baptism and the Being of the Church / 49
3. Baptism as a Sacrament / 68
4. Baptism and the Gathered Community / 87
5. Baptism and the Free Community / 116
6. Baptism and the Witnessing Community / 147

Conclusion / 182

Bibliography / 189

Acknowledgments

This book began its life as a dissertation at Baylor University. I am grateful to my committee for their guidance and careful reading. Ralph Wood's vision and guidance throughout this study made its completion a possibility. It was in Dr. Wood's seminar on Barth that an interest in Barth first became serious study. His hard work has made me a better writer and a better reader of Barth. I am also indebted to Barry Harvey. I learned much from him as theologian and teacher. They are both, of course, free from any responsibility for errors in this text.

Two weeks after I graduated with my PhD I moved to the Appalachian mountains of southwest Virginia to teach at Bluefield College. Bluefield College is a wonderful community within which to work. My colleagues in Christian Studies have been great to work with for the past six years. I am grateful to *Perspectives in Religious Studies* for permission to include my article in this book: "Free and Faithful Witness: Karl Barth on Believers' Baptism and the Church's Relation to the State," 33/2 (Summer 2006) 173–86.

My deepest gratitude, of course, is for my family. I am truly grateful to my parents for everything they have given me throughout my life. Their love and support is a debt I can never repay. I hope they can see my gratitude as I try to be a good parent to my own children. My wife Kristy has traveled with me faithfully through graduate work and now my first teaching position. In her beautiful way she has been my supporter, challenger, encourager, and motivator. A work such as this requires much time and energy that is thus not available for other things. I could not have finished such a project without her faithful presence. My children Alexandra, Ethan, Aiden, and Elias are my joy in life. They help me keep things in perspective. During the initial writing of this text the request "come play in my room" slowed this project down on a few afternoons. Those were days well spent.

Introduction

CONTEMPORARY THEOLOGY HAS TAKEN AN ECCLESIAL TURN. SOME OF the best contemporary theology has turned its attention to ecclesiology. Theology's focus has shifted from the autonomous, knowing or experiencing subject, as the center of much of the modern project, back to the community in which God's purpose and presence are made manifest. This shift is due to several reasons, including the "communal" and non-foundational orientation found in much of contemporary philosophy. Karl Barth's rejection of the anthropocentrism inherent in modern theology has also been no small influence.

Because of its central place in Barth's theology, Barth scholarship has given the doctrine of revelation, or the Word of God, the largest share of attention. Barth's theology has long been recognized as "Christocentric." For Barth the sole source of our theology is the self-revelation of God in Jesus Christ. Yet Barth's ecclesiology has not, until recently, received the careful study that the other elements of his theology have all seen.[1] Many interpreters have failed to discern the importance of his ecclesiocentrism. Critics have criticized Barth for what they take to be a lack of emphasis upon the human recipients of revelation.

That the church is the setting for theological reflection according to Barth is not a new insight. However, the importance of the church in Barth's thought and the importance of Barth's work on the church have not been sufficiently explicated. Critics and interpreters have begun to study Barth's ecclesiology following the lead of Roman Catholic theologian Colm O'Grady, who more than thirty years ago wrote what was until the last few years the only book length study of Barth's ecclesiology.[2] Most work on Barth's ecclesiology has been critical and has

---

1. Sheldon Sorge offers reasons why Barth's ecclesiology has been ignored. Sorge, "Karl Barth's Reception in North America," 223.

2. O'Grady, *Church in the Theology of Karl Barth*. A number of articles have been written since O'Grady's work. These studies have been mostly critical of Barth's ecclesiology. A couple of new books on Barth's ecclesiology have been published recently.

generally seen this doctrine as one of Barth's weakest areas. While I am not uncritical of Barth's ecclesiology, there is much to learn from Barth for those who seek to clarify the nature and purpose of the church in the twenty-first century. This study will help to refocus study of Barth's ecclesiology and bring forth what Barth has to offer to current ecclesiocentric theologies. I approach Barth's ecclesiology from the Baptist tradition. From this perpective, Barth's ecclesiology is fascinating when put into conversation with the Believer's Church tradition and insightful both when it has a corrective to offer the tradition and when that tradition can strengthen Barth's theology in places.

This book will focus on specific elements of Barth's mature ecclesiology as they relate to his doctrine of baptism. Its thesis, which the entire course of this study will attempt to demonstrate, is this: Barth's understanding of baptism is indispensable for his understanding of the church and thus both his acceptance of believers' baptism and his rejection of baptism as a sacrament are crucial and formative in his ecclesiology. This study is not a digest or summary of Barth's entire doctrine of the Church, but is limited to the specific aspects which are determined by Barth's view of baptism. These elements are, however, the central tenents of Barth's ecclesiology. I will primarily discuss the ecclesiology developed in the *Church Dogmatics,* and concentrated in volume four, but I will also include other relevant works regarding the Church.

Following the background discussion of baptism given in this introduction, chapter 1 offers a description of Barth's doctrine of baptism. It will detail Barth's development of the doctrine in *The Teaching of the Church Regarding Baptism* and in the final fragment of the *Church Dogmatics.* Barth caused a stir in the 1940s with his arguments against infant baptism and again in the 1960s with his denial of the sacramental nature of baptism. Barth's doctrine of baptism will provide certain key features of his ecclesiology, which I will examine.

The second and third chapters will address the being of the church in relation to Barth's treatment of baptism. Barth argues that the basis of the church is Christ. All ecclesiological reflection must stem from Christology. The Church is the earthly-historical existence of Jesus Christ in the present. I will ask whether the doctrine of baptism helps us to understand the relation of the Spirit to the church. This issue will

---

See Bender, *Karl Barth's Christological Ecclesiology* and Yocum, *Ecclesial Mediation in Karl Barth.*

be pressing in light of Barth's rejection of the sacramental nature of baptism. The nature of baptism as a sacrament will be examined.

Chapter 4 will address the visibility and concrete nature of the church. Baptism is itself a visible witness to the baptism by the Spirit which has come upon the candidate. Likewise, the church is a visible witness to Christ. Yet the true nature of the church is the work of God and the church is thus invisible as well. This chapter will also discuss two further elements of the concrete church. Barth's view of the church includes a congregational polity in which the concrete, local congregation is the true focus. This emphasis on the congregation will be studied to see the concrete nature of Barth's ecclesiology. Secondly, Barth's actualism presents an understanding of the church that is based in Barth's theological proclivity for thinking in term of actions, relationships, and history rather than static states. Though this is a place where Barth has been criticized, I will show that Barth actually presents a concrete picture of the visible church that exists as a history.

Chapter 5 focuses on the ecclesial implications of Barth's rejection of infant baptism. Barth rejected infant baptism because it supported the unhealthy relationship between the church and European society. In the first half of the twentieth century the church had no place from which to stand against the political events of the day because it had connected itself too closely to the life and interests of the states in which it lived. Barth rejected the Constantinian assumptions which undergirded the church's relationship to the state and, in his evaluation, infant baptism is inseparable from these problems. The church, he argued, as a result, should remain free from the state and the culture in which it lives. To understand Barth's vision of the free church I will study Barth's view of the state in its relation to the church. Barth rejected the state or national churches in favor of voluntary church membership. Yet, even in a free church vision, the church must relate to the city in which it lives. Barth held a strong, positive view of the state. I will thus look at Barth's view of the church's political and cultural involvement in light of believers' baptism.

In the sixth chapter I will examine the church as witness in light of Barth's thesis that baptism is initiation into the Christian community, an act which the Holy Spirit sanctifies and uses as a witness to God's work in the world. For Barth, the church always exists for the world. Its orientation and purpose are to be for the world. This chapter will identify two elements of Barth's ecclesiology which need to be seen together in light of baptism. Both sanctification and ethics involve the life of the community of God as it is being called and fitted by the Spirit to offer a provisional representation of the Kingdom of God. In his doctrine of sanctification Barth deals with the church as the baptized community that is made holy by God, even as it is also called to an ethical life of obedient discipleship.

Situating Barth's Doctrine of Baptism

The remainder of this introduction will set the stage for the discussion of Barth's view of baptism. This section will provide a brief overview of the various baptismal views that have produced the believer's church tradition: from Calvin and Zwingli to the Anabaptists and Baptists descending from the English reformation. The advocates of believers' baptism included are merely representative and are not meant to be the spokespeople for a tradition. They are included in roughly chronological order.

Calvin and Zwingli on Baptism

As the true head of the reformed tradition in which Barth is situated, I will examine Calvin's view of baptism first. Baptism for Calvin is, first, a sign, or enactment, of the fact that our sins are forgiven. It points to the cleansing which we receive through our union with Christ. Baptism is like a "sealed document to confirm to us that all our sins are so abolished, remitted, and effaced that they can never come to his sight, be recalled, or charged against us."[3] Calvin uses the symbol of cleansing in his treatment of baptism rather than Paul's images of death and burial.[4]

Only Christ's blood cleanses us from sin, therefore the cleansing which baptism denotes points us to Christ. The baptized participate in Christ's righteousness. Baptism is the testimony that we are "so united to Christ himself that we become sharers in all his blessings."[5] Our baptism is the token of our being cleansed from sin and is effective for future sin. Baptism points to our perpetual cleansing by Christ's blood.

---

3. Calvin, *Institutes*, IV, XV, 1.
4. Parker, *Calvin*, 151. See also Wendel, *Calvin*, 319.
5. Calvin, *Institutes*, IV, XV, 6.

When people baptized as an infant later sin, they need to remember that they have been baptized; they do not need to be rebaptized. "As often as we fall away, we ought to recall the memory of our baptism."[6]

Baptism is also a sign or token of our mortification in Christ and the new life that is offered to us. The sacrament is a sign that the old person has been put to death in Christ's death. Christ objectively accomplished our death in his own person. Christians share in the death of Christ, and in baptism the Holy Spirit's work renewing the human person is made known. So infant baptism contains the promise of the forgiveness of sins as well as the renewal of the person. It is the work of the Holy Spirit to regenerate and sanctify the sinner. Of course, human beings will never fully overcome the effects of sin. Baptism is assurance that the condemnation of original sin is removed, yet one is not freed from the sinful nature of human existence. For Calvin original sin refers to the depravity and corruption of humanity. Therefore Calvin says that baptism does not set the candidate free from original sin. Yet, the guilt and punishment are remitted because Christ's righteousness is shared with us. Mortification of the flesh receives its beginning in the promises of baptism, yet is an everyday process that must continue after baptism.

In addition to the remission of sins, baptism is the candidate's initiation into the people of God. Calvin's discussion of baptism begins with the statement that baptism is "the sign of initiation by which we are received into the society of the church" so that we can be named as one of God's children.[7] In this, at least, Calvin agrees with Zwingli in understanding baptism as an initiatory sign. Baptism is a public profession of one's desire to agree with and be counted as a member of the church.[8]

Calvin affirmed, of course, the practice of infant baptism. Like circumcision, infant baptism gives believers a sign that God accepts their children into the fellowship of God's people. Baptizing children is a means for perpetuating the covenant.[9] God's promise is greater than a child's faith or lack of faith. At baptism a child receives the promise of God for faith and renewal which later he or she is to affirm and em-

---

6. Ibid., 3.
7. Ibid., 1.
8. Ibid., 13.
9. Calvin, *Institutes*, IV, XVI, 32.

brace. "Infants are baptized into future repentance and faith, . . . the seed of both lies hidden within them by the secret work of the Spirit."[10]

Against the Anabaptists Calvin was forced to defend infant baptism. In contrast to the "re-baptizers" he affirmed that a person's baptism as an infant was valid and effective and thus that no one needs to be rebaptized as an adult when he or she comes to faith. Calvin states in his *Treatise against the Anabaptists* that "when a man has been outside the fellowship of believers and is converted to our Lord, the doctrine under which he is baptized is addressed to him. Therefore he is expected to understand and comprehend it before he receives the sacrament." That person's children are not expected to understand the sacrament before they receive it.[11] For the children who are born into the church, their parents have already received the promise and are within the covenant.

Looking for biblical rationale for infant baptism, Calvin uses analogies and inferences based upon circumcision and Christ's blessing of children.[12] Calvin makes a strong connection between baptism and circumcision. He argues that circumcision was a sign of repentance and forgiveness of sins, just as baptism is. Just as circumcision is commanded of children, so can baptism be administered to infants.[13] Like circumcision, baptism is a sign that God has entered into covenant with this entire people, not simply individuals. Calvin's concern was not with the response of the individual, but with the covenant of the entire community. Baptism connects Jesus and his community with the people of Israel.[14] Children born to Christian parents already belong to the covenant community.

Ulrich Zwingli broke with the church tradition in a way that Calvin was not willing to do.[15] Unlike Luther and Calvin, Zwingli did not think that the medieval sacramental theology could be reformed and retained. Calvin made the grace of baptism more cognitive than the

---

10. Ibid., 20. Martin Luther states: "Faith does not exist for the sake of baptism, but baptism for the sake of faith. When faith comes, baptism is complete." "Concerning Rebaptism," in Lull, *Martin Luther's Basic Theological Writings*, 358.

11. Calvin, *Treatises against Anabaptists*, 47. See also *Institutes*, IV, XVI, 24.

12. Wendel, *Calvin*, 328.

13. Calvin, *Institutes*, IV, XVI, 3. Also Calvin, *Treatises Against the Anabaptists*, 50.

14. Balke, *Calvin and the Anabaptist Radicals*, 222.

15. On Barth's treatment of Zwingli, see Courvoisier, "Zwingli et Karl Barth," 369–87, and Akira Demura, "Zwingli in the Writings of Karl Barth," 197–219.

Roman Catholic tradition, but did not lose the central emphasis of the tradition on baptism as a sacrament. Zwingli, in contrast, could say that "all the doctors have been in error from the time of the apostles."[16]

Baptism with water is an outward sign for Zwingli; it is not itself connected to salvation. The inner baptism which only Christ can give is our salvation. Baptism does not justify or confirm one's faith. No external thing can do either of those.[17] Baptism does not regenerate or cleanse the baptized. "Water-baptism cannot contribute in any way to the washing away of sin."[18] Rather, it dedicates the initiate into a life of repentance and mortification of the flesh. No one but God can provide the inner baptism and we do not know when God bestows inward grace.[19] The church does not wait for the inner baptism before baptizing with water. Zwingli taught that a sacrament was a covenant sign or pledge. Just as soldiers in the Swiss confederacy wore white crosses to identify themselves, so "baptism is a sign which pledges us to the Lord Jesus Christ."[20] In baptism one pledges loyalty to the community as a soldier swore his allegiance to his army.[21] The pledge is an initiatory sign given by fellow-believers for the sake of the church and not for its effect upon the baptized person. Those who receive it are dedicated and pledged to Christ.

The analogy of a soldier's pledge of allegiance to his army seems to require the one being baptized be able to make such a pledge. Zwingli said that baptism is a pledge "with which we bind ourselves to God."[22] The Anabaptists in Zurich pushed Zwingli to take this view further by insisting on believers' baptism. Yet Zwingli held tenaciously to the ancient practice of infant baptism. Indeed, he was not opposed to using the power of the city to force his views of infant baptism. Rebaptism was made a capital offence in Zurich.[23] For Zwingli, the pledge was made on one's behalf by the community into which he or she was born.

16. Zwingli, "On Baptism," 130.

17. Ibid., 36–38.

18. Ibid., 153. "The sacrament can never cleanse the soul, for it is only an external thing." Ibid., 154.

19. Ibid., 149.

20. Ibid., 131.

21. McGrath, *Reformation Thought*, 171.

22. Zwingli, "On Baptism," 148.

23. Lindberg, *European Reformations*, 216.

Like Calvin after him, Zwingli connected baptism with circumcision. Both are signs of belonging to a particular people or community. Thus, infant baptism is the pledge of the child to the church by his or her Christian parents.

Both Zwingli and Calvin upheld the church's practice of baptizing infants. For both, incorporation of the child into the church was central to baptism. Yet, they disagreed on the nature of baptism as a sacrament. For Zwingli, water baptism is a sign, an external pointer to, one's inner baptism which only Christ can give. Zwingli's memorial view of baptism, in which the work is entirely human in nature, can correspondingly be labeled an external sign. In Calvin's usage, baptism accomplishes, or at least participates in, the thing shown by the outward sign. For Calvin, baptism is a human work that stands in conjunction with God's work confirming or sealing the faith of the baptized. Even this view is to be distinguished from the Catholic view of baptism as the objective means of grace, *ex opere operato*. Yet, for Calvin, God does act in baptism, which is not merely a pointer to what God is doing or has done elsewhere. I will call this an effective or participatory sign. A clear view of this difference is necessary.[24] In line with Calvin and Zwingli, the baptist writers viewed below can be understood according to this distinction.

Believers' Baptism

In contrast to the majority of the Christian tradition, baptists have, in general, insisted that baptism is not a sacrament but a confession of faith, and thus must not be administered to infants.[25] In fact these groups originally suffered persecution and even martyrdom for insisting that true baptism, according to the New Testament, is only for those who have a conscious faith in Christ prior to being baptized. These

---

24. One could also employ Herbert McCabe's distinction of a "sign of" (for external, pointing signs) and a "sign for" (for effective, participatory signs). See McCabe, *God Matters*, 165–79.

25. Occasionally I will use the term 'baptist' in this study according the broader usage of James McClendon. McClendon refers to baptists in the lower case to refer to the larger Anabaptist or radical Reformation tradition as well as the Baptists descending from the English Reformation. He thus includes all of what is otherwise referred to as the Believers' Church or Free Church tradition. See McClendon, *Ethics*, 18–20. On the "baptist vision," see 27–35.

Christians took the Zwinglian position to its logical conclusion. The baptists of the various kinds have required a commitment on the part of the person joining the church through baptism.[26] As opposed to babies that are circumcised, candidates for baptism must make their own commitment. They must be free and able to give their consent to baptism. Each new generation must be converted and baptized. Infant baptism carries the Constantinian assumption that, by virtue of one's birth into Christendom, one is a Christian. The concern of these baptists was the well-being of the church as it lived in the world as a separate community. "The anchor of Anabaptist theology and spirituality was this community, formed first by the spiritual, and then by the water baptism of believers."[27]

The Anabaptists insisted that faith and commitment must precede baptism. For the Anabaptists, the external act of water baptism was to be distinguished from the inner surrender of the will to God. This surrender is the transformation and regeneration that makes water baptism necessary as an outward sign.[28] The Schleitheim confession, generally attributed to Michael Sattler, states:

> Baptism shall be given to all those who have been taught repentance and the amendment of life and [who] believe truly that their sins are taken away through Christ, and to all those who desire to walk in the resurrection of Jesus Christ and be buried with Him in death, so that they might rise with Him; to all those who with such an understanding themselves desire and request it from us; hereby is excluded all infant baptism.[29]

The Anabaptist insistence upon faith also usually includes the commitment to a life of discipleship, or as Sattler states echoing Paul to the Romans, "the desire to walk in the resurrection of Jesus Christ."

Balthasar Hubmaier was perhaps the greatest theologian of the Anabaptists. He taught that the baptism of Spirit and fire, which makes us alive and whole, must precede baptism. "The Spirit of God makes and effects this enlivening internally in the human being." Baptism then follows as a public confession of the faith and commitment of the

26. For this reason Robert Friedman has called Anabaptist theology "existential." Friedman, *Theology of Anabaptism*, 30–34.

27. Snyder, *Anabaptist History and Theology*, 90.

28. Friedman, *Theology of Anabaptism*, 138.

29. Yoder, *Legacy of Michael Sattler*, 36.

sinner to Christ.[30] Teaching precedes baptism. Hubmaier asserts that the apostolic testimony always presents preaching, faith, and baptism in that order.[31] You must be aware that you are a sinner and have faith in Christ to be baptized. You must know "that you confess yourself a miserable sinner and guilty, that you also believe the forgiveness of your sins through Jesus Christ, and that you give yourself into a new life with the firm resolution to improve your life and order it according to the will of Christ, in the power of the Father and the Son and the Holy Spirit."[32]

Of special importance is Hubmaier's notion that baptism was entrance into a covenant community to which one was responsible. A person must be willing to submit to the rule of Christ so that one can grow in faith.[33] He states: "By virtue of his pledge he has submitted himself to sister, brothers, and to the church so that when he transgresses they now have the authority to admonish, punish, ban, and reaccept him."[34] Discipleship is "absolutely linked" to baptism. H. Wayne Pipkin asserts that the link to discipleship may be the distinctive element in believers' baptism.[35] The ecclesiological motif grew stronger in Hubmaier as his work progressed. The church is a community of committed disciples following and witnessing to Christ. Hubmaier could assert that without proper baptism there is no true church.[36]

Among the English Baptists, Thomas Helwys taught that true baptism was "the baptism of amendment of life for the remission of sins."[37] The only way to come to Christ was to amend one's life and be baptized. He asks: "Can there be amendment of life for the remission

30. Hubmaier, "On the Christian Baptism of Believers," 100.

31. Ibid., 115.

32. Ibid., 120–21.

33. Ibid., 121 and 127. See Mabry, *Balthasar Hubmaier's Doctrine of the Church*, 129–37.

34. Hubmaier, "On the Christian Baptism of Believers," 127. Hubmaier expressly rejected as a misunderstanding the idea that Anabaptists sought a perfect church, without sin, by their practice of believers' baptism. Ibid., 97.

35. Pipkin, "Baptismal Theology of Balthasar Hubmaier," 94.

36. Ibid., 102. "Where there is no water baptism, there is no church nor minister, neither brother nor sister, no brotherly admonition, excommunication, or reacceptance." Hubmaier, "On the Christian Baptism of Believers," 127. See also Mabry, *Balthasar Hubmaier's Doctrine of the Church*, 150–54.

37. Helwys, *Short Declaration of the Mystery of Iniquity*, 103.

of sins in infants? And can infants be buried into the death of Christ to walk in newness of life? And can infants put on Christ by faith? If they can do none of these things, which is most plain they cannot, then may they not be baptized."[38] Helwys's primary concern was the liberty of conscience. Baptism is only for those who believe and can consciously undertake the act. This emphasis on liberty of conscience was in turn tied to religious liberty.

Calvinist Baptist John Gill wrote that baptism is only for the penitent, those who can acknowledge and repent of their sins. Teaching and faith are required before baptism. Subjects for baptism are to be enlightened about their sinful nature by God. One needs to know Christ before being baptized. Before baptism a person should have received the Spirit of God. One must be born again to be baptized. No children can meet these requirements to be a proper subject for baptism, "let their pretences to birthright be what they may."[39] Neither baptism nor faith effect one's salvation. That is solely the work of Christ for the elect. Baptism represents the burial of Christ, but it does not wash away sin, that was done by the sacrifice of Christ. People are baptized in obedience to the command of Christ. Yielding in obedience is "an evidence of love to God and Christ."[40]

In the eighteenth century the English pastor Andrew Fuller addressed the use of baptism as a practice of the church. He took for granted that it was by immersion and for those who made profession of faith. He said that baptism was "a solemn and practical profession of the Christian religion."[41] Those in the New Testament who were baptized "were voluntary agents, and submitted to this ordinance for the purpose of making a solemn and practical profession of the Christian faith."[42] Baptism is a sign of our salvation and of the remission of our sins by Christ. Baptism is also the disavowal of the privileges of one's birth in order to become the children of God. It is thus an oath of allegiance to our new King. "Its design is also to draw a line of distinction between the kingdom of God and the kingdom of Satan." Whatever the current

---

38. Ibid., 123.
39. Gill, *Body of Doctrinal and Practical Divinity*, 656.
40. Ibid., 666.
41. Fuller, "Practical Uses of Christian Baptism," 339.
42. Ibid., 340.

understanding of baptism, baptism "was originally appointed to be the boundary of visible Christianity."[43] According to Fuller, if this boundary had been remembered much of the confusion and corruption that had taken place in the church when the distinction was lost between the church and the world could have been avoided.

Typical of Baptist argument in his period, Alexander Carson's work, *Baptism: Its Mode and Its Subjects*, deals primarily with immersion as the proper mode and believers as the proper subjects of baptism. In his interpretation of New Testament passages, he says that baptism is the "bath of regeneration," but he also states that baptism is required for those who have already been renewed by the Spirit.[44] Carson says of the New Testament that "in general, it is quite apparent that baptism is not only a figure of the washing away of sin, but that it is always supposed that the sins of those who are baptized are already washed away. Now this can be supposed of none but believers." Baptism, he continues, "supposes sins already washed away."[45] It isn't clear whether Carson truly saw baptism as effecting our regeneration, since he insisted that Christians are saved prior to baptism.

In the American South, James P. Boyce denied that baptism has any regenerative power. Baptism symbolizes the inner change and renewal worked by the Holy Spirit; baptism does not produce such change. "Ordinances can only be signs of grace and cannot confer it.... Baptism is an act of obedience, symbolizing the death of believers to sin, and resurrection to new life, and setting forth their union with Christ in his death and burial." As was his method, Boyce strung together biblical references to argue that faith must precede baptism. He asserted that only the heart that has already been regenerated can understand the ordinances of Baptism and the Lord's Supper.[46]

John L. Dagg gives attention to baptism in his *Manual of Church Order*. There he argues that water baptism does not cleanse the flesh. "It figuratively represents the burial and resurrection of Christ, on which the believer relies for salvation."[47] The water of baptism represents the

---

43. Ibid., 342.
44. Carson, *Baptism: Its Mode and Its Subjects*, 211.
45. Ibid., 211–12.
46. Boyce, *Abstract of Systematic Theology*, 377–78.
47. Dagg, *Manual of Church Order*, 17.

washing of our sins. It represents our salvation which was accomplished in Christ's death and resurrection. He concludes that baptism, as representing burial, requires immersion. Christ's burial is exhibited in our "burial."[48] Because we have been buried and raised with Christ, the body leaving the grave will be purified and made incorruptible. Thus the symbol of baptism represents our burial with Christ in his death and our being raised with Christ as the two are tied together with the idea of purification by water.[49] Dagg affirms that only those who repent and believe are proper subjects for baptism. Baptism is the ceremony of public profession and devotion to service of Christ. We are raised from baptism to walk in newness of life. "The ceremony implies a vow of obedience, a public and solemn consecration to the service of God." In fact, he says, "The obligation to make a baptismal profession of faith, binds every disciple of Christ." Even those baptized as infants are required to make their own profession in baptism.[50]

E. Y. Mullins remarks that faith is the source of the Christian life. This faith is "intensely personal and individual." No one can believe for any other and thus infant baptism is excluded as a possibility.[51] He states that baptism is a symbol of our spiritual death and resurrection. It is "the initial act of outward obedience."[52] W. T. Conner taught that baptism and Lord's Supper do not convey grace. They are "acts of obedience and manifest the faith by which we appropriate grace and thus strengthen the consciousness of grace in the believer. But they are acts of obedience on the part of the believer, who has already been drawn into a living union with Christ in the act of believing."[53] Faith is always a voluntary matter. Administering baptism to anyone who has not submitted to the gospel, including infants, is foreign to Christian order.

This sketch of various views of baptism is meant to give some background to our discussion of Barth's view of baptism. The Anabaptists conceived of baptism as an external sign. Among the early English

---

48. Ibid., 38. Interestingly Dagg spends 47 of 60 pages discussing baptism by immersion. Baptists have too often gotten hung up on the issue of the mode of baptism and underemphasized the meaning and importance of baptism.

49. Ibid., 40–41.

50. Ibid., 72, 73.

51. Mullins, *Christian Religion*, 375.

52. Ibid., 427.

53. Conner, *Gospel of Redemption*, 273–74.

Baptists, baptism was most often understood as an external sign. Yet it is important to note that, among baptists, believers' baptism has not necessarily meant a rejection of baptism as a sacrament. This view will be discussed in chapter 3. I will show in the next chapter that Barth's view of baptism in the *Church Dogmatics* is closer to the view of baptism as an external sign highlighted here, in regard to both infant baptism and baptism as an external, pointing sign, than it is to the more strictly sacramental understanding of baptism held by Calvin and the Reformed tradition to which Barth belonged. In what follows, I will address the ecclesiology that is integrally related to his view of baptism. With this survey in place, I now turn to Barth's doctrine of baptism.

1

Karl Barth's Doctrine of Baptism

THIS CHAPTER WILL ADDRESS BARTH'S UNDERSTANDING OF BAPTISM. It will examine Barth's lecture *The Teaching of the Church Regarding Baptism* and then turn to the *Church Dogmatics*. The majority of the chapter will address the baptismal fragment published as Volume Four, Part Four of the *Church Dogmatics*. I will note the continuity and the change from the early 1940s to the material written at the end of Barth's life. The purpose of this chapter is primarily descriptive. The following chapters will evaluate central ideas raised in the doctrine of baptism as they are given flesh in Barth's ecclesiology.

The Teaching of the Church Regarding Baptism

Barth delivered a lecture to Swiss theological students in Gwatt in May of 1943. The lecture was published as a volume of the series *Theologische Studien*.[1] This lecture caused quite a stir, primarily for its critique of the practice of infant baptism. In this lecture he asserted that "Christian baptism is in essence a representation (*Abbild*) of a man's renewal through his participation by means of the power of the Holy Spirit in the death and resurrection of Jesus Christ, and therewith the representation of man's association with Christ, with the covenant of grace which is concluded and realised in Him, and with the fellowship of His church."[2] Water baptism represents, and joins us to, the death and resurrection of

---

1. Karl Barth, *Teaching of the Church Regarding Baptism*. On material before the 1943 lecture, such as Barth's lectures in Göttingen, see Migliore, "Reforming the Theology and Practice of Baptism," 494–96; and also Migliore's introduction to the English version of the Gottingen Dogmatics: "Karl Barth's First Lectures in Dogmatics," LIII–LVII.

2. Barth, *Teaching of the Church Regarding Baptism*, 9.

Jesus. By the work of the Holy Spirit (i.e., the true baptism of the Spirit), we are united with Christ. The Holy Spirit enables our participation in the death and resurrection of Jesus Christ, which is our justification and rebirth to new life.[3] Water baptism is a representation, or symbol, of "the divine-human reality which it attests."[4] Baptism testifies to the fact that God's awakening of the person to faith through grace, and making that person a member of his covenant and the life of the church, are an objective reality and not subjective fancy. Baptism implies a threat to one's life and a corresponding deliverance. Methods of baptism can be judged by how well they represent this death and rebirth.

According to Barth, baptism is a part of the church's proclamation, and as such it is a human act. Yet, by the action of Christ it becomes his own word and act. Baptism is a living, expressive act because of who Christ is, the true Baptizer and chief Actor in baptism. The "potency" of baptism derives not from the faith of the baptized nor from the proper administration of the rite, not *ex opera operato*. The power of baptism comes solely from the reconciling work of Jesus Christ completed once for all.[5]

The meaning and intention of baptism is the glorification of God and the building up of the church. We cannot assert that water baptism is as such the means for the forgiveness of sins. To do so would confuse Jesus Christ with the one baptizing in his name. "Let us remember that the power of baptism lies in the free word and deed of Jesus Christ. Our baptism is no more the cause of our redemption than is our faith."[6] Baptism is not the cause, but the recognition and representation of our redemption. Barth states:

> In baptism (as in Communion, as in preaching, as in all of the elements of the church's proclamation) the word and work of Jesus Christ are recognized as a gift of salvation, a confirmation of the revelation of the covenant of grace, of the rebirth, of the forgiveness of sins, as a confirmation to believers of the complete divine-human reality which supports and surrounds him, and as a summons and obligation of believers to correspond to

---

3. Ibid., 11–12.
4. Ibid., 14.
5. Ibid., 21.
6. Ibid., 27.

this reality in one's own being and to be obedient to the Holy Spirit in accordance with his gift.[7]

Barth affirmed baptism as a sacrament, in the sense that it is a symbol that participates in what it points to.[8] He developed a cognitive view of baptism as a sacrament which was in line with that put forth by Calvin. Baptism does not convey grace; it does however bring a person to realize the grace that he or she has been given.[9] Baptism is a public act, meant to speak to the church. In baptism candidates are told that their sins are forgiven and that they are children of God. Secondly, they are told that they no longer belong to themselves; they have no further ground for disobedience. They have a Lord. All allegiance has been pledged to Jesus Christ.

Unfortunately, in actual practice the order of baptism may be sufficiently inadequate that the church really does not comprehend what baptism means. Yet, Barth rejects any re-baptism. As opposed to the repetition required for the Lord's Supper, Barth emphasizes the once-for-all-ness of baptism.[10] Re-baptizing adults was a fundamental error on the part of the Anabaptists. Baptism without the willingness of the baptized person may not be correct or given in obedience, and therefore is "clouded," but it is still "true, effectual, and effective baptism" and is not to be repeated.[11]

The element of Barth's theology of baptism which shocked and even angered those in the Reformed tradition was his insistence that the baptized be an active partner. Barth called the church to move away from infant baptism. The baptized should not be a passive instrument. We can no longer assume that everyone born to Christian parents is a part of the Christian church. The New Testament, Barth argues, does not support infant baptism.[12] Barth asks: "What is baptism in itself and as such, if it has no reference to the conscious acknowledgement of regeneration and faith, to the complete divine-human reality, which

---

7. Ibid., 28. Translation revised. *Die Kirchliche Lehre von der Taufe*, 18–19.
8. Barth, *Teaching of the Church Regarding Baptism*, 16.
9. Johnson, *Mystery of God*, 167.
10. Barth, *Teaching of the Church Regarding Baptism*, 36, 64.
11. Ibid., 40.
12. Ibid., 42–45. For a critique of this essay arguing for infant baptism as a sign of prevenient grace leading to subsequent faith, see Cullmann, *Baptism in the New Testament*, 20, 33.

is portrayed within it; if it cannot be in a really intelligible sense the confirming and binding in allegiance of the second of the chief actors, the one baptized; if it cannot be a matter of decision and confession at all?"[13] In baptism a person receives the symbol of grace, but it is also a public affirmation of faith, an expression of the will. Baptism places an obligation upon the baptized; it is not meant to oblige parents or godparents.[14] Baptism is to be a responsible act; "the candidate, instead of being a passive object of baptism, must become once more the free partner of Jesus Christ, that is, freely deciding, freely confessing, declaring on his part his willingness and readiness."[15] Only if baptism is requested can it avoid "the character of an act of violence."[16] Barth thinks that the practice of infant baptism takes from the Holy Spirit the free movement and control of the calling and assembling of the church.

Barth recognizes the dangers of adult baptism, which presupposes free decision and confession: the forcing of conversions, perfectionism, false illusions of sanctity, and the rise of pharisaism. But perhaps perfectionism is not the church's greatest concern. The dangers of infant baptism are more serious. The real danger is the existence of a Christendom which can disclaim its responsibility for Christianity.[17] The greater threat is when all in a given society are baptized into the church by virtue of their citizenship in a Christian nation or in the culture-religion of even a pluralist nation.

> Am I wrong in thinking that the really operative extraneous ground for infant-baptism, even with the Reformers, and ever and again quite plainly since, has been this: one did not want then in any case or at any price to deny the existence of the evangelical Church in the Constantinian *corpus christianum*—and today one does not want to renounce the present form of the national church (*Volkskirche*)? If she were to break with infant-baptism, the Church would not easily be a people's church

---

13. Barth, *Teaching of the Church Regarding Baptism*, 47–48.

14. Ibid., 50. Also, "The person bound under this sign is engaged to a life of responsibility." Ibid., 63.

15. Ibid., 54.

16. Ibid., 47. "The theology and practices of seventeenth-century Baptists revealed a guiding conviction that God must be free to exercise divine prerogative in salvation. Their critique of and resistance to the state church were rooted in this theological intuition." See also Thompson, "Sacraments and Religious Liberty," 43.

17. Barth, *Teaching of the Church Regarding Baptism*, 51.

in the sense of a state Church or a church of the masses. . . . Are we so sure of the inner worth of the Constantinian system and of the present day form of the National Church—is our conscience in these matters so clear - that we ought and must resolve to hold fast to them, at whatever the cost—even at the cost of inflicting wounds and weakness on the church through a disorderly baptism?[18]

For Barth, infant baptism reflects a disorder in the sociological structure of the church. "Where does it stand written that Christians may not be in the minority, perhaps in the very small minority? Might they not be of more use to their surroundings, if they were allowed to be a healthy Church?"[19]

One other roughly contemporary treatment of baptism, by Barth, should be briefly noted. In his 1947 discussion of the Heidelberg catechism, Barth treated baptism in a similar way. There he stated that sacraments do not mediate grace to recipients, but they do mediate, in the sense that they point to something else. The sacraments should be understood as acts of the church, as "eventful witnesses."[20] As witnesses they are meaningful signs. The sacraments are acts that the church performs, which by the work of the Holy Spirit serve as a witness to those who observe. "Baptism is the action which eventfully bears witness to Christians that they have already entered into the fellowship of the death of Jesus Christ and may therefore once and for all be certain of their faith and in faith of the forgiveness of their sins."[21] Baptism is a sign that indicates something else. A sacramental union exists between the elements which signify the action of God, and the sacramental action itself. Thus there is a sacramental union between one's baptism and one's fellowship with Christ. Here Barth also says that in baptism one receives the confirmation of faith. Baptism "is an event in my life which testifies to me that I am set apart to be a member of Christ."[22] This treatment of the Heidelberg catechism contains the same cognitive understanding of baptism as a sacrament that confirms one's faith, as

---

18. Ibid., 52–53.
19. Ibid., 53.
20. Barth, *Heidelberg Catechism for Today*, 95.
21. Ibid., 98.
22. Ibid., 100. "Baptism simply attests to me: I am a believer." Ibid.,102.

well as the corresponding rejection of infant baptism, contained in *The Teaching of the Church Regarding Baptism*.

Church Dogmatics

Barth's treatment of baptism in the *Church Dogmatics* generally reflects what he wrote in 1943. The major distinction is that he came to reject the understanding of baptism as a sacrament. Other than brief references, Barth's discussion of baptism in the *Church Dogmatics* is contained in the fragment of Volume Four, Part Four. As in the three previous volumes, the doctrine of reconciliation was intended to climax in a volume on the ethics of reconciliation. In what was published, Barth treated baptism as the basis and beginning of the Christian life. The fragment posthumously published as *The Christian Life* offers a partial treatment of the Lord's Prayer. This ethics section was also supposed to have as its heart a discussion of the Lord's Supper. Chapter six of this study will show the importance of the fact that baptism is discussed chiefly in Barth's ethics, that is, his discussion of the life of the Christian community. In IV/4 Barth makes a distinction between baptism by the Holy Spirit and the baptism of water, the distinction that will also structure this treatment of his doctrine of baptism.

Baptism with the Holy Spirit

The beginning of the Christian life is the Christian's baptism by the Holy Spirit. Baptism with the Holy Spirit is a change brought about in the life of a person by God. The change is the free work of the gracious God. "The Christian life has its true source in this change which God brings about in man."[23] The striking biblical imagery for this change is varied: a new birth, putting on a new garment, raising from the dead. All of these metaphors suggest a radical change. The change, Barth says, is brought about in the life, death, and resurrection of Christ, and in a person it marks the beginning of the Christian life, a life in relation to God.[24] The change that takes place in the Christian is the liberation of

---

23. Barth, *Church Dogmatics*, IV/4, 6. Volumes of the *Church Dogmatics* will hereafter be cited as CD.

24. Barth, *CD* IV/4, 26.

that person from without as God sets free and awakens the person to the truth of his or her reality.²⁵

Baptism with the Spirit is the turning point in which a person can become faithful to God. The Holy Spirit makes it possible for human beings to be faithful to God, whereas before they were not, nor could they be, faithful. A person

> is enabled to participate not just passively but actively in God's grace as one who may and will and can be set to work too. It is God's power to draw and turn, so that this man will voluntarily and by his own decision choose that which God in His grace has already chosen for him, and in this choice he will be one who is converted to God instead of apostate from Him, one who confesses God instead of one who denies Him.²⁶

The freedom in which human beings can be faithful to God is the freedom in which God is faithful to humanity. It is the freedom in which the sovereign, transcendent God humbled himself in the person and the history of Jesus Christ.²⁷ The change that takes place in each person who is baptized with the Holy Spirit is the realization of what took place in Jesus Christ as the representative for all. Christians are brought to recognize that their own life is involved in the life of Jesus Christ. Their life history took place in the history of Jesus Christ.²⁸

As Barth puts it, the human person is the free subject who begins the Christian life, but this is itself done only on the basis of divine possibility. Barth rejects any Christomonist understanding of the Christian life in which human action is unnecessary.²⁹ In a Christomonist view, what Christ accomplished in his history makes our own history unnecessary. He similarly rejects the view of Protestant Orthodoxy, which argued for a grace that justifies a person but leaves that person entirely unchanged. Soteriology and anthropology are in this understanding subsumed by Christology.³⁰ Yet, Barth insists that even if the prior work

---

25. Ibid., 22.
26. Ibid., 6.
27. Ibid., 13.
28. Ibid., 13. "Christmas day is the birthday of every Christian." Ibid., 15.
29. Ibid., 19.
30. Unfortunately this is a view which has often been attributed to Barth by critics. See Berkouwer, *Triumph of Grace in the Theology of Karl Barth*, 12.

of God is necessary, the role of the person called to be faithful and obedient is not negated in the Christian life.[31]

Similarly an anthropocentric view is inadequate. In such a view the work of Jesus was an expression of what properly takes place in the experience of the human subject. Jesus Christ and his work are an instruction or an example, but the real change of the human person is within the person him or herself. Here Christology is lost in anthropology.[32] In this vein, Barth rejects the existentialism of Neo-Protestantism, which he equates with Pelagianism.

Barth argued that Christ's work was done without us, even if it was done for us, *pro nobis*. Christ's work was completed apart from any experience or acceptance on the part of others. Yet it was done so that it could be experienced and participated in by all others. The history of Jesus Christ is a "Word of universal salvation."[33] The work of Christ took place outside of us, objectively, yet it was done for us. "If he acts *extra nos pro nobis*, and to that extent also *in nobis*, this necessarily implies that in spite of the unfaithfulness of every man He creates in the history of every man the beginning of his new history, the history of a man who has become faithful to God."[34] What began apart from us was done for our sake. Christ, in his own life, liberated us and began the reorientation of human beings.[35] He liberated us for faithfulness to God. Barth asserts that it is the resurrection of Jesus which makes his history relevant to all other histories. His history, his life, is not simply past history. Jesus overcame death and the bounds of his history in order to include and to effect our history.

The Holy Spirit allows all people to participate in what Christ made a reality in his death and resurrection. The Spirit's manifestation of the history of Jesus Christ in human beings is not a second or different work. It is all part of the one divine work, the one divine movement.[36] Both the work and resurrection of Christ and the manifestation of that

---

31. John Webster has argued this persuasively in *Barth's Moral Theology*.

32. Barth, *CD* IV/4, 19–20.

33. Ibid., 25.

34. Ibid., 21. On Barth's use of the notion that God is *pro me* see Mangina, *Karl Barth on the Christian Life*, 57–58.

35. Barth, *CD* IV/4, 23.

36. Ibid., 27. On Barth's understanding of participation, see Mangina, *Karl Barth on the Christian Life*, 80–85.

complete work within people in the present are the one divine history of reconciliation. The baptism with the Holy Spirit thus involves two elements.

> We here presuppose the resurrection of Jesus Christ from the dead as the act of God in which His history was and is revealed as most properly the salvation history of all men. We also presuppose the work of the Holy Spirit as the act of God in which its revelation reaches certain men in such a way that they are opened up for it, and it for its part is disclosed specifically to them. The one act of God is the disclosure of His history to all men in the resurrection of Jesus Christ and the opening up of specific men for His history in the work of the Holy Spirit.[37]

These two factors together form the basis of the Christian life. Christ's revelation is accepted and affirmed by the Christian who is freed by the liberating power of the Holy Spirit. In being freed for faithfulness, the Christian is liberated from the drive to isolation. The Spirit joins us with God's holy people who have also been awakened by God and in whose faithful witness we can now participate.[38] The Holy Spirit calls people to participate in the life of the community and to be active in its ministry.[39]

Barth makes five summary points regarding baptism with the Holy Spirit. First, the Christian life has its beginning in the self-attestation of the living Christ. The Holy Spirit works in the present, creating the redemptive change in human beings. Thus the initiative in the Christian life lies with God.[40] Second, the foundation of the Christian life is the grace of God that reconciles the world to God. Grace is given to specific people. In Baptism with the Spirit the human person is changed and renewed by God. It is truly a sacramental event.[41] Third, this bestowal of grace demands gratitude from the recipient. Human beings are liberated for a life of thankful obedience. The human decision to be obedient is only possible because of the liberating work of the Holy Spirit. Yet,

---

37. Barth, *CD* IV/4, 29–30.

38. Ibid., 29.

39. Ibid., 32. The call to become a Christian and the call to participate in the Christian community are one in the same.

40. Ibid., 31–33.

41. Ibid., 33–35.

the human decision is a genuine one.[42] Fourth, the Christian life thus set in motion is lived in a distinctive fellow-humanity. The Christian is incorporated into the communion of the saints who are gifted for special tasks and ministries within the one body. Barth states that baptism with the Spirit is identical with reception into the church.[43] Fifth, baptism with the Spirit is the beginning of a forward movement. The work of the Holy Spirit continues the process of bringing in the new creation. The Spirit brings repetition of the beginning in a teleological movement. This means that the Christian life is never perfect, yet it is moving toward its eternal goal of sanctification. The Christian life is thus one of penance and possibilities. The pilgrim people of God are moving toward their future kingdom.[44]

Barth's discussion of the baptism of the Holy Spirit fits into the overarching pattern of his theology.[45] The prior work of God, in reconciliation as in revelation, is objective, that is, before and not dependent upon human experience and appropriation. It is then participated in and taken up subjectively, that is, in concrete human experience. Thus, conversion, or the change that takes place, is the work of God but does not exclude the work of the human participant. "The point is that here, as everywhere, the omnicausality of God must not be construed as His sole causality. The divine change in whose accomplishment a man becomes a Christian is an event of true intercourse (*echten Verkehrs*) between God and man."[46] The origin of this genuine relation is with God. Yet this work of God does not overpower the human person. It liberates a person so that he or she can be faithful to God. Barth says clearly that the faithfulness of the Christian is the person's own work. "It is truly his own faithfulness, decision, and act. He could not achieve it if he were not liberated thereto. But being thus liberated, he does it as his own act, as his answer to the Word of God spoken to him in the history of Jesus Christ."[47]

---

42. Ibid., 35–36.
43. Ibid., 36–38.
44. The Christian life is "one long Advent season." Ibid., 38–40.
45. See the treatments of objective revelation and salvation that are mediated to human beings in Hunsinger, *How to Read Karl Barth*, 76–151.
46. Barth, *CD* IV/4, 22. *Kirchliche Dogmatik*, IV/4, 25.
47. Barth, *CD* IV/4, 23.

Here Barth shows a sophisticated approach to divine power and activity which avoided some of the problems inherent in the univocal metaphysics of modern thought. Through his remembrance of the difference between creation and God, Barth avoided the zero-sum game in regards to the power and activity of God that resulted from the adoption of a univocal ontology by the medieval nominalists and subsequent modern theology.[48] Barth can say:

> God is *Spirit*, and therefore He truly awakens man to freedom. That He causes His divine power to come on him does not mean that he overtakes and overwhelms and crushes him, forcing him to be what He would have him be. He does not dispose of him like a mere object. He treats him, and indeed establishes him, as a free subject.[49]

Or again, "The work of the Holy Spirit, then, does not entail the paralyzing dismissal or absence of the human spirit, mind, knowledge and will."[50] As was just noted, God's omni-causality is not a sole-causality in which God alone acts without free and meaningful human action. In his ethics of reconciliation Barth's whole intent is to show that Christian ethics are the free answer of the human agent in response to, and enabled by, the work of God's grace.[51]

When the Holy Spirit liberates a person that person "is granted the true and genuine freedom to acquiesce in God's will." He or she "is no longer free to reject God's will," this false freedom no longer being available.[52] Freedom is not the modern notion of the maximization of choice. As Hans Urs von Balthasar noted, Barth has an Augustinian concept of freedom. True freedom is not neutral choice, but orientation

---

48. Univocal language speaks of God in the same way that it speaks of created, finite beings. God is wholly different from creatures so we cannot speak of God and the world univocally. On this problem in the nominalists, see Milbank, *Word Made Strange*, 41–49, and Blond, *Post-Secular Philosophy*, 6–9. On God's power and human freedom, see Tanner, *God and Creation in Christian Theology* and McCabe, *God Matters*, 10–24.

49. Barth, *Church Dogmatics*, IV/3.2, 941.

50. Barth, *CD* IV/4, 28.

51. Ibid., ix. "Ethics seeks to determine what can be called good human action. This search must take place in a theological context." Barth, *Christian Life*, 3.

52. Barth, *CD* IV/4, 142. For good treatments of human freedom in Barth see, Webster, *Barth's Moral Theology*, and Gunton, "Barth, the Trinity, and Human Freedom," 316–30.

toward God.⁵³ In the Christian tradition human freedom is obedience to God. True freedom is not to have to choose to do God's will. It is the ability (the God gifted ability) to be obedient to God's command without having to weigh and choose between alternatives. "Human freedom is not about a capacity to choose between good and evil. Human freedom occurs when our desires are so turned toward God and the good that no choice is necessary."⁵⁴

The Relation of Baptism of the Holy Spirit to Water Baptism

Human decision, while essential and irreducible, is not in itself the beginning of the Christian life. The divine change, which is the initiative of Christ, enables people to be faithful to God. Human faithfulness corresponds to the divine decision, but the human decision does not make the divine change take place.⁵⁵

> The baptism of the Spirit certainly calls for the baptism with water which is requested of the community and administered by it, which is received by the man who accepts the Word of Jesus Christ. But it is not identical with this, nor is water baptism identical with it. Baptism with the Spirit does not take place in a man either with or through the fact that he receives water baptism. He also becomes a Christian *in* his human decision, in the fact that he requests and receives baptism with water. But he does not become a Christian *through* his human decision or his water baptism.⁵⁶

Water baptism is not equated, by Barth, with baptism by the Holy Spirit. Baptism with the Holy Spirit demands a human decision in response. Christ calls for a life of obedience which should begin with water baptism. Barth's view of baptism reflects a dominant theme of the *Church Dogmatics*: God and humanity in covenant. Barth insists that the Christian life begins with genuine human endeavor even if this is secondary to the work of the Holy Spirit. The human response to God's prior activity is an emphasis in Barth's later work.⁵⁷

---

53. Balthasar, *Theology of Karl Barth*, 129.
54. Long, *Goodness of God*, 46.
55. Barth, *CD* IV/4, 32.
56. Ibid., 32–33. Emphasis mine.
57. John Webster states that this emphasis continues in Barth's discussion of the invocation of God as the basic form of the Christian life. Prayer demonstrates God's prevenient grace and the human's response in obedience. Webster, *Barth's Ethics of*

Barth clearly states that baptism involves two elements, or the work of two distinct subjects. Baptism with the Holy Spirit is the divinely-wrought change (*göttliche Wendung*) in the human being which makes decision and conversion possible. At the same time, baptism must include the human decision that is a result of the change which God brings about in a person. "Baptism is, therefore, to be understood against the background of an understanding of an ordered correspondence between a prevenient, causative divine act of saving grace, and a subsequent human act of confession, thanksgiving, and obedience."[58] Only with both of these elements involved can baptism serve as the foundation of the Christian life and the formation of a person who is faithful to God.[59] These two elements are not to be confused or separated. Barth is thus distinguishing without separating baptism with the Holy Spirit from the act of water baptism. One is the action of God, and the other is action of human beings which is made possible by the action of God. This act of obedience to God's calling is the foundation of the Christian life. For Barth, at the essence of the Christian life there is a unity, which does not sacrifice the distinction, of grace and responsible action done in gratitude.

Is such a distinction an unnecessary dualism as T. F. Torrance has asserted?[60] Believers' baptism, which Barth will endorse, requires a conception of the Holy Spirit active in the Christian both independent and prior to baptism and also linked with baptism. In the practice of believers' baptism faith precedes baptism, thus the Holy Spirit must be active in the life of a person who is brought to faith prior to being brought to baptism. Barth's mistake was not in making the Holy Spirit active independent of baptism; the misstep was in saying that the Holy Spirit is *not* active in the human act of baptism. The moment of baptism with the Holy Spirit can't be pinned down too absolutely. In the whole process of becoming and being made a Christian the Holy Spirit is active, before, during, and after baptism. Even so baptism, as ordained by Christ, is one's public reception into Christ and thus into his body.

Reconciliation, 157–58. See also Jüngel, "Invocation of God as the Ethical Ground of Christian Action," 154–72.

58. Webster, *Barth's Ethics of Reconciliation*, 117.

59. Barth, *CD* IV/4, 41. *KD* IV/4, 45.

60. T. F. Torrance, *Theology in Reconciliation*, 99. On this see also, Jüngel, "Karl Barths Lehre Von Der Taufe," 263–68.

John Webster has countered Torrance's criticism of Barth's distinction of baptisms. According to Webster, Barth does not create a dualism, but a differentiated unity that does not threaten the importance of either element. Barth's Chalcedonian pattern is strained, Webster concedes, because Barth does ultimately stress the distinction of Baptism with the Spirit and Baptism with the water at the cost of their unity. Yet, Barth's intention is to keep them united without separation or confusion. Webster's assessment is that Barth needs a more carefully stated conception of sacramental mediation.[61] Barth may need more than just a better conception of mediation.

Baptism with Water

Because of his rejection of the sacramental character of baptism, baptism is, for Barth, a human work. It is an obedient response to God's gracious activity. Baptism is a human response to divine grace and thus a person's free choice is not purely arbitrary nor is human decision made out of its own power.

> That a man has himself baptised is something which . . . he owes wholly and utterly to the free resolve of the divine word and work of salvation which has or will come upon him; he owes it to this just as certainly as it is the free act of his own resolve and work for which he is liberated and to which he is summoned by that divine resolve. . . . His desire for baptism, and the step which he takes in being baptised, springs wholly from the fact that he is who he is through God's free grace and revelation in Jesus Christ.[62]

Receiving baptism is an answer to this divine summons to which the liberated Christian cannot say no. Stated in this double negative we see that baptism is no shallow matter of "personal choice." It is rather submission to, participation in, the eternal will of God.

Receiving baptism is not simply a human decision or choice that a person makes as one makes consumer "lifestyle" choices. Barth's discussion of baptism does not bear any of the consumer-oriented misunderstandings of baptism which plague some contemporary churches that

---

61. Webster, *Barth's Ethics of Reconciliation*, 170–72. Barth's understanding of baptism as a sacrament and its implications for the being of the church will be discussed in the next couple chapters.

62. Barth, *CD* IV/4, 48.

practice believers' baptism. The one seeking baptism does so by his or her own decision. "Yet this is no capricious act. He does it because he is invited and commanded to do it by the grace of God which has come upon him, by the history of Jesus Christ which has taken place for him, by the manifestation of this history which has occurred for him in the resurrection from the dead, by the work of the Holy Spirit in which that history and manifestation became an event in his own life, in short, by Jesus Christ Himself."[63] A person is summoned and called to baptism.

The notion of correspondence is central to this discussion. Correspondence of human action to God's action is central to Barth's theology. Humanity does not synergistically co-operate with God's grace, nor does grace need supplementation, yet our activity corresponds to God's activity. God's grace itself enables us to receive and respond to it. Regarding baptism Barth says that the human decision "corresponds (*entsprechende*) to the divine turning to man."[64] In proper correspondence we are enabled to participate in Christ's completed work. The being of the church is the life of the community which lives in correspondence to the work of Christ.

The Basis of Baptism.

Barth does not place the basis for Christian baptism upon the command of Jesus in Matthew 28:19. In Barth's argument the basis for baptism is, rather, Jesus's own baptism. The unity of divinity and humanity in the person and work of Christ is the basis for Christian baptism.

> The baptism of Jesus, as His baptism, is in a sense the point of intersection of the divine change and the human decision.... Here the baptism with the Holy Ghost, which may be regarded as the epitome of the divine change effected on a man, meets baptism with water, which represents here the first concrete step of the human decision which follows and corresponds to the divine change.[65]

In his doctrine of baptism the representative humanity of Jesus is baptized in obedience to the divine work and summons. Barth is arguing

---

63. Ibid., 43–44.

64. Ibid., 102. *KD* IV/4, 112. On correspondence in Barth, see Bender, *Karl Barth's Christological Ecclesiology*, 138, 273.

65. Barth, *CD* IV/4, 53.

that the basis for the church's baptism is the baptism of Jesus Christ as God and at the same time as representative human being. At the beginning of his vocation, Jesus is baptized. In his baptism the divine activity and human obedience are a complete unity. According to Barth, the fact of Jesus baptism becomes a command for the church. The baptism of Jesus is the "true baptismal command."[66] Thus, the incarnation is the basis for Barth's theology of baptism. The human action corresponds to the divine action in a manner analogous to the incarnation.

Barth makes three points clarifying the baptism of Jesus as the basis for baptism. First, in baptism Jesus wholly placed himself under the Lordship of God. His baptism was in complete submission to the will of God.[67] He heard the word of God that had come to all of Israel in John the Baptist and was obedient in baptism. John came announcing the drawing near of the kingdom. He proclaimed the coming of an act of God that would change the reality of Israel. The *metanoia* demanded by John is acceptance of the coming kingdom. It is the turning, the reorientation of the human will towards the kingdom. Repentance and conversion are one's readjustment to the kingdom.[68] A doctrine of Christian baptism must remember the character of submission to the kingdom, which is present in Christ's baptism as the basis for our own.

Secondly, Jesus's baptism was an expression of his solidarity with humanity. His acceptance of baptism placed him in fellowship with a fallen humanity. "He accepts solidarity with them in their great perversion. He is one of them, and confesses them as His brethren, when He has Himself baptised."[69] Jesus thus shared in the sinfulness of humanity; he fully accepted humanity's judgment for its sin. In this way, Jesus was truly baptized for repentance from sin as John preached. His baptism was the point where Jesus began to take on the task of bearing the sins of the world as our representative.[70]

Third, in the baptism of Jesus two lines converged, that of God for man and of man for God. It was the commitment of divinity to humanity and the subjection of humanity to God. This "twofold service" was

---

66. Ibid., 53.
67. Ibid., 54–55.
68. Ibid., 56–58.
69. Ibid., 60.
70. Ibid., 58–59.

the beginning of his ministry. The baptism is, therefore, a proclamation of Jesus's activity as the mediator between God and humanity. "The baptism of Jesus is quite plainly the act of obedience in which he entered upon His ministry and way of life in a manner typical and decisive for all that was to follow."[71]

Yet, one might ask, how is the gospel proclamation of Jesus's baptism a reason for the baptism of every Christian? Barth himself mentions that the Gospels do not make Jesus' baptism normative for Christian practice. According to Barth, the community baptizes members into solidarity with Christ who was baptized into solidarity with humanity in his role as mediator.

> The community certainly did not have to enter upon a new Messianic and saving office of its own. But it did have to enter on the way of those who are called to be His witnesses, and who are thus called to fellowship with Him.... It [Jesus' baptism] became exemplary, normative, and binding in respect of the form of the beginning of their new life. When in faith in Him the beginning of a life of fellowship with Him was at issue, it had to follow His act of obedience, His subjection to God, His solidarity with men, His acceptance of service both of God and men. It had to submit to this, to integrate itself into it. It had to perform the same act of acknowledgement and commitment as that with which He began His work as Man.[72]

Barth thinks that this basis for baptism gives grounding to the baptismal command in Matthew 28. Without this foundation, the order to baptize disciples is left without purpose.

The Goal of Baptism

The goal, the *telos*, of baptism is beyond the action of the rite itself. The goal of baptism is neither the administration of the rite nor the creation of human faith. According to Barth, "the goal of baptism is God's act of reconciliation in Jesus Christ through the Holy Spirit."[73] In the church, baptism is both a looking backwards in recollection of Christ's work and a looking ahead to the coming of Christ. Jesus Christ, the basis for

---

71. Ibid., 64.
72. Ibid., 68.
73. Ibid., 72.

baptism, is also the goal of baptism.[74] Baptism sets the baptized on a journey. It is an initiation into the company of pilgrims who are moving ahead, towards the full realization of what Christ accomplished in his life, death, and resurrection.

Another way of stating the goal of baptism is that baptism is an expectation of the coming Kingdom of God.[75] Baptism is initiation into a teleological movement toward Jesus Christ and the Kingdom of his reign. It is the foundation of the Christian life as a life lived toward the Kingdom. Jesus came with the announcement in the Gospels that the kingdom has drawn near. The kingdom has not been fully consummated, but a new reality has broken into our own. The kingdom was inaugurated on Easter, and it presses for completion and consummation. In baptism one's citizenship is transferred into this kingdom. According to Barth the entire Christian life is an expression of the petition, Thy Kingdom Come, in the Lord's prayer. Baptism is the beginning of this life lived in invocation of God's kingdom.[76]

Christian baptism is a human action directed toward its divine fulfillment. The Kingdom of God cannot be brought about by the church or its baptism. The baptized together seek the Kingdom and witness to its coming. Baptism "points forward" to the "future baptism with the Holy Spirit."[77] Now in addition to the divine change which leads to baptism, baptism with the Holy Spirit is referred to as the future goal and fulfillment of baptism as well. It is both the presupposition and the goal for baptism, Barth has stated this fact in both christological and pneumatological terms.

As initiation into the Christian life lived in view of the Kingdom, the goal of baptism is lived out in Christian ethics. Baptism is the first step in human obedience to God made possible by the Holy Spirit. "Christian baptism is the first form of the human answer to the divine change which was brought about in Him who was and is and is to come."[78] It is the act in which Christians publicly confess and commit themselves to Christ. In baptism a Christian enters solidarity with the world and

---

74. Ibid., 89.
75. Ibid., 70.
76. Ibid., 76. See the treatment in *Christian Life*, 233–56.
77. Barth, *CD* IV/4, 71.
78. Ibid., 90.

with God in correspondence to Christ's own portrayal of commitment to God and humanity in his baptism.[79] The human answer of baptism is a confession of faith. "Without the faith of the Christian community and of those who join it there would be no Christian baptism."[80] Of course, the confession of baptism is not a confession of the efficacy of one's own faith, but of that of Jesus Christ. The ethical sphere in which Barth has placed baptism is evident. Baptism is initiation into a life of discipleship. In Barth's doctrine of reconciliation, baptism is a matter of the Christian life and vocation. As John Webster states, baptism for Barth is

> best seen not as the point at which cleansing from sin takes place, but as the beginning of life-long obedience to the situation in which the candidate has been placed by the effective work of Christ and its self-presentation. In sum, once remission from sins is located in the work of Christ whose merits are distributed by the Holy Spirit, water-baptism is most naturally associated with vocation.[81]

Barth argues that in the New Testament references to baptism occur primarily in ethical contexts.

Baptism is also the act in which one confirms commit to the community of fellow Christians. Baptism is the work of a person who is professing faith and commitment in Christ. Yet, baptism confesses that being in Christ means joining with the body of Christ.[82] The personal confession of baptism necessarily involves affirmation and confession by the community which baptizes the candidate. "It is a specific action taken in concert by those who are already serious Christians and those who seek to be such, by the Christian community and those who newly confess their Lord."[83] Baptism after Pentecost can never be taken individualistically. Thus Barth can say that baptism proclaims fellowship. A person is baptized into Christ, who is the head of a community in which

---

79. Ibid., 72.

80. Ibid., 73. Such language of baptism of a confession of faith is typical Baptist language.

81. Webster, *Barth's Ethics of Reconciliation*, 153.

82. Barth, *CD* IV/4, 82–83.

83. Ibid., 101.

he or she now participates. Candidates for baptism are received by the company who go before them.[84]

The Meaning of Baptism.

The meaning of baptism must be sought in its nature as a human action. Its meaning must cohere with Barth's rejection of the idea that baptism is a sacrament, or a means of grace. Water baptism is

> the human decision which corresponds to the divine turning to man.... It is the work and word of men who have become obedient to Jesus Christ and who have put their hope in Him. ... Baptism responds to a mystery, the sacrament of the history of Jesus Christ, and of his resurrection, of the outpouring of the Holy Spirit. It is not itself, however, a mystery or sacrament.[85]

Baptism is the obedient work done in response to God's command by those who have been liberated by God. It is performed by the community that believes in, loves, and is committed to Christ. Barth argues that to rob baptism of this human element is to lose the importance of the Christian life established in the act. Baptism must be a human decision in response to, and thus distinct but inseparable from, the baptism of the Holy Spirit. The church should baptize in recognition and confession of the prevenient grace of God which has already called us. To make of baptism a divine action alone is to lose the importance of both baptism by the Holy Spirit, which is the act of God, and water baptism, which is the corresponding human action.

Barth is concerned that we not confuse divine and human action. The notion of correspondence is again important in Barth's correction of what he sees as mistaken in a sacramental notion of baptism. Water baptism "corresponds" to the baptism with the Holy Spirit. This correspondence is itself made possible only by God, not by anything inherent in the human work. Thus not just any human action would correspond to the work of Christ. In Barth's trinitarian theology, the Holy Spirit makes the work and words of human beings a witness to Christ. Similarly, the practice of baptism corresponds to that of Christ through the work of the Holy Spirit. Even so, the actions that correspond to God's activity are truly human works. Barth is trying to insure that the human decision

---

84. Ibid., 82–83.
85. Ibid., 102.

and action are not robbed of their significance. "Our objection to the sacramental interpretation of baptism is directed against this conjuring away of the free man whom God liberates and summons to his own free and responsible action."[86] Our action is truly our own; God's primary activity in creation and providence do not determine and make human action irrelevant.[87] A grace that overwhelmed and negated human existence would not be grace. Grace makes possible and demands human action. With the notion of correspondence, human action in baptism is free human activity and yet is still given its meaning by God.

According to Barth's exegesis the New Testament term *musterion*, mystery, (sacramentum) refers to an event directly brought to pass by God alone. Baptism and faith are not called a mystery in the New Testament. In the New Testament usage the term refers to God's work, particularly in Christ, and never to human reactions.[88] Barth claims that references to baptism have an ethical character, not the understanding of mystery that developed in Greco-Roman mystery religions. In the Hellenistic mystery religions, a mystery was a secret rite in which candidates were initiated into the secret knowledge of the cult. The rite was meant to mediate a share in the God being worshiped. According to Barth, the church adopted this Hellenistic notion at the expense of the New Testament ethical understanding.[89]

In contrast, Barth argues that in the New Testament baptism is not understood as a divine work or a dispensation of grace that cleanses or renews the recipient. Rather, "man's cleansing and renewal take place in the history of Jesus Christ which culminates in His death, and they are mediated through the work of the Holy Spirit."[90] Christ's history does not need to be repeated or supplemented. Thus, baptism is a genuine human action in response to God's word and work.

---

86. Ibid., 106.

87. See Webster, *Barth's Moral Theology*, 106. "Those who participate in baptism are summoned, empowered and in the full sense ordered by God to take the decision as such. Hence they are not engulfed and covered as by a divine landslide or swept away as by a divine flood. They are taken seriously as God's partners. At issue is their own answer to his work and word, a joyful and confident answer which is to be given quite voluntarily and with full awareness of what is entailed." Barth, *CD* IV/4, 163.

88. Barth, *CD* IV/4, 108.

89. See Ibid., 112–27. Barth refers to the treatment by Bornkamm, "μυστήριον, μυέω," 802–28.

90. Barth, *CD* IV/4, 128.

After addressing the idea of sacrament Barth turns to the positive task of explicating the meaning of baptism. He gives three statements that need to be remembered to understand baptism. The first indispensable element is a "recollection of the technical administration of the act."[91] Baptism needs to be remembered. Baptism is a visible action, a concrete event. It takes place in public so that participants can hold one another accountable on the basis that it has taken place. We cannot rid ourselves of the rite of baptism holding only to the inner, 'spiritual' happening along the lines of Caspar Schwenkfeld in the sixteenth century.[92]

Second, to understand baptism we have to consider the social character of the act. The Christian life initiated in baptism is "a participation in the life of the Christian community."[93] The one baptized and the one who baptizes are equally important. It is a confession of faith by the community and an acknowledgment by the community of this new member's faith.[94] Third, we must remember the principle that baptism should be a free action for all involved. This faithful life, made possible by the liberating work of the Spirit, must begin in free obedience. Baptism is a "first and exemplary answer" which commits Christians for their entire future life.[95] This commitment can be entered into only freely and with a good conscience. The community should never force baptism and should only baptize those who seem to be ready for it. Baptism is not a part of any given culture or pattern of life to be administered to all at a given time or at a certain age.[96] It is a mistake to domesticate baptism so that it is simply what everyone does. This fact is no less true for believers' baptism in areas where groups such as Southern Baptists are numerically the largest denomination. Baptism "must be a breaking

---

91. Ibid., 130.

92. "An Answer to Luther's Malediction," 165–78. He is dealing with the Supper but his view of baptism can be inferred.

93. Barth, *CD* IV/4, 131. Barth asserted previously in the Dogmatics that baptism was the beginning of one's life within the Christian community. For Barth the active life is co-operation in the service of the Christian community. Presenting oneself for baptism is one's acceptance into the community. Barth, *Church Dogmatics*, III/4, 490.

94. Hartwell's claim that Barth makes the community inferior to the candidate does not hold up. "Karl Barth on Baptism," 29.

95. Barth, *CD* IV/4, 132.

96. Ibid., 133.

of all rules, customs, sequences and arrangements, a completely new and special event in relation to them."[97]

The meaning of baptism lies in the correlation and appropriate distinction between "the human action as such and the divine action from which it springs, on whose basis it is possible, and towards which it moves."[98] Barth describes the act of baptism as one of obedience in regard to its basis, and of hope in regard to its goal. Baptism is, then, a matter of command and of promise. Neither the command which is obeyed in baptism nor the promise which is grasped belong to or come from the community or the act itself. They are from Jesus Christ. Obedience in baptism is obedience to his command. The hope that comes in baptism is from the promise that Christ fulfilled in himself.[99]

Obedience and hope together constitute the meaning of baptism. That baptism is done in obedience again shows that the decision to be baptized is not arbitrary or capricious. "A man does this act because he wants to, but he wants to do it in obedience, so that he could not just as well not want to do it."[100] It is obedience in which a person submits to the will of God expressed in Christ. This obedience is not submission as a slave, but the establishment of true freedom. Barth can say that "obedience is freedom and freedom is obedience."[101]

Jesus Christ is both the basis for baptism and the goal and hope for the future which goes beyond it. Obedience to the living word is at the same time an expectation. Those baptized into Christ's death are raised with Christ to a new, living hope. The Christian life is a life moving towards the fulfillment and manifestation of Christ's kingdom. In this interim time, the children of God are only moving towards the consummation, not living in its fullness.[102] "On the basis of their baptism they have freedom only to stride forward in the direction of the Lord who comes in His new, final and comprehensive revelation, of the Lord

---

97. Ibid. One might recall Andrew Fuller's description of baptism as the line of distinction between the Kingdom of God and the Kingdom of Satan, as the boundary of visible Christianity.

98. Ibid., 134.

99. Ibid., 134–35.

100. Ibid., 154.

101. Ibid.

102. Ibid., 198.

and His dominion."[103] Striding forward is the freedom which comes from obedience, the life of the liberated children of God. Baptism is the decision which begins this new life of obedient hope. Thus, baptism is an eschatological, or teleological, act done with a view to the future consummation of all things.

The freedom and hope given to the church are not for its own possession. The baptized community lives as a witness to the world's reconciliation with God and the future glorification of the cosmos.[104] It is the task of this community to declare the greatness of God and his salvation. Baptism into the church is not baptism into privilege or status; it is baptism into a common ministry. Every new member of the church is initiated into a responsibility for the task of the church.[105] God calls this community out of the world so that they may witness to the world. This proleptic, prophetic ministry is central to Barth's understanding of the church that follows after the prophetic Christ.[106] The Christian life is a mission from baptism forward. This mission is to witness to God's grace in a world that does not even know it needs grace. A person becomes, in baptism, an active member of the people of God who mediate the covenant to all of the world. "Within this teleology of the will of the God who loves the world, the Church is also specifically a baptismal community. In each individual baptism it documents God's universal will of grace and salvation."[107] Baptism is thus an act of proclamation. Every baptism opens the community to the fact that God's salvation is open for all humanity.

As the initial step of obedience in the Christian life, baptism is the first step of many. Baptism is "the first step of the Christian life which is a model for all the steps that follow. . . . A whole life, longer or shorter, attaches itself to baptism. Lived under this as its sign, it is the Christian life."[108] Further decisions and choices made in life should all repeat the

---

103. Ibid., 199.

104. Ibid.

105. Ibid., 200. "All those baptised as Christians are *eo ipso* consecrated, ordained and dedicated to the ministry of the Church." Ibid., 201.

106. Barth, *CD* IV/4, 200. See prophetic office of Christ in *Church Dogmatics*, IV/3.1, 86-109, and 191-93. Also the discussion in Webster, *Barth's Moral Theology*, 125-50.

107. Barth, *CD* IV/4, 200. In Yoder's phrase, baptism is a practice before a watching world. See Yoder, *Body Politics*.

108. Barth, *CD* IV/4, 201-2.

decision made in baptism. The fact that one is baptized should set the standard according to which one lives his or her life thereafter. The Christian life is "a being from baptism."[109] Baptism is the beginning of a life of gratitude. The obedience in which the Christian lives is the true freedom of the creature reconciled to God. It is obedience out of gratitude and love, not compulsion. Barth is not naïve or idealistic about the sinfulness even of the baptized. No guarantee, of course, exists; one's life can either affirm or deny one's baptism. He understands that the Christian life will often not correspond to the church's baptism.[110] Yet, we should not lose our hope; baptism rests upon the word and command of God.[111]

One's conversion "summons, drives, and impels" one to baptism. Baptism is a confirmation of conversion. The meaning of baptism is the conversion of all who are involved.[112] Baptism is conversion because in it a concrete sign that the candidate, and the congregation, "are leaving an old path and entering upon a new."[113] A person's baptism is flanked on each side by a definite Before and After. Prior to baptism one was outside of the community and after baptism one has entered into it. To employ Wolfhart Pannenberg's phrase, baptism is "the constitution of Christian identity." Baptism is the once-for-all transfer of oneself to God's possession.[114] This fact, Barth says, is missed in national churches that assume one is a part of the church by virtue of birth. Conversion as expressed in the act of baptism is "the transition from self-will to obedi-

109. Ibid., 202. "The human step at which all that God willed from eternity and did in time was primarily aiming, and with which the answer of man thereto primarily begins, is baptism. This is the step in which the stage of the provisional and the non-obligatory, of mere preparation, is overhauled and left behind, in which looking at Jesus Christ becomes necessary instead of contingent, fixed instead of vacillating, in which faith becomes solid in spite of unbelief, in which it rings out as man's response, in which his conversion becomes an act which is visible to God and irrevocable, an irreversible event." Ibid., 151.

110. On the need to recognize the sinfulness of the church, see Healy, *Church, World and the Christian Life*, 7–11.

111. Barth, *CD* IV/4, 205. The act of baptism can be entered into and performed in confidence because it is a prayer that Christ be responsible for our mistakes. Ibid., 208–10.

112. Ibid., 145, 138.

113. Ibid., 135.

114. Pannenberg, *Systematic Theology*, 239. For Pannenberg baptism is a sign of one's eschatological election.

ence to God, from anxiety before Him to hope in Him."[115] Baptism is a profession before the world that one has entered upon the new way.

Upon baptism the person is bound to the Christian community and it is bound to him or her. Now this person is responsible for the ministry and witness of the community. Both in the church's glory and its shame the baptized are united in sharing the life of the church. Together candidate and congregation are traveling this new path. Baptism is a profession of faith by the congregation no less than the one being baptized. The community, together with the new member, declares at baptism that they will be obedient to God. Baptism and the Christian life are not a private affair, yet the person does not lose his or her individuality. As Barth says "in all its [a human life's] individuality, however, it becomes the life of a member of the community."[116] The church is not a collective in which a member becomes something less than human.

"A specific renunciation is made and a specific pledge is made" by a person presenting his or herself for baptism.[117] In baptism the community places itself under the justification and sanctification of sinful humanity completed by Jesus Christ. Baptism is thus a recognition of God's No and God's Yes to humanity that were pronounced in Him. In Christ God's No was spoken against sinful humanity in their pride, sloth, and falsehood. Christ was also God's Yes to the new life that God has declared for humanity because of Christ's faithfulness. Jesus was the sanctification of humanity for a new way of life, a new path. The renewal of humanity took place in his life.[118] Baptism as a burial of the old person is also one's embrace of the new. Baptism

> bears witness to the boundary line which God has drawn between a passing age and a coming age, a passing personal life and a coming personal life. Ventured with a look at Jesus Christ and in obedience, it is man's tracing of the divine act of judgment which is also as such the divine act of reconciliation. It is not, then, an autonomous decision. It is a free and responsible act, but as such it simply follows the justification and sancti-

---

115. Barth, *CD* IV/4, 136.

116. Ibid., 149. Baptism is not a private affair, but it is a personal one. These terms are not synonymous.

117. Ibid., 158.

118. Ibid., 161.

fication, the cleansing and renewal of sinful man which God has accomplished and revealed in Jesus Christ. Controlled by God's own renunciation and pledge, it receives and has in all its humanity the character of a valid and effective renunciation and pledge.[119]

Baptism is thus the burial of those who died with Christ on the cross (Rom 6:4 and Col 2:12). At the same time the sin and guilt which are confessed in baptism are also understood to be forgiven and pardoned and a new life begun.

Barth emphasizes that the pledge and renunciation are, again, a communal activity. The community together confesses its old state and the new reality that has come into the world in Jesus Christ.[120] The baptized and the congregation look back upon this pledge to remember their commitment to live faithfully. Both this renunciation of the old and the pledge to the new must be undertaken by free and responsible agents. God's grace affirmed in the renunciation and pledge does not reduce the freedom of decision given to the human being.[121] We could say rather that God's free grace demands decision. This central assertion guides Barth's view of baptism, both in his rejection of the idea of sacrament and his rejection of infant baptism.

Since the meaning of baptism is conversion, the life that follows will naturally be different than before. It will be, Barth says, a life of daily repentance. "If baptism means this conversion, then what can take place after baptism, and on the basis of it, but the turning of man's whole life into a daily repentance?"[122] The Christian life is a life of continual *metanoia*, remembering the renunciation and the pledge made in baptism. This, again, is not for the sake of the individual Christian, but so that the Christian community can be a witness to the world around it.[123]

Conversion marks the turning point in which, by the power of the Holy Spirit, the Christian turns to a life of obedience and hope based upon baptism. The candidate submits to baptism in obedience to God's

119. Ibid., 159.
120. Ibid.
121. Ibid., 163.
122. Ibid., 203.

123. The Anabaptist concern for a community of believers was this same concern. The idea of the ban in Mennonite communities is for the health of the church, especially as it witnesses to the world around it. See Menno Simons, "On the Ban," 261–71.

command. It is thus the first step of the Christian life begun in one's conversion. Baptism is at the same time a hope that one's conversion is only a part of what awaits God's creation in his eschatological kingdom, which is the goal of baptism.

Barth on Infant Baptism

All discussion thus far has centered around conversion, obedience, responsible decision, and the confession of Christ. Thus, no place has been made for people who come unconsciously to baptism through the faith of others. The developing assumption has been that one should be able to make a free decision. Because believers need to be capable of commitment, decision, and action before receiving baptism, Barth rejected the baptism of infants. Baptism is the beginning of the Christian life and the Christian life can only be entered upon in responsible commitment and with a good conscience.[124] Being baptized by proxy is no better for Barth than being made a "Christian citizen" because one is in a "Christian State." Barth's opposition to infant baptism was not the center of his theology of baptism, for his opposition to the baptism of infants was based upon his understanding of the meaning of baptism, not the reverse.[125]

Barth's insistence on baptism as an act of obedience corresponding to one's baptism with the Holy Spirit stands as the key element in Barth resistance to infant baptism. Barth argues, like most baptist theologians, that faith should always precede baptism. Faith is the gift of the Holy Spirit whose baptism comes prior to the baptism of water.[126] The obedience given in faith must be responsible and free. As Barth said in Basel in 1963, "the point at issue here is that of responsibility, both that of the baptizing congregation and that of the future Christian who is to be baptized."[127] The life of the church is its obedience and response to the Word it has heard. For this reason, it is important to Barth that

---

124. Through volume one of the *Church Dogmatics*, Barth apparently accepted infant baptism. In a seminar in 1938 Barth came to negative conclusions regarding Calvin's arguments for infant baptism. See Busch, *Karl Barth*, 286. As seen above, by the 1943 lecture Barth rejected infant baptism as a mistake.

125. Hartwell, "Karl Barth on Baptism," 14. Barth's critique of the Constantinian assumptions of infant baptism will be dealt with in chapter five.

126. Barth, *CD* IV/4, 156.

127. Barth, *Fragments Grave and Gay*, 85.

one being baptized receive some instruction prior to being baptized. Candidates for baptism need to have an understanding of the Word that the church proclaims.[128]

According to Barth, adherents to infant baptism cannot provide evidence of its inherent necessity. On the contrary, the Reformers' defense of infant baptism was not based upon their general doctrine of baptism. Their defense only arose under the pressure of Anabaptist practice and critique. Barth states that the Heidelberg Catechism speaks of a believing person who confesses faith in Christ, and yet this emphasis is ignored when the Catechism affirms the baptizing of infants. In addition, Barth asserts that there is no New Testament command or permission for infant baptism.[129]

This emphasis on personal faith raises an important issue, which Colin Gunton expresses well. In his stress on the communal and public nature of baptism Gunton argues that baptism is not about the faith of the individual being baptized. Baptism has become too individualistic and is no longer focused on the community of salvation. He recognizes the problem of Christendom, but the answer is not rejecting infant baptism but reforming the indiscriminate baptism of infants, which is the real problem.[130] Baptism, as a communal act, is the means by which we are brought into the community, into the body of Christ. It is not meant as an expression of faith. "It is not first of all the expression of the faith of an individual or some invisible inner cleansing but is public and communal: it is the means by which a person is brought into relation with Christ through the medium of his body, the Church."[131] Infant baptism emphasizes what is received, not the faith of the one baptized. Baptism is therefore not an ethical act.[132]

Gunton also offers an important challenge to churches which insist upon believers' baptism. Restricting baptism to those who have a personal faith—"adults or near adult believers who have qualified themselves for membership by virtue of a particular experience or

---

128. Barth, *CD* IV/4, 151–52.

129. Ibid., 179. Compare the exegetical discussion of Baptist scholar Beasley-Murray, *Baptism in the New Testament*.

130. Gunton, "Baptism," 204–5.

131. Ibid., 208–9.

132. Gunton, "Church as a School of Virtue," 224. See John Colwell's assessment of this assertion in *Promise and Presence*, 132–33.

decision"—will impoverish the community of the church. He criticizes any notion of church which does not include children.[133] Gunton is right about the communal nature of baptism, and Barth also insisted upon this aspect of baptism. Here Gunton and Barth can offer a corrective to much Baptist practice. Yet, at its best, the baptist emphasis upon the faith of the individual, as with Barth, is not overly individualistic, but for the sake of the congregation. Also, to suggest that baptist churches do not have a place for children does not match the life of any Baptist church that I have experienced. True, unbaptized children are not voting members, yet they are a vital part of the life of the church. They are formed and shaped by the community so that they might continue in the church's life and witness as adults. Many churches practice baby dedications for infants, which are in reality the church dedicating itself to the child.[134]

One of the strongest arguments for infant baptism is its nature as a depiction of the free grace of God, prior to human decision.[135] Having Christian parents is surely a form of prevenient grace, as supporters of infant baptism argue, yet the grace lies in the presence of the church, that is, having parents and a Christian community who will nurture the child in the faith. Even these children must be awakened by the Holy Spirit.[136]

> The Christian life cannot be inherited as blood, gifts, characteristics and inclinations are inherited. No Christian environment, however genuine or sincere, can transfer this life to those who

---

133. Gunton, "Baptism," 210–14.

134. On this, see Gilmore, *Baptism and Christian Unity*, 58–73 and 90–103. Colwell argues in response to such a view that the withholding of Lord's Supper from a baptized child until that child has been confirmed by a distinct sacrament invalidates baptism and effectively excludes the child from the sacramental life of the church. Colwell, *Promise and Presence*, 140–45.

135. This argument is used by those who support infant baptism in response to Barth. See Migliore, "Reforming the Theology and Practice of Baptism," and Jennings, "Grace Without Remainder," 201–16.

136. I am convinced by Moltmann that infant baptism is not a sign of prevenient grace as usually understood, but rather prevenient grace that will be at work through the faith of the parents and the church. He points out the important role that parents play as missionaries and evangelists for their children. This places an even greater role on the community in the formation of Christians. In a sense, the church is God's prevenient action. Moltmann, *Church in the Power of the Spirit*, 230. Compare McClendon, "Conversionist Spirituality," 23–32.

are in this environment. For these, too, the Christian life will and can begin only on the basis of their own liberation by God, their own decision. Its beginning ... cannot be made for them by others through the fact that, without being asked about their own decision, they receive baptism.[137]

The children of Christian parents become members of the church through faith and the call of God no less than their parents. The basis of the new covenant does not change from one generation to the next.

According to Barth, no one's faith can substitute for another's, and as noted above, faith is indispensable for Christian baptism. "Believing is something which no one else with his faith can do for us: not even the most believing parents, the strongest Christian brother, the most vital community."[138] As Moltmann notes, the faith of the community is necessary, but in a way which challenges the child to believe, not in a way that diminishes the child's need for faith.[139] According to Barth, even Luther and Calvin's treatments of baptism in general emphasize the faith of the candidate.[140] Barth does not think much can be made of the Reformation argument that the Holy Spirit has given the infant faith or planted a seed for faith. Baptism performed in hope, or even expectation of faith that will later be confirmed, is still an attempt to Christianize people without their desire or their confession.[141] The rite of confirmation is required as a supplement for infant baptism, yet in Barth's evaluation the necessity of confirmation devalues baptism.[142]

---

137. Barth, *CD* IV/4, 184.

138. Ibid., 186.

139. Moltmann, *Church in the Power of the Spirit*, 230.

140. Barth, *CD* IV/4, 189. Aquinas's treatment of baptism makes a distinction regarding the "necessity" of faith for baptism. Faith is necessary for grace to be received, and in that sense faith is necessary for Baptism. Faith, on the other hand, is not necessary for the baptismal character or seal to be imprinted on the one baptized. Aquinas, *Summa Theologica*, III.68.8. He does say in the previous article that "those who are to be baptized ask of the Church that they may receive Baptism: and thus they express their intention of receiving the sacrament. The one coming for baptism must "of his own will, intend to lead a new life, the beginning of which is precisely the receiving of the sacrament. Therefore, on the part of the one baptized, it is necessary for him to have the will or intention of receiving the sacrament." *Summa Theologica*, III.68.7. Yet he procedes to argue for the baptism of children because of original sin.

141. Barth, *CD* IV/4, 187–88. Such attempts were, of course, at the heart of the failed Constantinian project.

142. Ibid., 188. Baptist theologian John Colwell agrees that confirmation often does render baptism invalid. However, he develops a position which includes a sacrament of

One could not charge Barth's doctrine of believers' baptism as an individualistic, consumer approach to baptism. Yet, adherents of believers' baptism must remember Luther's essential warning regarding the practice. "We are not to base baptism on faith. There is quite a difference between having faith, on the one hand, and depending on one's faith and making baptism depend on faith, on the other."[143] Insisting on the faith of the baptized could run the risk of basing one's baptism upon his or her faith. As in his theology as a whole Barth insists on the realization of God's work by the individual Christian without making this subjective appropriation dominant over the objective work of God in Christ. "Without the *pro me* of the individual Christian there is no legitimate *pro nobis* of the faith of the Christian community and no legitimate *propter nos homines* of its representative for the non-believing world."[144] But Barth quickly goes on to say that the *pro nobis* and *propter nos homines* can not be subsumed under the *pro me*. The *pro me* must never be made a governing or systematic principle. It is always Jesus Christ *pro me*. Christ is still the center of a personal faith, not the person of faith or the faith itself.

Barth sees the community and the person as dwelling in a relation, corresponding to the objective ascription and subjective appropriation of salvation. "Salvation is ascribed to the individual in the existence of the community, and it is appropriated by the community in the existence of the individuals of which it is composed."[145] Barth makes it clear that baptism must be objective and subjective. Yet the objective truth precedes the subjective appropriation. Because of the problems inherent in infant baptism, believers' baptism is the best recognition and confession of God's prevenient grace. Only God's Spirit at work in human beings makes human decision possible, yet this wholly gracious, divine origin does not reduce the necessity of human commitment.

---

confirmation to supplement the irregular baptism of an infant, so that infant baptism is not declared invalid. Colwell, *Promise and Presence*, 135–54.

143. Lull, *Martin Luther's Basic Theological Writings*, 364.

144. Barth, *CD* IV/1, 755.

145. Ibid., 149.

Conclusion

Paul McPartlan argued in dialogue with Henri de Lubac and John Zizioulas that the Eucharist makes the church, so I can perhaps say for the Believers' Church tradition, baptism makes the church.[146] Baptist scholar H. Wheeler Robinson similarly declared: "The Baptist stands of falls by his conception of what the Church is; his plea for believers' baptism becomes a mere archaeological idiosyncrasy, if it be not the expression of the fundamental constitution of the Church."[147] Below it will be seen that, when understood correctly, this can be said of Barth's ecclesiology as well. Four key elements of Barth's doctrine of baptism will be important for examining Barth's ecclesiology. In fact, it is my claim that Barth's doctrine of baptism sheds an important light, perhaps even gives us a key, for understanding his doctrine of the church.[148] First, Barth's treatment of the relation between the baptism of the Spirit and water baptism will help to understand the being of the church according to Barth. His rejection of the sacramental nature of baptism, held equally alongside his insistence on the prevenient grace of God, will help us to understand the church as the presence of Christ in the world and the work of the Spirit in the church. Second, Barth's emphasis on baptism as a visible sign, as 'eventful witness,' sheds light on Barth's treatment of the church as visible and yet invisible. Barth stresses the visible nature of the church while remembering that the true being of the church is God's doing. Barth's congregationalism and his actualism emphasize a concrete, embodied congregation which also fits this element of his doctrine of baptism. Third, Barth's forceful argument that the candidate for baptism must be a free responsible agent led him to reject infant baptism. In examining his ecclesiology, I will show that

---

146. McPartlan, *Eucharist Makes the Church*. Barth probably would not have accepted the statement "baptism makes the church" any more than the "Eucharist makes the church." Saying that baptism makes the church is not meant to exclude the work of the Holy Spirit in any way. Only God can bring about the existence of the church, but the argument here is that God does so through baptism as ordained by Christ. See *CD* IV/2, 616.

147. Robinson, *Life and Faith of the Baptists*, 73. Colwell argues that the church is defined in and through baptism. Colwell, *Promise and* Presence, 72–73.

148. Eberhard Jüngel asserts that the doctrine of baptism is a test of how one understands all of Barth's theology. Jüngel, "Karl Barths Lehre Von Der Taufe," 287. On Jüngel's affirmation of Barth's view of baptism and the avoidance of Jüngel's assessment, see Richardson, *Reading Karl Barth*, 176–208.

Barth insisted that the church must be a free community that is not captive to any state or culture. Barth's rejection of infant baptism springs from his rejection of the Constantinian assumptions that he identifies in the practice. Finally, Barth's doctrine of baptism was cast in an ethical context. I will argue that, hand in hand with this, Barth's ecclesiology is ethical in nature. Thus the church does not exist for its own sake; people are baptized into a task and a mission. Barth's discussions of sanctification and discipleship offer the picture of a teleological community, which exists for the sake of the world. Both Barth's ethics and his view of baptism center around the church as witness. The community is sent into the world by the Holy Spirit as a witness to Jesus Christ.

2

Baptism and the Being of the Church

BARTH'S ECCLESIOLOGY IS AN ELEMENT IN HIS LARGER DOCTRINE OF reconciliation. It is not separated off as the next doctrine in a system. To treat his understanding of the church in such a manner would be to miss the drama of reconciliation and redemption which he describes. We are approaching the doctrine from a different angle, but ecclesiology is another dimension of the one mystery of the doctrine of reconciliation.[1] Barth's intention in the ecclesiological sections of the doctrine of reconciliation is to discuss the "active participation of man in the divine act of reconciliation."[2]

Barth questions the normal order of the doctrine of reconciliation. Is it "actually the case that what we have to say concerning Jesus Christ can be gathered together in the one section on Christology, over against which there is a completely different section which includes what we have to say concerning man and the Church?"[3] For Barth, these "topics" are all interrelated. All are related to the center which is Christ. The New Testament does not give an explicit Christology in the abstract, nor does it separate Jesus from Israel or from his followers. We cannot do Christology without its implications for humanity and for the Church. In the same way, we cannot leave Christology behind and move on to ecclesiology.

Like the doctrine of revelation, reconciliation consists of both an objective and a subjective element. Both of these elements are essential for the understanding of the doctrine. The doctrine of reconciliation involves first the prevenient divine act and only then an active human

---

1. Barth, *CD* IV/1, 644.
2. Ibid., 643.
3. Ibid., 124.

participation in that prior act of God. What Christ accomplished in incarnation, death, and resurrection is complete and sufficient in and of itself. Human beings are allowed to participate in and witness to what Christ finished and made possible for us. Barth's doctrine of baptism fits the structure of his doctrine of reconciliation: the prior act of God makes possible human response and participation.

This chapter will examine the existence of the church in relation to Christ and the Holy Spirit. I will then ask what light Barth's doctrine of baptism sheds on the being of the church. Barth says that two names are necessary to understand the church: Jesus Christ and the Holy Spirit. Both a christological and a pneumatological statement need to be made about the church. The Christian community is called and maintained in existence by the Holy Spirit so that it can be a witnessing people who are bound and committed to Christ.[4]

The Basis of the Church in Christology

From the beginning of the *Church Dogmatics*, Barth makes it clear that the heart of his understanding of the church is his Christology. In I/1 Barth points out the divine-human character of the church. It exists by the action of God and the appropriation of this action by human beings. "The being of the church is Jesus Christ."[5] Barth also says that "anthropological and ecclesial assertions arise only as they are borrowed from Christology. That is to say, no anthropological or ecclesiological assertion is true in itself and as such. Its truth subsists in the assertion of Christology, or rather in the reality of Jesus Christ alone."[6] Ecclesiology is derived from and understood in the context of reflection upon the person and work of Christ.

It is only when he reaches volume four of the *Dogmatics* that Barth offers extended discussions of ecclesiology. Of course, Barth has not heretofore neglected the church; it has arisen in discussions of revelation, election, and ethics. Yet because of its internal relation to the person and work of Christ, he offers a developed view of the church

---

4. Barth, *CD* IV/3.2, 752. Compare Lossky's two aspects of the church: the christological and the pneumatological. Lossky, *Mystical Theology of the Eastern Church*, 174–95.

5. Barth, *CD* I/1, 15.

6. Barth, *CD* II/1, 148–49.

only as he explicitly engages his Christology and soteriology. In Barth's logic the Holy Spirit and the Church are both gathered together under the larger picture of the person and work of Christ. Christology is the governing concept which provides the content of pneumatology and ecclesiology. As Hans Urs von Balthasar states the matter, "Christology is the inner form of ecclesiology; it alone determines the nearness and distance that must obtain between the obedience of Christ the Head and the obedience of the Church, his Body and members."[7]

In his helpful book on Barth's ecclesiology Kimlyn Bender identifies the basic structure according to which Barth develops his ecclesiology. The pattern is Christological and "is articulated in terms of the patristic *anhypostasia/enhypostasia* formula in Christology."[8] This formula states that the human nature of Christ in the incarnation did not have its own independent existence apart from the divine Logos. The human nature has its existence *in* the hypostasis of the Word. "When applied by analogy to designated divine and human relationships, then, this Christological formula entails that the human partner and work has no independent existence apart from the divine initiative, but at the same time ensures that the human subject does have a real and true existence and activity as established by and in relation to the divine Subject and activity."[9] Niether the priority of the divine nature nor the reality of the human can be sacrificed.

Working with the Christological pattern, Christ is to the Church what the Logos is to the human nature of Christ. Also the invisible church, which is the work of the Holy Spirit, is thus related to the visible institution of the church.[10] The visible, historical church is secondary and dependent upon the Holy Spirit, but its reality, within Christ, is given and secure. This logical and ontological order is irreversible. "Christ remains Lord, as the church must remain servant, for the church's election is a reality only a it partakes in the prior election of Jesus Christ."[11] The Church's being is a predicate of Christ's.[12] In the

---

7. Balthasar, "Christology and Ecclesial Obedience," 139.
8. Bender, *Karl Barth's Christological Ecclesiology*, 4.
9. Ibid., 5.
10. Ibid., 157–58.
11. Ibid., 104.
12. Barth, *CD* IV/3.2, 754.

doctrine of reconciliation Barth unequivocally states that the being of the church has its basis in Jesus Christ. Barth can say in fact that, "Jesus Christ is the community."[13] This is a christological statement which is only secondarily an ecclesiological statement. It cannot be reversed.

For Barth as for the Reformers, the work of Christ is permanent and unrepeatable. According to Hunsinger, "since we are given a share in this event by grace through faith, having been baptized into Christ's very death (Rom. 6:3), the substance of our salvation, and not just the source, is Christ himself and Christ alone."[14] Barth derived his radical Christocentricity from the Reformers as they attempted a critical recovery of the Catholic tradition.[15] The church exists where the Spirit acts to create witnesses to who Christ was and what he did. Rather than continuing the work of Christ, the church participates by grace in his completed but not yet consummated work.

Barth casts Christ's uniqueness in a trinitarian understanding of God's dealings with the world. Thus the being and work of Christ inherently involve the Spirit-formed community which follows from them.

> The being of the community is a predicate or dimension of the being of Jesus Christ Himself. In this full and strict sense it belongs to Him and is His property. This is the source of its life and existence. Hence it has no option but to exist in faith in Him, love for Him and hope in Him. It exists as He exists. For He doesnot exist without it. He alone is who and what He is. But He is not alone as who and what He is.[16]

The true existence of Christ must be understood as the *totus Christus*, which is "Christ including all those who are elected and justified and sanctified and called in Him.... To Christ there belong all His own."[17]

For Barth, the church is necessary because Christ meets us in the church. To be withdrawn from the church is to be separated from its savior.[18] He states: "the true Church ... is savingly necessary.... The salvation addressed to man by God, and therefore in particular the eleva-

13. Barth, *CD* IV/2, 655.
14. Hunsinger, *Disruptive Grace*, 285.
15. Mangina, "Bearing the Marks of Jesus," 302.
16. Barth, *CD* IV/3.2, 754.
17. Barth, *CD* IV/2, 624. "The crucified Jesus lives ... as the *totus Christus*." Ibid., 658.
18. O'Grady, *Church in the Theology of Karl Barth*, 247.

tion and establishment of man, of all men, as it has taken place in Jesus Christ, is not a self-enclosed saving fact either far behind us or high above us. It is a living redemptive happening which takes place."[19] Barth tends to speak primarily of the resurrection in this connection.[20] The living Christ has a living community that continues in the world. The church exists because Christ died and rose again. "She is the human, the temporal, the earthly fact corresponding to the Christological reality of his death, of his resurrection, of his ascension, of his reign and return."[21] The church is the work of the living Christ who makes possible and necessary the community which follows after him.

The strength of the church lies in the fact that it comes from Easter. The church "exists in the light of Easter Day."[22] Living from Easter, the church is the community to which the reconciling and justifying work of Jesus Christ has been revealed. "The Church has its origin in the completed self-declaration of God. As this took place in the world, it not only became true and actual that the whole world was confronted with it, but there arose within and across the other peoples of the world a people in which it took root, in which it was perceived and accepted."[23] The church is this people who remember and proclaim the new reality that God has brought about and revealed to the world. The church lives in light of Good Friday and Easter.

What will one day be known by all is confessed by this gathered community that exists in the meantime. "The Christian community which is His body is the gathering of those men whom already before all others He has made willing and ready for life under the divine verdict executed in His death and revealed in His resurrection from the dead."[24] By its existence and by its proclamation in the world, the church witnesses to what has been done in Jesus Christ for all of humanity. The Christian community is the first, the first of many, who acknowledge and live in response to the work and revelation of Christ. It exists es-

---

19. Barth, *CD* IV/2, 621.

20. Cochrane, "Markus Barth—An Un-Barthian Barthian," 46–47. Cochrane argues that, for Barth, Christ is truly present because of the resurrection and does not need sacramental mediation.

21. Barth, *Faith of the Church*, 123.

22. Barth, *CD* IV/1, 726.

23. Barth, *Christian Life*, 133.

24. Barth, *CD* IV/1, 661.

chatologically, "i.e., in correspondence with the 'already' of Easter Day, which was the dawning of the Last Day within earthly history."[25] The being of the church is its participation in the New Life that will ultimately be revealed to all.

The "essence" of the church is the event in which Christ gives himself to human beings that they may fulfill a certain task.[26] They are to be witnesses; having received they are to become givers. As noted, the church does not add to the work of Christ nor, strictly speaking, does it continue the work of Christ. Witnessing to that which it is not, Jesus Christ, is the true visible being of the Church. The church's "true invisible being . . . is that it is elected and called to be a people alongside and with Jesus Christ and with a share in His self-declaration, that it is given to it to be appointed His witness, to be set in service to the eternal Word of God spoken in Him, to be ordained to follow the Son of God incarnate in Him."[27] Lest we think this visible task too small, let us be reminded that an ontological connection exists between Jesus and all Christians. "In the New Testament the gathering and upbuilding of the community, of those who know Him, is depicted as a necessity grounded in Himself," for "this community is sent out, again with a necessity grounded in Himself, and entrusted with the task of mission in the world."[28]

Barth states that when the church misunderstands itself and its place in God's work, it can exist in either excess or in defect. The church in excess exceeds the limit within which it is the church. That limit is its determination that Jesus Christ is its sovereign; and to Christ it owes its origin and constitution. The church in excess serves its own needs instead of serving Christ. It becomes its own means of life and glory. The church in defect is the church that does not take itself seriously enough. The church in defect is only half sure of its cause and takes up this cause with hesitancy and reservation. It pursues its task only timidly. It fails to see the importance of the church.[29]

---

25. Ibid., 662.
26. Barth, *God Here And Now*, 62–63.
27. Barth, *CD* IV/3.2, 729.
28. Barth, *CD* IV/2, 275.
29. Barth, *Christian Life*, 136–37.

The Earthly-Historical Existence of Jesus Christ

In the present time, between incarnation and consummation, Christ is present both with the Father and in the world through His body the Church. "He can have an earthly-historical form of existence as well as a heavenly-historical. He can create and sustain and rule the *communion sanctorum* on earth. He can exist in it in earthly-historical form."[30] Without locking and limiting Christ within his earthly body, Barth affirms the activity of the church in making Christ present to the world. "The community is the earthly-historical form of existence of Jesus Christ himself."[31] The church is the embodied representation of Christ in the world. As an element in the being of Christ, the Church is, precisely in its historical finite being, Christ in the world.

Barth affirms and utilizes the Pauline language of the church as the body of Christ. "The Church is His body, created and continually renewed by the awakening power of the Holy Spirit."[32] This statement need not be taken metaphorically. "The community is His body, His body is the community."[33] What Christ is and has done in eternity takes on a historical dimension in the physical body of Christ and in the church as Christ's body. Christ gathers, shapes, and upholds this body as his own. The body has its existence only from Jesus Christ its head.[34] As Paul taught, the multiple gifts all work in a common unity for the well-being of the community. Those who have received the Spirit work together for the good of the community. A promise for the unity of all humanity can be foreseen in the one united community. The emphasis upon the church as the body of Christ in the world will have ramifications for the visibility of the church upon which Barth is insistent.[35] As Christ's body the church exists in space and time. It is visible by its very nature. Barth uses the concept of the body of Christ because the church in its concrete, historical occurrence can be identified with Christ's presence in the world.[36]

---

30. Barth, *CD* IV/2, 653.
31. Barth, *CD* IV/1, 661.
32. Ibid.
33. Ibid., 666.
34. Barth, *CD* IV/2, 655.
35. See chapter four.
36. Healy, "Logic of Karl Barth's Ecclesiology," 256–57. Healy's strong critique of

The Church in the Doctrine of the Word Of God

According to Barth, people become recipients of God's revelation in a definite, specific tradition. God's making himself known in Jesus Christ is not a context-free, generalized imposition of knowledge upon humanity. Revelation "is not an issue of men universally or of man in general but very concretely and specifically of man in the Church."[37] Revelation occurs within the Church, the community that recollects what God has done in Christ.[38] A definite ecclesial context exists in which God's revelation, while available to all, is specifically and historically focused. The Christian community recollects God's revelation. The recipients of revelation are "bound" to the church. "By belonging to Christ, we belong to all who belong to Him—not secondarily but *a priori* . . . not by accident or disposition or choice, but in the strictest possible sense, by necessity."[39] In God's economy of salvation the reconciling work of Christ naturally includes the work of the Church as his body existing through the impartation of his Spirit. "The existence of the Church involves a repetition of the incarnation of the Word of God in the person of Jesus Christ."[40] The Church is a non-identical repetition of the incarnation. The church follows the work of Christ in the world, but not in an identical fashion. It exists, by the Spirit, to witness to the incarnation. The work of Christ and the impartation of the Spirit to the Church cannot be separated, nor can they be confused, yet they are together apart of the one work of God in creation and redemption.

Barth affirmed the notion of *extra ecclesiam nulla salus*. Only in the Church can believers both know God and participate in the practices within which God's revelation is concretely embodied. "The Church is the reality which arises and continues wherever the revelation of God in Jesus Christ has made itself known."[41] The Church is the location for truly and fully encountering God because it is the community within

---

Barth's ecclesiology, that he does not actually allow the concrete community to be the church, will be dealt with in chapter four.

37. Barth, *CD* I/1, 189.
38. Barth, *CD* I/2, 210.
39. Ibid., 217.
40. Ibid., 215.
41. Karl Barth, *Against the Stream*, 225.

which God's revelation is received and celebrated.[42] The body of Christ exists to remember, retell, and thus to live the Christian story, and to love and obey the God made known in that story.

The Church in the Doctrine of Election

Von Balthasar asserts that Barth's doctrine of election is the center of his theology.[43] Barth's doctrine of election was a drastic refiguring of the Augustinian-Calvinistic tradition. Election is the very heart of the gospel as Barth tells it; it is the sum of the gospel.[44] Election is first of all the election of Jesus Christ. God in his eternal election declares himself to be for humanity. All of God's dealings with his creation arise out of his free and unchanging grace. That God is for humanity and that sinful humanity is elected to participate in God's glory reveals the eternal will of God. No divine will exists outside that which is fulfilled and revealed in Christ. God in his absolute freedom has bound himself to humanity.[45] Election, according to Barth is the eternal being of God for humanity in the person of Jesus Christ; it is not an absolute decree given apart from the triune life of God.[46] God's election of all in Christ is God's eternal act of self-determination.[47]

---

42. Barth cites with agreement Calvin's notion that the church is the "mother" of all believers. The community is the "definite historical context" in which people become Christians. *CD* IV/2, 614. This is a practical meaning of Cyprian of Carthage's response to Novation and his followers, who led a puritanical schism in Rome: "He can no longer have God for his Father, who has not the Church for his mother." Cyprian, "On the Unity of the Church," c.6.

43. Balthasar, *Theology of Karl Barth*, 172–74.

44. See Barth, *CD* II/2, 3, 10, 13–14, 34. For a fuller discussion of the church in the doctrine of election than is necessary here, see Bender, *Karl Barth's Christological Ecclesiology*, 95–159.

45. Barth, *CD* II/2, 155.

46. The discussions of human freedom in the previous chapter should be remembered in this statement of Barth's doctrine of election. Barth's strong doctrine of election founds human freedom; it does not negate it. This point reveals Barth's basic disagreement with Calvin, whose doctrine of the double decree is derived apart from the Trinity.

47. Bruce McCormack has argued that, for Barth, the Logos does not exist apart from the eternal decision for humanity and the decision to become incarnate. McCormack, "Grace and Being," 95. Such an assertion, McCormack argues, is more radical than Barth even realized. The very being of God is eternally determined by God's decision to be for his creation and to reveal himself in Jesus Christ. In Barth's actualistic ontology

In the two natures of Jesus Christ, he is at once the electing God and the elected human being, and conversely he is the rejecting God and the rejected man. In the person of Jesus Christ God declared both his yes and his no. Both our acceptance by God in grace and our rejection by him in judgment have been borne in the person of Jesus Christ. All of humanity was elected in the election of the humanity of Jesus Christ. All of humanity was judged on the cross.[48] Christ stands on our behalf as the full and true human being in election and rejection. The two antitheses of election and rejection are not equal, but together they constitute the one statement of grace.

The Church is central to Barth's doctrine of election. Israel and the Church are the two parts of the elect community. These two forms of the community of God are the means of witness to God's eternal election in Christ.[49] The church is the gathering of those who must now witness to the eternal mercy and grace known in the election of Jesus Christ.[50] "The Church form of the community reveals the scope of what God wills for man when in His eternal election of grace He elects him for fellowship with Himself."[51] As a fellowship elected for service, the church is not an end unto itself. By their very existence Israel and the church point beyond themselves. As seen before, the primary task given the church in the doctrine of election is witness. At the heart of Barth's theology, the unique Christ leads to the *totus Christus*, identifying himself with the Church as his witness. The asymmetrical unity and difference of Barth's Christological logic still shapes the notion of the totus Christus.[52]

Barth thus discloses the relation between Christology and ecclesiology to be inseparable. First, the church is essentially related to the

---

God's being is in act. God *is* in this eternal act of being for humanity. McCormack, 98–99. The doctrine of the Trinity is logically dependent upon this understanding of eternal election and actualistic ontology. This elicited a response from Paul Molnar in *Divine Freedom and the Doctrine of the Immanent Trinity*. See Hector, "God's Triunity and Self-Determination," 246–61.

48. Barth, *CD* II/2, 453.

49. For Barth's view of Israel's role in election, see Sonderegger, *That Jesus Christ was Born a Jew*, 81–133.

50. Balthasar, *Theology of Karl Barth*, 181. See also O'Grady, *Church in the Theology of Karl Barth*, 106–8.

51. Barth, *CD* II/2, 265.

52. Bender, *Karl Barth's Christological Ecclesiology*, 204.

person of Christ. In revelation, election and reconciliation, the work and being of Christ lead to the work and being of the church. The *totus Christus* includes the church as witness. Secondly, to look ahead, the doctrine of baptism creates a concrete, embodied understanding of the church. Barth's emphasis on the body of Christ depends on his understanding of believers' baptism as initiation into the body. Baptism is one's union with Christ.

The Spirit in the Church

To treat the baptismal being of the church in Barth's ecclesiology I must address the relationship between the Spirit and the church. The completed work of Christ does not eliminate the need for human activity and obedience. According to Barth, it is precisely the finished work of Christ which makes human faithfulness possible. As shown above, the Church exists by the work of Christ; "because He is, it is."[53] Christ makes it possible for human beings to do what they cannot do of themselves, to will what they otherwise would not will: "men are called by the Holy Spirit to participation in Christ's word and work."[54] In Barth's trinitarian doctrine of reconciliation, the Holy Spirit is the quickening and awakening power which awakens human beings from their pride and sloth to a life of freedom in obedience to God. "God in this particular address and gift, God in this awakening power, God as Creator of this other man, is the Holy Spirit."[55] Fundamentally what we can say of the Spirit is that "He is the power of Jesus Christ in which it takes place that there are men who can and must find and see that He is theirs and they are His, that their history is genuinely enclosed in His and His history is equally genuinely enclosed in theirs."[56] The Holy Spirit enables believers to appropriate as their own the conversion, liberation, and orientation that place in Christ. The Holy Spirit proclaims to humanity the reconciliation and justification which Christ accomplished for us.[57]

---

53. Barth, *CD* IV/1, 661.
54. Barth, *Dogmatics in Outline*, 141.
55. Barth, *CD* IV/1, 645.
56. Ibid., 648. Below I will deal with the charge that Barth turns the person of the Holy Spirit into a force or power of Christ. This quote suggests that reading.
57. See Barth *CD* IV/2, 304, and *CD* IV/1, 647.

In George Hunsinger's term, the Holy Spirit is the mediator of communion. The Spirit creates communion within God and within the church. Following the Augustinian tradition, Barth conceives of the Holy Spirit as the fellowship and the love between Father and Son. The essence of the Spirit's work is the building of *koinonia*.[58] The Spirit is at times spoken of as the agent of that communion and at times as that communion itself. Either way, the Spirit is a distinct hypostasis of the one God.[59]

> The Holy Spirit is the power, and His action the work, of the co-ordination of the being of Jesus Christ and that of His community as distinct from and yet enclosed within it. Just as the Holy Spirit, as Himself an eternal divine "person" or mode of being, as the Spirit of the Father and the Son (*qui ex Patre Filioque procedit*), is the bond of peace between the two, so in the historical work of reconciliation He is the One who constitutes and guarantees the unity of the *totus Christus*.[60]

The doctrine of redemption is the particular work of the Spirit in Barth's theology. The doctrine of reconciliation is christocentric, but this does not exclude or render unnecessary the work of the Holy Spirit. For Barth, "Christ's reconciling work was not to be devalued but rather upheld as 'intrinsically perfect,' yet no 'subordinationist' displacement could be allowed of the Spirit's own special work of redemption."[61]

The Spirit's unique work within the life of the Trinity is to point to the other members of the Trinity. The Spirit witnesses to Christ. "The Holy Spirit . . . is the Lord who acts on us in revelation as the Redeemer, who really sets us free and really makes us the children of God, who really gives His Church the words to speak God's Word, because in this work of His on us He simply does in time what He does eternally in God."[62] The Holy Spirit comes to us only by and as a result of the Word, never by an independent way which goes around or acts apart from the Word.[63] The Spirit's role in revelation and reconciliation is not secondary or dispensable, yet it never exists independent or given as something

58. Hunsinger, *Disruptive Grace*, 185.
59. Ibid., 153.
60. Barth, *CD* IV/3.2, 760.
61. Hunsinger, *Disruptive Grace*, 150.
62. Barth, *CD* I/1, 471.
63. Barth, *CD* I/2, 236.

new. For Barth the Holy Spirit is always and only the Spirit of Christ. It has its role in relation to the work of Christ as the teacher of the Word.

As I have already shown, the witness of the Spirit always includes the concrete, historical witness of the community which the Spirit gathers, upbuilds, and sends into the world. In the power of the Spirit, human beings are made to be witnesses to Christ's proclamation in the world. As Barth states the matter, "our 'I believe in the Holy Spirit' would be empty if it did not also include in a concrete, practical, and obligatory way the 'I believe one Holy Catholic and Apostolic Church.' We believe the Church as the place where the crown of humanity, namely, man's fellow-humanity, may become visible in Christocratic brotherhood."[64] The human community is converted into the body of Christ by the work of the Spirit. By the Spirit's activity human beings share in the work of Christ in the form of this new community.[65]

The objective work of Christ becomes subjective by the operation of the Holy Spirit. The subjective appropriation is realized in the sphere of the church by the Holy Spirit. The process of the objective becoming subjective is actually identified with the life of the body of Christ.[66] This subjective revelation is not something to be added to revelation and reconciliation in Christ as a secondary reality. "There is no special or second revelation of the Spirit alongside that of the Son."[67] The revelation of God *to humanity* is the particular work of the Holy Spirit. The Spirit is the power of God as God awakens human beings to his truth and his new reality. Human beings are caught up by God in the event of revelation. Revelation exists for us. We can receive the revelation of God only by the Spirit which brings the Word to our hearing.[68] Of ourselves human beings have no capacity to receive God's revelation. The Triune God's (objective) revelation of himself also creates the people who are able to accept it (subjective revelation). In Barth's understanding, this is the particular and absolutely essential role of the Holy Spirit.

---

64. Karl Barth, *Humanity Of God*, 65.
65. Thompson, *Holy Spirit in the Theology of Karl Barth*, 89–91.
66. Barth, *CD* I/2, 248. See Thompson, *Holy Spirit in the Theology of Karl Barth*, 93.
67. Barth, *CD* I/1, 474.
68. Barth, *CD* I/2, 246–47. Eberhard Jüngel asserts that the Holy Spirit makes the history of Jesus Christ an existential reality for Christians. Jüngel, "Karl Barths Lehre Von Der Taufe," 273–74.

The church exists only through the activity of God the Holy Spirit making sinful human beings into the servants and witnesses of God—something, of themselves, they could never be. The Holy Spirit creates the fellowship in which witnesses become brothers and sisters in Christ. It is the particular work of the Spirit to create community. Thus the Holy Spirit is the direct line from Christ to his community.[69] Everything which we can say about the community assumes that it is founded by the Holy Spirit and must continue to be so founded in each moment.[70] Barth fully affirms the activity of the Holy Spirit in the formation and existence of the church. According to the three ecclesiological sections of volume four, the Holy Spirit is the awakening, quickening, and enlightening power in which Jesus Christ gathers, upbuilds, and sends the community as the earthly-historical form of His existence. In short, "The Christian community, the true Church, arises and is only as the Holy Spirit works—the quickening power of the living Lord Jesus Christ."[71]

At the same time, the Holy Spirit remains Lord in relation to the church and to humanity itself. The Spirit is never given over to or confined within the institution of the church. The church is not the incarnation of the Holy Spirit in the ontological sense of this phrase. Barth is concerned that notions of the incarnation of the Spirit in the church will ultimately sacrifice the free sovereignty of God. He says that, if the church is a continuation of the incarnation,

> then manifestly the lordship of Jesus Christ and the power of God's providence would have fallen under the sovereign power and administrative control of Christendom and enslaved mankind would have to expect its salvation from us—from our clear grasp of the world's historical situation, from the progress and action and hoped-for future triumphs of the church as the embodiment and representative of Jesus Christ and God himself.[72]

Barth was overly concerned not to identify the practices of the church, such as baptism, with the activity of the Holy Spirit. He did not wish to confine the free Spirit to the works worked by the church. This led him to react against the notion of sacrament as seen in the discus-

---

69. Barth, *CD* IV/2, 319–23.

70. Barth, *CD* IV/1, 647. As we declare the church's freedom and its voluntary nature in subsequent chapters we must remember this prior assumption.

71. Barth, *CD* IV/2, 617.

72. Karl Barth, "No Christian Marshall Plan," 1330.

sion of baptism. The "sacraments" are human works, not divine works. Thus, in his doctrine of baptism, baptism with water remains distinct from the baptism with the Holy Spirit for Barth. Ultimately, Barth says, we have very little information regarding the work of the Holy Spirit.[73] Barth affirms Calvin's reference to the *arcana operatione Spiritus*, the hidden work of the Spirit.[74] He concludes that it is the work of the Holy Spirit through which "there are men who can and must find and see that He [Christ] is theirs and they are His, that their history is genuinely enclosed in His and His history is equally genuinely enclosed in theirs."[75]

The Spirit and the Practices of the Church

A crucial question remains: what is the relationship between the being and work of the Holy Spirit and the being and work of the church, such as the practice of baptism? Whether we understand baptism in sacramental or in non-sacramental fashion is central to how the work and being of the Spirit in the Church are also understood. Barth's critics have alleged that he has either ignored or at least left pneumatology largely underdeveloped. The hesitancy on Barth's part to relate the Spirit to the practices of the church is credited as a failure in pneumatology. It is thought that, in his emphasis upon the centrality of Christ, Barth did not allow for the work of the Holy Spirit as a fully active member of the Trinity. According to Reinhard Hütter, "For Barth . . . the Church's practices remain, as witnessing responses, radically distinguished from the Holy Spirit's activity."[76]

Robert Jenson and Joseph Mangina have both sought to point out the ecclesiological consequences for what is to them an underdeveloped

---

73. He states: "how gladly we would hear and know and say something more, something more precise, something more palpable concerning the way in which the work of the Holy Spirit is done. . . . The confession *credo in Spiritum Sanctum* does not tell us anything concerning this How." Barth, *CD* IV/1, 648. On the anonymity of the Spirit see Rogers, "Mystery of the Spirit in Three Traditions," 243–60.

74. See the small print in Barth, *CD* I/2, 240–42. Calvin, *Institutes*, III.1.4. In fact, some of Calvin's main emphases in the little chapter 3.1 of the *Institutes* are central to Barth's development of pneumatology. These include the notion of the Holy Spirit as the bond which unites Christians with Christ and faith as the work of the Spirit in believers. According to Calvin, faith is the principle work of the Holy Spirit. This emphasis is evident in Barth's main pneumatological discussions in volume one.

75. Barth, *CD* IV/1, 648.

76. Hütter, "Karl Barth's 'Dialectical Catholicity,'" 150.

pneumatology in Barth. Jenson argues that Barth's commitment to the western understanding of the Spirit, as the love between Father and Son involving the Filioque, excludes the Spirit from the relation because it is the relation itself.[77] This understanding of the Spirit, he argues, leaves Barth with, in essence, a binitarian conception of God. In practice, Barth speaks only of the Spirit in impersonal terms as a force or power. The result of the avoidance of the Spirit is an avoidance of a robust doctrine of the Church in Barth.[78] In response, George Hunsinger has asserted that Jenson requires saving work on the part of the Spirit in addition to that of Christ. He faults Jenson for questioning the accomplishment of our salvation completely at Golgotha.[79] For Barth, any effort to make the Holy Spirit's work necessary apart from or to complete the cross of Christ is inadequate. "In Barth's theology it is Jesus Christ who constitutes the saving significance of the Holy Spirit in a way that is not true in reverse. . . . It is the saving significance of the Holy Spirit to impart and bear witness to Jesus Christ."[80]

Joseph Mangina also asserts that Barth refuses to recognize the Spirit's presence in the practices of the church. He argues that this refusal makes the church's life episodic and, as a result, that Barth's ecclesiology lacks persistence in time.[81] He identifies the main problem with Barth's ecclesiology as Barth's refusal to identify the work of the

---

77. Jenson, "You Wonder Where the Spirit Went," 301.

78. Ibid., 302–3. Others have similarly critiqued Barth for reducing distinct personhood of the Holy Spirit. In particular Moltmann has critiqued the Augustinian understanding of the Spirit as the bond of love between Father and Son in Barth. See Moltmann, *Trinity and the Kingdom*, 139–44.

79. Hunsinger, *Disruptive Grace*, 162. As the context of Jenson's statement shows, he was arguing, not that the work of Christ was insufficient, but that Christ's death without Christ's resurrection is incomplete. Jenson says, "Much theology has proceeded as if the Crucifixion were by itself the encompassing burden of the message, as if 'Jesus died for us' were itself the defining claim. Theologians have too often constructed their systems as if *Christ fully accomplished our salvation at Golgotha*, and was raised only because, being immortal God, he could not remain dead, or as the consequence for the human Jesus of what he did on the cross." Words in italics are those quoted by Hunsinger. Jenson, *Systematic Theology*, 179. See further the exchange between Hunsinger and Jenson regarding Jenson's *Systematic Theology* in the *Scottish Journal of Theology*, Hunsinger, "Robert Jenson's Systematic Theology," 161–200 and Jenson, "Response," 228–32.

80. Hunsinger, *Disruptive Grace*, 157.

81. Mangina, "Stranger as Sacrament," 333.

Spirit with the social forms and practices of the church.[82] He repeats the charge of Jenson that the ecclesiological problems arise from a 'short-circuiting' of the Spirit's work. In his reading, Barth does not give the church a positive role in the economy of salvation because the Holy Spirit is given little to do after the crucifixion.[83]

Reinhard Hütter has also argued that Barth's pneumatology has two problems. "What is lost in this pneumatological account is (a) the Holy Spirit as distinct trinitarian "identity" (hypostasis) and (b) the Spirit's distinct economy as enacted through the Spirit's works."[84] With Jenson, Hütter thinks that in Barth's trinitarian theology "the Holy Spirit, as the mode of God's self-manifestation, is rather identical with God's action."[85] Hütter critiques Barth for giving the Spirit "no real work of its own within the framework of the trinitarian economy of salvation."[86]

These critics have identified a problematic element of Barth's theology. Barth's view of the Spirit in the church is not wholly adequate, precisely in line with the late rejection of sacramental mediation. And yet we cannot dismiss Barth out of hand. A helpful term is offered by Eugene Rogers who states that the Spirit is "eclipsed" by the Son in Barth's theology. He claims this is a rhetorical move on Barth's part to turn the question of the Holy Spirit into a question about Christ. Thus he never speaks of the Spirit apart from the Son. In Barth's theology the interval between the work of Christ and the work of the Holy Spirit is closed.[87] Barth makes this move because of his hesitancy regarding the subjectivism of the nineteenth century which Barth sees aligned with the existential, participatory work of the Holy Spirit as opposed to the objective work of Jesus Christ.[88] Barth's hesitancy is also rooted in his

82. Ibid.

83. Mangina, "Bearing the Marks of Jesus," 270–82.

84. Hütter, "Church," 30–31. This essay is a compact version of his argument in *Suffering Divine Things*; see especially pages 103–15.

85. Hütter, *Suffering Divine Things*, 112.

86. Ibid.

87. Rogers, "Eclipse of the Spirit in Karl Barth," 173–90.

88. As Rogers states: "It is true that the Holy Spirit is *responsible* for the human reception of revelation. But the Holy Spirit is not therefore *reducible* to the subjective. Precisely if the Holy Spirit is the (relatively) independent *witness* to the revelation by the Father of the Son, then the Spirit has its own objectivity. Yet we can recognize this objectivity as such only if we see the Spirit as an actor united to the other persons, not their act. The Spirit has the objectivity of a witness, not the subjectivity of a response." "Eclipse of the Spirit in Karl Barth," 184.

insistence upon the freedom of the Holy Spirit. The Spirit could never be controlled by the church. In this light the eclipse is understandable, but still has problematic effects for ecclesiology.

That the Holy Spirit does not function as Mangina and Hütter would have it in Barth's dogmatics does not mean that Barth denies either the identity of the Spirit or the activity of the Spirit in God's salvific economy. The assertion that Barth does not give the Spirit its own existence cannot be held.[89] As seen above the role of the Holy Spirit in creating the Body of Christ as witness to Christ, is essential in the economy of God's reconciling the world. Such interpretations tend to overlook "the trinitarian dramatics of the doctrine of reconciliation" as Barth develops it.[90] We must remember the work of the Spirit as the mediator of communion and the enabler of witness to Christ.

Yet, on a basic level these critiques of Barth do point to a shortcoming in Barth's ecclesiology. Barth's separation of the Spirit from the practices of the church, would leave the visible church as a purely human institution, despite his desire to avoid such a conclusion. Given his insistence that the Spirit makes the church, his disconnection of the Spirit from the practices of the church seems like a strange move. Protecting both the freedom of the Spirit and the ethical nature of the church's practices led him to sever those practices from what makes them meaningful, the work of the Spirit. "In 'ethicizing' baptism he desacramentalizes the Church."[91] Yet, this need not have been the case. Theology after Barth has seen the need to make room for a "concrete pneumatology" where the Spirit works in the concrete practices and structures of Christianity.[92] Such an understanding would have to retain the free activity of the human being without excessively separating divine and human action.

---

89. To cite one example: "Within the deepest depths of deity, as the final thing to be said about Him, God is God the Spirit as He is God the Father and God the Son. The Spirit outpoured at Pentecost is the Lord, God Himself, just as the Father and just as Jesus Christ is the Lord, God Himself." Barth, *CD* I/1, 466.

90. Webster, "Translator's Introduction," ix.

91. Yocum, *Ecclesial Mediation in Karl Barth*, 174.

92. Mangina, "Bearing the Marks of Jesus," 301–2. Mangina states that he borrows the term from David Yeago.

Conclusion

In Barth's theology the Holy Spirit is always in the church making it what it is, which makes the separation of Spirit and baptism all the more puzzling. Barth's understanding of the Spirit's indispensable role in the life of the church is held in spite of his non-sacramental understanding of baptism. The question remains, therefore, whether Barth needed to reject baptism as a sacrament? How do we hold to a sacramental view of the church so that the work of the Spirit is embodied in church practices without sacrificing the ethical nature of those practices? Can we affirm that the life of the church is a participation in the life of the triune God without losing the freedom of God by at once tying God to a sinful, human institution and thus making grace automatic? One can fully affirm both the freedom of God and the ethical nature of the church's life and practices without denying the Holy Spirit a part in the church's practices. Barth could have found a clear instance of this in the sacrament of believers' baptism.

3

Baptism as a Sacrament

THIS CHAPTER WILL RETURN TO THE NATURE OF THE SACRAMENTS IN Barth's theology. It will highlight Barth's understanding of the sacraments in earlier portions of the *Dogmatics*. Subsequently it will detail the views of theologians in the baptist tradition who were able to retain the understanding of baptism as a sacrament in their insistence upon believers' baptism. It will then rethink Barth's position on baptism as a sacrament and thus baptism's relation to the church.

Barth on the Sacraments

Barth's understanding of the sacraments developed over the course of writing the *Dogmatics*.[1] His account of the Spirit's action in the practices of the church is much stronger in earlier volumes. In volume one, Barth spoke of baptism as a sign of revelation. The subjective reality of revelation which is realized by the Holy Spirit consists of "definite signs" of the objective reality. Through these signs, the Word which entered the world continues to speak. They are instruments through which God has His Word heard. They are a creaturely reality which veils the Word to bring it close to humanity. These signs point to revelation.[2] Creaturely realities, events, orders, and relations become, not in and of themselves, but, through the activity of God, signs of His revelation. God's objective revelation reaches human beings "by means of the divine sign-giving."[3]

---

1. See Schlüter, *Karl Barths Tauflehre*, 33–56. John Yocum offers a good treatment of Barth and the larger notion of "sacramental mediation" across the *CD*. Yocum, *Sacramental Mediation in Karl Barth*.

2. Barth, *CD* I/2, 223.

3. Ibid., 233.

Barth states, "God's revelation comes mediately to man in that it actually never does come without creaturely mediators or media, and it always occurs in a creaturely area and framework."[4] In the biblical witness these signs include the election of the people of Israel, circumcision, the activity of the prophets in Israel, the sacrificial system, and the Temple. All Old Testament signs were replaced when Christ was made manifest on earth. The Church takes the place of the ancient sign-world. The signs after Christ, after the messiah has come, are preaching, baptism and the Lord's supper. The entire existence and history of the church belong to the sign-world of the New Testament.[5]

In volume II/1, Barth again says that revelation is the giving of signs. In his own self-witness God represents His truth to the knowledge and existence of creatures. We can say quite simply that revelation means sacrament, i.e., "the self-witness of God, the representation of His truth, and therefore of the truth in which He knows Himself, in the form of creaturely objectivity and therefore in a form which is adapted to our creaturely knowledge."[6] In this earlier material, the incarnate Jesus is absolutely unique as God's revelation. Jesus is the "first sacrament," not in the sense that he is the beginning of a similar series, but because the incarnation is

> a beginning of which there are continuations; a sacramental continuity stretches backwards into the existence of the people of Israel, whose Messiah He is, and forwards into the existence of the apostolate and the Church founded on the apostolate. The humanity of Jesus Christ as such is the first sacrament, the foundation of everything that God instituted and used in His revelation as a secondary objectivity both before and after the epiphany of Jesus Christ.[7]

In relation to Jesus as the true sacrament, all other signs are therefore "secondary" but do truly signify the truth revealed in the incarnation. By the grace of God the creature can be the "instrument and sign of God Himself."[8] This shows that earlier in the *Church Dogmatics*, before

---

4. Barth, *CD* I/2, 224.
5. Ibid., 227.
6. Barth, *CD* II/1, 52.
7. Ibid., 54. See Yocum, *Ecclesial Mediation in Karl Barth*, 33–34.
8. Barth, *CD* II/1, 54.

Barth denies the sacramental nature of baptism, baptism was truly a sign, but still only a secondary sign of the true sacrament, i.e., the humanity of Christ. The connection of these secondary signs to the true sacrament seems to be functional. They give testimony to the incarnation as true sacrament.[9] Barth's understanding of Christ as the one true mediator between God and humanity will later be developed in a way which makes it difficult for him to allow any other finite signs to thus mediate, even in a secondary manner.[10] Doing so seems to undermine the view of creaturely media developed here.[11]

By volume four of the *Dogmatics* Barth had come to deny that baptism is a sacrament. He gave the credit for this primarily to his son Markus's work on baptism in the New Testament.[12] As Webster notes, Barth moves from a "sacramental continuity" between the humanity of Jesus and all creaturely signs to a concept of "attestation." The creaturely signs attest or witness to the complete person and work of Christ.[13] The perfection of the incarnation is effective for all human history and does not need to be repeated or supplemented. Jesus Christ is the only true sacrament and baptism with the Holy Spirit, which is the enablement of faith in believers, is the one sacramental sign. The humanity of Jesus is the only true mystery, the only place where the finite world truly bears the presence of God.[14]

William Stacy Johnson argues that Barth's strong stance regarding the non-sacramental nature of baptism does not necessarily constitute a radical break with his earlier theology. He argues that Barth's rejection of the sacramental does not mean that Barth rejected all understanding of "sacramental reality whatsoever."[15] Thus, he asserts that Barth's work in IV/4 was not intended to eliminate the sign-giving function

---

9. Buckley "Christian Community, Baptism, and Lord's Supper," 201–3; and Johnson, *Mystery of God*, 166–70.

10. See Yocum, *Ecclesial Mediation in Karl Barth*, 56–57 and 92, and Bender, *Karl Barth's Christological Ecclesiology*, 280–81.

11. Yocum, *Ecclesial Mediation in Karl Barth*, 41.

12. Karl Barth, *CD* IV/4, x. Markus Barth's work was: *Die Taufe ein Sakrament?*

13. Webster, *Barth's Ethics of Reconciliation*, 128.

14. Johnson, *Mystery of God*, 168.

15. Ibid., 168. The incarnation "both encloses and transcends the secret of creation, that is the great Christian mystery and sacrament beside which there is, in the strict and proper sense, no other." Barth, *CD* IV/2, 40.

of baptism and the Lord's supper as signifying the true humanity and divinity of Jesus Christ. Barth can say, in *The Christian Life*, that baptism belongs "to something that God has permitted and entrusted and commanded to Christians, namely the answering, attesting, and proclaiming of the one act of revelation of salvation that has taken place in the one Mediator between God and humanity (1 Tim 2:5) who himself directly actualized and activates and declares himself in the power of the Holy Spirit."[16] Baptism is clearly not meant to repeat or add to the true sacrament of Christ. Yet it does bear a continuity with Christ, even if a "symbolic continuity." Thus, Johnson concludes, Barth's late understanding of baptism is not inconsistent with what he has been doing throughout his entire theology. Barth's view is in keeping with his non-foundationalist approach to our knowledge and experience of God. Barth worked with the assumption that no ground or foundation, either empirical or rational, can be found outside of God's self-revelation upon which to construct a theology with absolute certainty. "Barth's revision of traditional sacramental theology reflects his primary conviction that God is not simple 'given' or 'present' to human disposal, otherwise than in the hiddenness of the human life of Jesus Christ."[17] The beginning of the Christian life remains God's work and cannot be controlled or made a human possibility.

In Paul Molnar's evaluation Barth's late rejection of sacrament is a change in his theology, but not a radical break because it was based on presuppositions he was working with throughout the *Church Dogmatics*.[18] He argues that Barth's rejection of the notion of sacrament fits his doctrine of God, in which he rejected any monism, dualism, or synthesis. Monism sees an identity between God and creation where the difference is lost. Dualism posits an unbridgeable gap between Creator and creature in which real relation is made impossible. Barth also rejects any idea of synthesis between God and the world. God freely enters into relation or fellowship with a world that remains different and other to him.[19] Thus in baptism Barth wants a distinction between divine and

---

16. Barth, *Christian Life*, 46. Quoted in Johnson, *Mystery of God*, 169.

17. Johnson, *Mystery of God*, 170. Where Johnson does fault Barth is for what he considers to be an overly individualistic turn in his rejection of infant baptism. As seen in chapter one, such a critique is not accurate.

18. Molnar, *Karl Barth and the Theology of the Lord's Supper*, 3, 233, and 304.

19. Ibid., 231–33. According to Molnar, Barth's view of sacrament in his late theology is based on his consistent distinction (but not separation) between the immanent

human action. "God does not hand over his divine self-disclosure to the form in and through which he chooses to reveal himself."[20] While there is a true unity, Barth would not let the Church's action be identical with the acts of the Holy Spirit.[21]

The real change in Barth's theology of Baptism is that he "has removed from the visible historical sphere one of the signs to which he previously believed we could refer in an attempt to find assurance that we are living in the Spirit." Barth protected the free work of the Holy Spirit but at times did not take into account the concrete work accomplished by the Holy Spirit. By moving away from his earlier notion of secondary objectivity in signs Barth was left with an ambiguous stance regarding the Spirit's relation to the practices of the church.[22] The issue is "when we speak of the sacraments as symbols we cannot allow their symbolic nature to be dictated *by* any ontology of symbolic reality which can be discerned apart from faith in Christ."[23] Barth could have affirmed an understanding of sacraments based on his previous theology, but following another stream in his theology choose to reject the sacramental nature of these church practices.[24]

John Yocum's recent work on Barth's development of sacramental mediation suggests that there is a more fundamental change in Barth's theology when he rejects the sacramental nature of baptism. It was a radical change which, while not hard to see coming, still comes as a significant shift.[25] Barth moves from the sacramental view of symbolic actions and the notion of sign-giving in the first volumes to an increasingly strained relation between God's action and human action. Early in the *CD* the relation between divine action and human action was asymmetrical but Barth did offer some space for a secondary form of sacramental mediation.[26] According to Yocum a strain between human

---

and the economic Trinity. God is the same *ad intra* and *ad extra*, but what God does in the world is always enclosed in the immanent life of God. The distinction between immanent and economic Trinity must be remembered. Ibid., 210–11.

20. Ibid., 229.
21. Ibid., 136.
22. Ibid., 237.
23. Ibid., 301.
24. Ibid., 238, 301.
25. Yocum, *Ecclesial Mediation in Karl Barth*, xii, 69, and 145.
26. Ibid., 33, 41, 92.

and divine action characterizes Volume IV of the *Church Dogmatics*.[27] He notes that "in discussing the uniquely effective divine action and the imperative corresponding action of the community, there is a marked concern with clarifying and distinguishing who is operating effectively at any given time."[28] Even so there was nothing in Barth's theology that made his late development necessary and it effected the coherence of his entire theology.[29] To move from baptism as a mediating sign of revelation to denying any sacramental mediation in baptism is a significant shift, even if elements in his work suggested this possibility.

Baptist Sacramentalism

It is generally assumed that baptist theology has followed the Zwinglian understanding of a memorial or pointing sign, and this is largely correct, but recent scholarship has argued that Baptist theology, particularly in Britain, has also included a stream of theologians who viewed baptism as an effective, or participatory sign.[30] It will be helpful here to briefly examine the views of some of these proponents of a sacramental believers' baptism.

General Baptist Thomas Grantham published, in 1678, a work entitled *Christianismus Primitivus*. In it he criticized the baptism of infants, and yet he spoke of baptism for the remission of sins.[31] For Grantham, the experience of forgiveness of sins was an effect of baptism.[32] Thus did he link baptism with grace and the forgiveness of sins. Baptism is made effective only by faith, and thus he would not have accepted a notion of baptism working *ex opere operato*. Baptism is the way in which we "sacramentally" receive forgiveness, the gift of the Holy Spirit and the

---

27. Ibid., 83, 96, 175.

28. Ibid., 103.

29. Ibid., 69, 145.

30. Fowler, *More Than a Symbol*. I am indebted to Fowler's important work for leading me to most of the quotes from these historical sacramental Baptists. The works of Grantham and Keach were accessed through the Early English Books Database. See also Cross, *Baptism and the Baptists*, and "Dispelling the Myth."

31. Grantham, *Christianismus Primitivus*, Book 2, second part, ch 1, sect. V, page 19. He wrote that "baptism is joyned with this Gospel repentance, that as repentance being now necessary to the admission of Sinners into the Church of Christ, even so Baptism being joyned thereto, by the will of God, is necessary to the same end."

32. Fowler, 28.

washing of the conscience.³³ Benjamin Keach, in 1689, also argued that baptism was effective for the remission of sins. Baptism is a "lively Sign or Symbol" for the "washing of regeneration."³⁴ Like Grantham, Keach argues that baptism is not effective in a mechanical way, or without the faith of the candidate. Thus baptism is not effective merely as a rite performed; but rather the Spirit acts upon those who come in faith, regenerating them. Baptism is a medium or instrument of divine grace.³⁵ Both Keach and Grantham thus held a sacramental understanding of baptism that attempted to avoid a mechanical view of the sacrament. Stanley Fowler concludes that a significant trend within seventeenth century Baptist thought urged an instrumental view of baptism in which the Spirit "bestows spiritual benefit through baptism."³⁶

One other prominent example, this time from the nineteenth century, is Robert Hall Jr. Hall dealt with baptism in the context of debates over whether or not Baptist churches should allow people to their communion tables who were baptized as infants. Hall argued for an "open" communion in his 1815 work *On Terms of Communion*. Within this context he says that "the effusion of the Spirit" was not given during the earthly life of Christ but at Pentecost. "In the subsequent history, we perceive that this gift was, on all ordinary occasions, conferred in connexion with baptism."³⁷ Christian baptism is different from John's baptism because of the "superior effects with which it was accompanied," including the "supply of supernatural gifts and graces."³⁸ Hall clearly states that "the baptism with the Holy Ghost, or the copious effusion of spiritual influences, in which primitive Christians were, so to speak, immersed, was appointed to follow the *sacramental* use of water, under the Christian economy."³⁹ Hall insisted that at baptism the believer is

33. Grantham, *Sigh for Peace*, 87–88.

34. Keach, *Gold Refin'd*, 82–83.

35. Vaughn, "Benjamin Keach," 63. All three persons of the Trinity are present in baptism: "1. The Father seals it and honours it. 2. The Son is there, and subjects it, shewing what an honourable respect he has to it. . . . 3. The Spirit also *descended like a Dove, and rested upon him*; the Holy Ghost puts his Seal upon it, and in a glorious manner owns it." Keach, quoted in Vaughn, "Benjamin Keach," 63.

36. Fowler, 32. These two Baptists are only part of the larger trend that Fowler demonstrates.

37. Hall, *On Terms of Communion*, 298.

38. Ibid., 297.

39. Ibid., 298. Italics added.

gifted with the Holy Spirit. Baptism effects that donation, not as a mere rite but by prompting for union with Christ that occurs by faith alone.

Some representative twentieth century sacramental baptists show that a sacramental understanding of baptism which insists on the importance of faith is still an important theological position.[40] George Beasley-Murray has been one of the strongest Baptist voices arguing for the sacramental nature of baptism. Beasley-Murray stands at the head of a twentieth century movement among British Baptists who sought to regain a sacramental understanding of baptism.[41] He states: "the idea that baptism is a purely symbolic rite must be pronounced not alone unsatisfactory but out of harmony with the New Testament itself."[42] According to his interpretation of key biblical passages, baptism is said to bestow many gifts: forgiveness of sins, union with Christ, membership in the church, possession of the Spirit, regeneration, grace to live, inheritance of the Kingdom, and a pledge for the coming resurrection. Ultimately, in baptism the church is "concerned less with water than with the Living God."[43] In the New Testament, "baptism is thus represented as the occasion when *the Spirit* brings to new life him that believes in the Son of Man lifted up on the cross to heaven."[44] Beasley-Murray, like all these other baptist figures, insists on the baptism of believers. He argues for the inseparable connection between faith and baptism. "God's gracious giving to faith belongs to the context of baptism, even as God's gracious giving in baptism is to faith."[45] The same gifts of grace are associated both with faith and with baptism. The New Testament connection between faith and grace is key to the sacramental view of believers' baptism.

---

40. In addition to the earlier movement mentioned in the next note, see the more recent efforts in Fiddes, *Reflections on the Water*; and Cross and Thompson, *Baptist Sacramentalism* and *Baptist Sacramentalism 2*.

41. Fowler, *More Than a Symbol*, 89–155. Included in this movement are Clark, *Approach to the Theology of the Sacraments*; White, *Biblical Doctrine of Initiation*; Gilmore, *Baptism and Christian Unity*. See also, Gilmore, *Christian Baptism*. The precursor to this movement was the work of Baptist Old Testament scholar H. Wheeler Robinson.

42. Beasley-Murray, *Baptism in the New Testament*, 263.

43. Ibid., 266.

44. Ibid., 278.

45. Ibid., 272. "Baptism is the divinely appointed rendezvous of grace for faith." Ibid., 273.

John Howard Yoder, a Mennonite theologian, has been the strongest theological voice for the Anabaptist tradition in contemporary theology. In his little book *Body Politics*, Yoder offers a discussion of baptism from this perspective. Baptism, Yoder writes, is an initiation into life within a new people. The church is a new social reality into which people are introduced in baptism. This new social reality consists of a united people who are from different nations and peoples brought together in a new community that cuts across these old boundaries. Yoder argues that infant baptism becomes a celebration of birth. The baptism of infants does not serve as an initiation which crosses boundaries, but actually reinforces given identities. Baptism must involve conversion, the transfer of citizenship. Yoder critiques the 'Baptist' view in which baptism is an outward symbol that affirms or signifies an inward experience. On the contrary "Baptism *is* the formation of a new people whose newness and togetherness explicitly relativize prior stratifications and classification."[46] Not simply a symbolic act, baptism is a political act. It is the establishment of a radically egalitarian society.

James McClendon identifies baptism as a remembering sign. It involves five elements: entrance into a community awaiting the new age, conversion to the newness as a condition of entrance, God's forgiveness of sins, the name of Jesus as identifying mark on baptized, and gift of the Spirit to the community and to each member upon baptism.[47] With these elements involved, baptism is a convergence of one's own baptismal story with that of Jesus. Our baptism is a recapitulation of Jesus's baptism. "The story of the baptized is of entry into a realm where the old has passed away, the new has come."[48]

Baptism is a "sign," rather than a "mere" symbol or an objective sacrament. A sign, McClendon argues, does something. The action done in baptism is performed by the community, the candidate, and God. Thus baptism is a "triply enacted sign, a deed in which God and candidate and (through its designated minister) church all act to effect a turn in one life-story (the candidate's) on the basis of Jesus's crucified and risen life."[49] Baptism is a sign of salvation that is tied to faith.

46. Yoder, *Body Politics*, 33.
47. McClendon, *Doctrine*, 386–87.
48. Ibid., 387.
49. McClendon, *Doctrine*, 390. See McClendon, "Baptism as a Performative Sign," 403–16.

Yet when baptism became an infant rite the "privilege of Christian initiation was effectively revoked . . . for the child of many a Christian home."[50] McClendon links the loss of baptism as an effectual sign to the Constantinian compromise when the church was assimilated into culture. When society was itself Christianized, the turn or conversion signified in repentant baptism no longer seemed necessary.

British Baptist John Colwell offers a significant theology of the sacraments from a Baptist perspective. His affirmation of the sacraments is first a doctrine of God and of God's creation of the world. The Trinitarian relations are the basis for our understanding of sacramental mediation. The relatedness of the persons of the Trinity is mediated relatedness, this is what maintains the distinctness between the persons of the Trinity who mutually interpenetrate and fully indwell one another. For this reason he criticizes the Western tradition for depersonalizing the Spirit.[51] This diminishing of the Spirit causes problems within the doctrine of the Trinity as well as sacramental theology. He relates the Western (Augustinian) tendency to reduce the Spirit to the love between the persons of the Father and Son to the Western focus on absolute will. When the loving relations of the persons of the Trinity are collapsed, God becomes a single monarchical sovereignty.[52] In turn, Colwell argues that there is "no unmediated presence or action of God within or toward creation; the relatedness of God to creation is mediated in the Son and through the Spirit. Or to put the matter more *theo*logically: God related to creation as the One that he is, as the Father, the Son, and the Spirit, as the One whose free, loving relatedness is itself mediated. And herein, I believe, lies the possibility for a proper understanding of a sacramental dynamic and of sacramental particulars."[53] Having freely created the physical world, mediated through the Son and Spirit, God relates to his creation mediated through that creation itself.[54]

In particular, God has promised his own presence and gracious action on our behalf through the physical signs of the sacraments. God effects this promise through particular, ordained means. "We therefore

50. McClendon, *Doctrine*, 391.
51. Colwell, *Promise and Presence*, 21.
52. Ibid., 22–24.
53. Ibid., 48.
54. Ibid., 56.

come to the sacraments in the prayerful expectation of the fulfillment of this promise."[55] In this way baptism is neither purely human act, though the human element is irreducible, nor a prison for God. God remains free to lovingly act as he has promised. Colwell develops this view of baptism with an explicit critique of Barth's theology. Baptism is the means by which the Holy Spirit mediates our inclusion into Christ and thus into his Church. This is both ethical and eschatological. We are incorporated into an eschatological union with Christ and as the community of Christ we are to live as his witnesses.[56] Colwell's goal is not to argue for believers' baptism over against infant baptism. He refers to infant baptism as irregular, but never invalid. While faith does not establish baptism, faith is an important part of baptism understood as a prayer for God's grace. "We are not brought to baptism," he explains, "we come to baptism."[57] Only the gracious promise of God makes baptism a sacrament, but the normal practice of this sacrament, as the New Testament affirms, includes the faith and prayer of the one being baptized.

These theologians in the baptist tradition show how a sacramental understanding of believers' baptism is possible. Just as importantly they reveal that such a view is not outside of the baptist tradition in history and recent theology. According to these theologians, God is acting in baptism; something essential happens through the rite. This can inform a rethinking of Barth's rejection of the sacramental nature of baptism. To retain his ecclesiology Barth did not need to reject the sacramental nature of baptism. On the contrary a proper view of the sacrament would have strengthened his understanding of the Spirit in the church.

Rethinking Baptism as a Sacrament

Barth's denial of sacramental mediation was not a necessary move given his earlier theology. A sacrament need not reduce the freedom of the creaturely world, nor enslave God to a mechanistic process. The sac-

---

55. Ibid., 115. Following the traditional understanding, Colwell states, "a sacrament is the instrumental means of God's promise."

56. Colwell, *Promise and Presence*, 124.

57. Ibid., 133. "Those coming to baptism do so repentantly, prayerfully, and expectantly. They come expecting this rite to be the means through which they receive the Spirit and through which they are incorporated into Christ through being incorporated fully into his Church and its sacramental life." Ibid., 144.

raments would be better understood as the Spirit led practices of the church in which God acts and meets the church as he promised to do. What Barth needs is a better understanding of sacramental mediation in the life of the church.[58]

Part of the problem lies in Barth's definition of a sacrament in IV/4. As was seen above, a sacrament for Barth is entirely God's action.[59] This definition is problematic even on Barth's account. Barth's thin account of the Spirit in the church can be overcome only by rethinking his understanding of the Spirit's role in the sacrament. Barth sought to protect the freedom of God and the freedom of the human being. Both of these can and must be affirmed in a sacramental theology. As Christopher Ellis states,

> God's freedom refuses to allow grace to be dispensed on demand or as the result of correctly followed procedures. However, that freedom is the freedom of the God who freely gave His son for our salvation, the freedom of the one who laid out his hands to be pinned to a cross, the freedom of one who lay bound in a borrowed tomb. Here is no capricious deity refusing to be held accountable or truculently ignoring the plea for justice. Here is the freedom of one who freely loves and freely gives and who promises to meet us both in the waters of baptism and in the world to which we are sent.[60]

The freedom of God exists as the freedom of love. God's freedom is the freedom in which God has committed himself to human life. This commitment is the heart of Barth's doctrine of election in which the church is fundamental to God's dealings with the world. In baptism, God condescends to humanity as he lovingly promised to do, without losing his own freedom to the institution of the church.[61]

---

58. Webster, *Barth's Ethics of Reconciliation*, 172.

59. A sacrament is "an event in the world of time and space which is directly initiated and brought to pass by God alone, so that in distinction from all other events it is basically a mystery to human cognition in respect of its origin and possibility." Barth, *CD* IV/4, 108.

60. Ellis, "Baptism and the Sacramental Freedom of God," 42.

61. Molnar finds in Barth's theology an understanding of sacraments based on the promise and command of God. God's promise meets us in the phenomenological realm and is there effective, but not in such a way that God is "dependent upon the phenomena." The divine promise cannot be institutionalized, only held to in faith. Molnar, *Karl Barth and the Theology of the Lord's Supper*, 165. See also Colwell, *Promise and Presence*, 111.

Stanley Fowler argues that Barth's exegesis of the New Testament passages upon which he based his rejection of the sacramental nature of baptism is inadequate.[62] According to Fowler, Barth's exegesis of these baptismal passages is not the natural interpretation of the texts. Barth, in Fowler's view, has theological concerns that lead him to interpret these texts in ways other than what seems to be the plain sense of the text. As such, his separation of water baptism from Spirit baptism is the result of his insistence upon the sovereign freedom of God and not, Fowler argues, the result of good exegesis. In several cases that seem to suggest baptism for forgiveness of sins, Barth asserts that it is the invocation of God and the prior work of the Spirit producing faith that bring forgiveness, not baptism (such as Acts 22:16; Gal 3:27; and Titus 3:5). Barth interprets Heb 10:22 and Eph 5:25–26 as saying that Christ's completed work, not baptism, effects our cleansing. Fowler takes each of Barth's anti-sacramental readings as being, while in several cases possible, not necessary.[63] Fowler notes that Barth omitted a few important texts for understanding the sacramental nature of baptism, such as Acts 2:38 and 1 Cor 6:11 and 12:13. Ultimately Barth's exegesis does not provide him with an adequate ground for his denial of baptism as sacrament.[64] Fowler is correct in asserting that Barth's rejection of the sacramental nature of baptism was directed only at a certain form of sacramentalism, in which the divine act overshadows and basically excludes the human act or in which the church seeks to mechanically control the Spirit. Yet neither of these is necessary for an adequate sacramental understanding of believers' baptism.[65]

Affirming with Barth that baptism is a human work, I also contend, with the tradition, that God acts in baptism. Baptism is an effective, participatory sign, not merely an external, or pointing, sign. Yet Barth

---

62. For this material see Barth, *CD* IV/4, 112–27.

63. Fowler, *More Than a Symbol*, 178–92. It is not my intention to reproduce the treatment and critique of these passages individually, but Barth explains the following: Acts 22:16; Heb 10:22; Eph 5:25–26; Titus 3:5; Gal 3:27; Rom 6:3–4; Col 2:12; John 3:5; Mark 16:16; 1 Pet 3:21. Fowler addresses each of these in turn.

64. Compare the interpretations with those of Beasley-Murray, *Baptism in the New Testament*; White, *Biblical Doctrine of Initiation*, and the writers in Alec Gilmore, *Christian Baptism*. All of these are Baptist interpreters who argue for believers' baptism and for a sacramental understanding of baptism.

65. Fowler, 194. For other critiques of Barth's exegesis see Yocum, *Ecclesial Mediation in Karl Barth*, 162–64 and Dinkler, "Die Taufaussagen des Neuen Testaments," 61–153.

was correct that no confusion should occur between the action of God and human action. As Molnar noted, Barth always rejected any identity, separation, or synthesis between divine and human action.[66] With an adequate notion of sacramental mediation, God can act in baptism without negating the human act. The human act of baptism requires the faith enabled by the Spirit and is used by God as a sign of his activity in the world. The human act thus takes place within the act of God. Sacraments do not have of themselves any innate capacity to mediate God's grace. "They may become true participants in grace in the power of the Holy Spirit as they actually point to the being and activity of the triune God himself. But their limitation is that they cannot do this if they are confused in any way with the action of God."[67] For an adequate account of baptism as a sacrament and thereby for an adequate understanding of the being of the church, Barth's earlier sacramental theology is helpful.[68]

In volume one, Barth detailed his understanding of the three-fold Word of God. George Hunsinger argues that "given the logic of Barth's conception of the threefold Word, no compelling reason would seem to exist why Jesus Christ could not be the one true sacrament Barth insists upon while yet allowing also for secondary and dependent sacramental forms."[69] The three forms of the Word are the revealed Word Jesus Christ, the Written Word of Scripture, and the preached Word.[70] Hunsinger proposes that Barth's understanding of Christ as the one true sacrament could correspond to this framework, with the church and baptism and Eucharist serving as the secondary forms of the sacrament. The Bible and preaching are not in themselves revelatory, but they are used by God as a means of revelation. In like fashion the sacraments do not achieve reconciliation, but the Spirit can use them as a Word or sign participating in Christ's finished work in the incarnation and the cross. Barth could have argued that, like preaching and scripture, the sacraments attest to the Work of God in Christ. As "revelation engen-

---

66. Molnar, *Karl Barth and the Theology of the Lord's Supper*, 35, 238.
67. Ibid., 229.
68. Hunsinger, "Baptism and the Soteriology of Forgiveness," 266.
69. Ibid., 254–55.
70. See Barth, *CD* I/1, 88–120.

ders the Scripture which attests it," so reconciliation engenders church practices which attest it.[71]

Baptism can become "derivatively and indirectly" a sign of reconciliation.[72] Like the eucharist, it becomes an eventful witness and signifier by the power of the Holy Spirit. Thus a "sacramental continuity" exists between the objective work of Christ and the church's "subjective" practice of baptism as participation in his work.[73] Baptism signifies and, by God's activity, becomes our death and burial with Christ, and is thereby our initiation into the church, and our cleansing from sin and beginning of a new, resurrected life. All of this was completed objectively in Christ. The grace bestowed in baptism, as in the being of the church as the body of Christ, allows us to live within Christ's completed work. Baptism is an eventful witness or a performative sign which points to and participates in God's reconciliation of the world to himself in the person and work of Christ. Baptism is an acted sign of salvation.[74] The Holy Spirit works to enable a proper response in a person and that response is expressed in baptism. As Fowler states, "if the Spirit is given to all those who believe, as both Jesus (John 7:37–39) and Paul (Rom. 8:9) affirm, and baptism is the vehicle by which faith comes to expression, then it is appropriate to think in terms of the bestowal of the Spirit through baptism."[75] In the human act of confessing salvation, conversion, and commitment, God is also acting to enable and affirm that confession.

---

71. Barth, *CD* I/1, 115. Barth says in IV/1, "The death of Jesus Christ on Golgotha: no other event, no earlier and no later, no event which simply prepares the way for it, no event which has to give to it the character of an actual event. This is the one *mysterium*, the one sacrament, and the one existential fact before and beside and after which there is no room for any other of the same rank." Barth, *CD* IV/1, 296. Baptism could be a sacrament clearly not "of the same rank" as the death of Christ.

72. "Revelation is originally and directly what the Bible and Church proclamation are derivatively and indirectly, i.e., God's Word." Barth, *CD* I/1, 117.

73. Barth, *CD* II/1, 54.

74. See McClendon, *Doctrine*, 388–91, and "Baptism as a Performative Sign," 403–16. This language of participation may be too strong for even the earlier Barth, but I use it with 1 Cor 10:15–17 and 2 Cor 5:17–19 in mind.

75. Fowler, *More Than a Symbol*, 194. "Baptist sacramentalism is generally rooted in the concept of baptism as the vehicle of faith, the means by which faith becomes a conscious, tangible reality." Ibid., 201.

The New Testament evidence is clear that faith must precede baptism.[76] Because the Holy Spirit gifts us with faith, the Spirit must bring a person to baptism. Thus, a sacramental view of believers' baptism does not mechanically produce salvation or dispense grace. We cannot deny the faith of the human being or the gracious activity of the Spirit in baptism. As George Beasley-Murray states:

> Baptism is the embodiment of the Gospel. The objective givenness of baptism lies in its being a representation of the redemptive act of God in Christ, whereby life from the dead became possible for men, and the means of participation in that act and life through participation in the Christ. God Himself must grant this participation, even as He gave the Christ on the cross and raised Him from death. Yet the very term 'participation' (κοινωνία) is meaningless without the assenting will of the human κοινωνός.... From the human side baptism is a confession of that faith in Jesus as Lord, a joyful committal of self to Him unto the sharing of his death and resurrection, and an appropriation by faith of the boundless grace the Lord has brought through his redemption.... [Baptism is] at one and the same time an act of grace and faith, an act of God and man.[77]

A conception such as the baptist sacramentalism described by Beasley-Murray could have enabled Barth to retain the necessary elements of human and divine action and not reject the sacramental nature of baptism. Faith is the gift of the Holy Spirit and baptism is where faith and confession of Christ are expressed. In this divinely enabled human act the Spirit also meets that faith with grace.[78]

Barth's Kingdom-Oriented Ecclesiology

Given this corrective to Barth's unnecessarily anti-sacramental understanding of baptism, the positive elements of Barth's ecclesiology, as seen in his understanding of baptism, need to be drawn out for contemporary ecclesiology. First, Barth teaches that the church exists as a representation of the kingdom of God. The teleological thrust of Barth's ecclesiology should bring to mind the fact that baptism is entrance into an eschatological movement. We are baptized into the transition

---

76. See Beasley-Murray, *Baptism in the New Testament*, esp. 266–75.
77. Ibid., 271–72.
78. Fowler, *More Than a Symbol*, 201.

from the old age to the new age. The church is the community which proclaims this transition. This historical, teleological thrust links the doctrine of baptism with the heart of Barth's ecclesiology. The goal of the church is the kingdom of God.[79] Baptism is initiation into the community that has as its goal the kingdom of God. As McClendon notes, baptism is a future-oriented rite.[80]

Baptism is related to the vocation of the Christian and the life of the Christian community. The life of the church, which is gathered, upbuilt, and sent into the world by the Holy Spirit, is its primary witness to the world regarding Jesus Christ.[81] Barth's doctrine of baptism, his ecclesiology, and his ethics are inseparably united in his emphasis on witness. Again, we cannot take the idea of witness too lightly. Baptism is the birth into a life of discipleship. Barth's conception of baptism gives his ecclesiology a robust, embodied sense of the task and responsibility of the church. The mission of the church is at the heart of Barth's ecclesiology. "What Barth 'shows' with regard to the Spirit and the Church," writes James Buckley, "is quite simply that the Spirit is in the Church for the world only insofar as the Church is in history, a people of God in world-occurrence whose hope is the new coming again of the same One who has come before."[82] Alongside with what Barth "says," he also "shows" a rigorous estimate of the indwelling of the Spirit in the church as regards the mission and task of the church. What he needed was a concrete pneumatology, where the Holy Spirit acts in the ordinances of the church as well.

Baptism is initiation into this community which is the body of Christ in the world. Through baptism the Holy Spirit creates a community that, as the body of Christ, the earthly-historical form of his existence, is embodied and present in the world. The vocation of the church as a witness must be entered into with a sense of purpose and commitment. The decision to join this community must be a free one involving commitment on the part of the new member. This decision to

---

79. Colwell, *Promise and Presence*, 73.

80. McClendon, *Doctrine*, 386.

81. Sacrament as witness and sacrament as mediation are not exclusive of one another or in opposition. See Hunsinger, "Baptism and the Soteriology of Forgiveness," 258–60.

82. Buckley, "Field of Living Fire," 91. The distinction between what Barth says and what he shows is borrowed from Hans Frei.

join the church is, of course, consequent upon the Holy Spirit's activity in gathering the church. As with the doctrine of baptism, in which the one baptized is following the Spirit's baptism, the church exists because of the activity of the Spirit. Yet the work of the Spirit in no way reduces the task of the church in the world. Its conduct, its service, and its varied witness are all necessary and demanded of the church because of the grace the Spirit has bestowed upon it.

The Chalcedonian emphasis on distinction within unity needs to be retained in relating Spirit-baptism to water baptism, especially in light of Barth's emphasis on the distinction between them. In this corrective, the action of the Spirit in baptism is to make it a sign of and participation in Christ's reconciliation of us to God. The Spirit calls to baptism and the Spirit acts in the human practice of baptism. Baptism is not the forcing of God's hand or the dispensing of God's grace as if it has been deposited for the church's use. Baptism is, in this view, a participation by faith in the grace of God through this God-given medium. As Barth discerned, baptism is the beginning of one's vocation; the taking up of the freedom for which we have been set free. The life of discipleship is the common life created by the Spirit.[83] It is a communal following after Jesus. This common, human life in Christ is itself grace. It is God's doing. Grace demands obedient, thankful discipleship working for the kingdom of God. Indeed only grace makes discipleship possible. Thus baptism, as initiation into this "way," is both the work of God and the work of the Spirit-led, free church. Perhaps this conception is not enough to be called a sacrament by Barth's late definition, or it may be seen as too thin to satisfy his critics, but it keeps together the essential notion of sacramental mediation and Barth's view of baptism as related to the vocation of the community.

Conclusion

Barth's development of the doctrine of baptism sheds light upon Barth's conception of the being of the church. Positively, I have said that the emphasis on the human act in baptism highlights the concrete existence of the Body of Christ in the time and place where it finds itself. Embodied, human commitment is necessary for baptism and for a healthy church. The prior work of the Spirit makes baptism and the church possible; it

---

83. See McClendon, *Doctrine*, 366.

indeed demands and makes them necessary. The Spirit in the church has a distinct and indispensable role to play in God's economy of salvation both as witness and as provisional representation of the Kingdom. I also have noted that Barth's emphasis solely upon the human work in baptism led to an unnecessary separation of the Holy Spirit from the concrete practices of the church. The shortcomings in sacramental mediation in baptism has its impact upon the being of the church. Without the sacramental action of God in the practices of the church, its task as witness is itself impossible. The embodied life of the church is endangered by the removal of the Spirit from the concrete practices of the church, especially baptism. However, when we affirm the work of the Spirit in baptism and the other practices of the church, the church can truly be the body of Christ witnessing to the Kingdom of God.

4

Baptism and the Gathered Community

BAPTISM IS AN ACTIVE WITNESS TO THE WORLD ABOUT ITS RECONCILIAtion in Christ. As practices such as baptism show, the church constitutes a visible witness in the world. This chapter deals with three elements of Barth's ecclesiology that fit with the embodied church created through baptism. Because Barth stated that the church is both visible and invisible, I will first elaborate the nature of this distinction. To further this discussion I will then deal with two elements that disclose the visible, concrete nature of the church. The first of these is Barth's congregationalism. Barth regarded the church as the local, gathered congregation. The final section will then treat Barth's actualism. Barth said that the church is an event. I will argue that the event is a history, giving the church both visibility and concreteness. The chapter will also reveal that these elements of Barth's ecclesiology are reflected in Barth's doctrine of baptism.

The Visible Yet Invisible Church

The Church exists as a nexus of human activities. "The Church is visible." It is not merely a *"civitas platonica,* the pure idea of a Christian community and therefore only an invisible Church."[1] Barth seeks to avoid any form of "ecclesiastical Docetism" that overlooks the visible church, "explaining away its earthly and historical form as something indifferent, or angrily negating it, or treating it only as a necessary evil, in order to magnify an invisible fellowship of the Spirit and of spirits."[2] The church is thus, in a certain sense, a sociological, historical phenom-

---

1. Barth, *CD* IV/1, 652, 653.
2. Ibid., 653.

enon like any other community.³ We should not define the church so as to lose its visible, historical character as the Body of Christ.

We cannot avoid the visible church. The individual Christian must always take part in a historical community. Barth parts ways with some of the ecclesiological emphases of the magesterial Reformers, who largely regarded the true church as hidden within the mass of Christendom.⁴ The true church for Calvin is the secret number of the elect ensconced within the body of the church.⁵ In contrast, Barth insists that the church is and must be a concrete, historical, visible reality in the world. "The Church is visible.... It is essential to it to be so.... The work of the Holy Spirit to which it owes its existence is something which is produced concretely and historically in this world."⁶

Barth thought that to take the church seriously was to affirm the church as the concrete body of Christ in the world: "without a discriminate but serious participation in the historical life of the community, its activity, its upbuilding, its mission, in a kind of purely theoretical and abstract churchliness, no one has ever seriously repeated the *credo ecclesiam*."⁷ This is because, "The Christian community as such cannot exist as an ideal commune or universum, but—also in time and space—only in the relationship of its individual members as they are fused together by the common action of the Word which they have heard into a definite human fellowship; in concrete form, therefore, and visible to everyone."⁸ To be in the church is to invest one's life within a particular gathering of the people of God in a particular place and time. As the Creed affirms, to believe in the triune God, to believe in Christ, is to believe in the Spirit in the church. Indeed, no one can be a Christian apart from the body of Christ. And as Barth states, this means the visible church: "*Credo ecclesiam* means that I believe that the congregation to which I belong, in which I have been called to faith and am respon-

---

3. O'Grady, *Church in the Theology of Karl Barth*, 311.

4. On a strain of congregationalism in Luther, see "On the Councils and the Church—Part Three" in Lull, *Martin Luther's Basic Theological Writings*, 540–75 and Durnbaugh, *Believer's Church*, 3–4.

5. Calvin, *Institutes*, IV.I.7 and Wiley, "Church as the Elect," 96–117.

6. Barth, *CD* IV/1, 652.

7. Ibid., 654.

8. Ibid., 653.

sible for my faith, in which I have my service, is the one, holy, universal Church. If I do not believe this here, I do not believe it at all."[9]

The multitude of the churches should not drive us to take refuge in an invisible unity. We cannot escape the divided church into the invisible.[10] This escape is the option of the hermit's retreat, the ivory tower, or the individual with a private faith—all of which entail individual withdrawal from the concrete church. "We are either in the *communion sanctorum* or we are not *sancti*. A private monadic faith is not the Christian faith."[11] Barth rightly also identifies the problematic attempt to put away any characteristic features of a particular Christian tradition in order to hold to "a kind of nondescript Christianity." The particular feature of such separation is "its featurelessness as a Church."[12] In a "post-denominational" age Barth would not suggest that the different strands of Christian tradition set aside their distinctives for a bland, generic unity which ignores those differences and the theological reasons which undergird them.[13]

The visiblity of the church, while real and wholly essential to understanding the church, is not the only dimension of the existence of the church. The church, even in its free human activity, is always the work of the Holy Spirit. The visible community is not its own foundation. While fully visible and earthly, the church is also a spiritual reality. It is invisible without losing the full truth of its visibility in history.[14] No contradiction is involved here. The church is both a human activity and a divine activity. It is both in its entirety. This spiritual reality is the hidden, invisible center of the existence of the church within all its visible activity. This invisible dimension of the church is not accessible to all,

---

9. Barth, *Dogmatics in Outline*, 144. "The concrete congregation to which I belong and for the life of which I am responsible, is appointed to the task of making in this place, in this form, the one, holy, universal Church visible." Ibid., 145.

10. Barth, *CD* IV/1, 677. See also Barth, *Church and the Churches*, 25–30.

11. Barth, *CD* IV/1, 678. "In a sense it would be true to say: *extra Christum nulla salus*. But the Church as His body is only the form of existence in which He encounters the world historically, the community of those who know and confess their salvation and that of the world in Him. . . . There is no legitimate private Christianity." Ibid., 688–89.

12. Barth, *CD* IV/1, 678.

13. Barth, *Church and the Churches*, 49–54.

14. Barth, *CD* IV/1, 656. See Busch, "Karl Barth's Understanding of the Church as Witness," 99.

but can be understood only by faith.[15] The church should take comfort and learn humility from the fact that its visible existence is founded in a mystical, spiritual reality.[16]

To understand the church as only visible is to misunderstand the church, even in its visibility.[17] Barth stresses the human dimension of the church only, in turn, to stress its incompleteness. As Barth notes, "we cannot look abstractly at what a human work seems to be in itself."[18] The Holy Spirit, the Spirit of the living Christ, constitutes the church. It is the divine operation in the human action which makes the true church. If taken alone, human institutions and activity are abstract phenomenon and may be only "the mere semblance of a Church (*Scheinkirche*)."[19] The human institution, Barth says, does not reveal the true church in the way that the citizens, officials, and laws reveal a state. Yet, this particular statement is not very helpful because it suggests that the visible church is always merely the appearance of a church. It leads some interpreters to misunderstand the relation between the visible and invisible in Barth's ecclesiology.[20]

Nicholas Healy has criticized Barth's ecclesiology on this point. According to Healy, Barth's ecclesiology causes a bifurcation of the church. He objects to descriptions of the church which depict the church as a twofold entity.[21] Healy rightly questions Barth's description of the human element of the church as *die Scheinkirche*.[22] This is, admittedly, a problematic term. Healy asserts that the human church, for Barth, is never more than merely an apparent church, since the true church is beyond the human church. If Healy is correct, this is an important critique that reveals a fundamental problem in Barth's ecclesiology. Barth defi-

---

15. Barth, *CD* IV/1, 656. According to O'Grady, Barth's ecclesiology "provides a welcome return to the idea of the Church as a divine institution, a creation from above." O'Grady, *Church in the Theology of Karl Barth*, 36.

16. Barth, *CD* IV/1, 660.

17. Barth, *CD* IV/3.2, 727, 731.

18. Barth, *CD* IV/2, 616.

19. Ibid., 617. Barth, *Die Kirchliche Dogmatik*, Vierter Band, Zweiter Teil, 698.

20. Bender might be right that Barth is ultimately better at expressing the distinction between Spirit and church than he is at expressing their true unity. Bender, *Karl Barth's Christological Ecclesiology*, 274.

21. Healy, *Church, World, and the Christian Life*, 29.

22. Healy, "Logic of Karl Barth's Ecclesiology," 258–63. Healy has come to reconsider some of this critique. See Healy, "Karl Barth's ecclesiology reconsidered," 287–99.

nitely states that the true church only exists by the activity of the Holy Spirit.[23] The human church apart from the Spirit is only the semblance of a church, a church in appearance only. Yet, this is not where Barth ends his discussion of the human church. Healy seems to cut off Barth's dialectic at this point. While the human church is not the basis for its own being, it is neither unnecessary nor unreal. Barth clearly states: "It is not the case . . . that only to the extent that it is invisible . . . is it the real Christian community."[24] The visible, human form of the church is absolutely essential for Barth and becomes the true church.

Speaking of the visible and invisible churches does not denote for Barth two distinct elements within the church, let alone two churches. The visible is real only because of the invisible, and the invisible only exists within the visible church. The invisible church for Barth is not the elect who are hidden in the vast numbers of the church. The invisible church, the secret of the existence of the church, is the work and presence of the Holy Spirit. The visible and invisible while not identical are inseparable, and the visible in some sense bears the invisible as the earthly-historical form of the existence of Christ himself. The visible church is the form and the invisible is the mystery of the one church. The mystery is hidden in the form and is to be sought in it.[25] The church is both visible and invisible in its election, calling, illumination, justification, and sanctification. It is the invisible church which turns the visible children of God into who they are.[26]

Credo ecclesium, Barth insists, is a confession of faith. The church exists as a visible community, yet its true reality and its true identity are known only by faith. Its institutions and organization are available to all, but not what it truly is.[27] To understand what the Christian community really is requires "the perception of faith." Only in the power of

---

23. Barth, *CD* IV/2, 617.

24. Barth, *CD* IV/3.2, 723. Miroslav Volf has more recently also noted that two factors give the assembly its configuration as a church: the presence and work of the Spirit as well as the external conditions that identify the church. Volf, *After Our Likeness*, 129–30.

25. Barth, *CD* IV/1, 669.

26. Barth, *CD* I/2, 219. "The church is, of course, a human, earthly-historical construct, whose history involves from the very first, and always will involve, human action. But it is *this* human construct, the Christian Church, because and as God is at work in it by His Holy Spirit." Barth, *CD* IV/2, 616.

27. Barth, *CD* IV/1, 654–55.

Christ can we know the concrete community for the reality that it is. If understood as merely visible, as only a matter of historical and social concern, the church is merely two-dimensional.[28] The church, however, has a third dimension, i.e., its spiritual reality.

Barth criticized *Mystici Corporis* from Pius XII for reducing the line between the visible and invisible church.[29] In its concrete, historical existence the church was understood as sinless and perfect. Its sinfulness was attributable only to individuals. In her sacraments and teaching the church is without fault. If, Barth says in contrast, the historical church is enough to truly be the church, believing in the church is not a matter of faith.[30]

It is interesting to note how Henri de Lubac similarly spoke of the two aspects of the one church. The two aspects are the visible, temporal, institutional church and the inner, spiritual, mystical church. He resists viewing the two aspects as two distinct elements or as two churches. They are a true unity—at once visible and mystical. In de Lubac's explanation, "the church is "human and divine at once even in her visibility, 'without division and without confusion,' just like Christ himself, whose body she mystically is."[31] The church is "*Ecclesia convocans et congregans. Ecclesia convocata et congregata;*" it is both "the divine calling-together and the community of the called together."[32] Both are united and both belong together. According to de Lubac both of these aspects are a part of the classic definition of the church. It is the view of Augustine and Aquinas and ultimately comes from Paul.[33]

Barth would have had reservations about this mystical understanding of the body of Christ. The visible community is ever in need of God's grace and cannot itself serve as the foundation of its own being. The historical community is sinful and fallen, therefore, the true be-

---

28. Ibid., 655–56.

29. The encylcial *Mystici Corporis Christi* was issued by Pius XII on June 29, 1943.

30. Barth, *CD* IV/1, 659.

31. Lubac, *Splendor of the Church*, 102. Of course, Barth does not go this far. Barth would part ways from de Lubac over his view of the mystical body of Christ. He would not accept this mystical identity of Christ and church. I am bringing de Lubac in at this point to show the similar description of the two elements of the church.

32. Ibid., 104.

33. Ibid., 103–5.

ing of the church is the work of God. This third, secret, dimension is required for the true church.[34]

> The glory of the community consists in the fact that it can give God the glory, and does not cease to do so. Its glory can appear only where there appears the glory of Jesus Christ and the sinner justified by Him. But as long as time endures, until the final manifestation of God and man in the future of Jesus Christ, the place where this takes place is hidden in its concrete form, with which it is only indirectly and not directly identical. For this reason this occurrence must be believed in the concrete form of the history which is visible to all.[35]

The statement that the relationship between the true church and its concrete form is not directly identical may present a problem. Of course what we actually believe in is Christ and not the church, or perhaps only Christ in the church. We do not want to place the institution of the church on the same level with God so we would not want to say the visible church is identical with Christ. Yet, to say that there is no direct identity between the true church, here the "glory of the church," and the concrete church as the earthly historical form of Christ suggests a denial of the reality of the visible church as the body of Christ. Because of the continuing work of the triune God there must be a direct relation, if not identity, between Christ and his church called into existence by the Holy Spirit, but this does not place the church on the same level, either ontologically or theologically, as Christ himself, nor does this direct relation make the human church sinless. The danger, Barth warns, is for the church to assume that its own doctrines, practices, and organizations, apart from its continual constitution by the Holy Spirit, constitute the true being of the church.

Barth clearly confesses that the human church is, by its own being and activity, a human construct. Yet, when brought to life by the Holy Spirit, this same human community becomes the true church. Barth's follows this logic throughout his theology. From the beginning, human beings have no capacity for God in and of themselves, but when God acts in them they become witnesses, bearers of revelation and grace. The existence of the invisible church is not a second essence, but an event within the one visible church. It takes place as the Holy Spirit is active

34. Barth, IV/1, 657.
35. Barth, *CD* IV, 1, 658.

in the earthly-historical body of Christ.[36] As in preaching when the human proclamation becomes, by the work of God, God's own speech, the human church is made the true church by God.[37]

The activity of God gathering, upbuilding, and sending his church is not done in separation from, or over against the humanity of the church, but through the human activity and work of the community. Because of the prevenient activity of God, the church's being and activity are possible. It is the mercy of God which makes the human institution and congregation the body of Christ, just as earlier in the Dogmatics it is the mercy and grace of God that allow human beings to know and speak of God at all. The grace of God makes sinful human beings into witnesses to the work and Word of God in the world. The history in which the being of the church becomes the true church is the "the divine inauguration and control and support of the human action which takes place in the community and in which Christianity exists in the world."[38]

The proper visibility of the church in the world is based upon the Christological orientation of the church.[39] As the glory of Christ was hidden within his humble humanity, so is the invisible nature of the church hidden within its human, visible existence. By the presence and action of the Spirit the church attests its invisible glory even in its sinful visibility.

> It is totally and properly both visible and invisible. The christological background should be remembered. Jesus Christ is not visibly but improperly true man and properly and invisibly true God. In the one being He is both visible as true man and invisible as true God, and both properly. *Thus it is in the totally visible being of the community that the totally invisible lives and moves as its secret. And the totally invisible calls for manifestation and declaration in the totally visible.* It is as this particular people

---

36. See O'Grady, *Church in the Theology of Karl Barth*, 286.

37. Barth, *CD* I/1, 93. Also, "The Bible is God's Word to the extent that God causes it to be His Word, to the extent that He speaks through it." *CD* I/1, 109.

38. Barth, *CD* IV/2, 619–20.

39. As Bender explains, the Christological framework for the invisible-visible church "entails that the human partner and work has no independent existence apart from the divine initiative, but at the same time ensures that the human subject does have a real and true existence and activity as established by and in relation to the divine Subject and activity." Bender, *Karl Barth's Christological Ecclesiology*, 5.

that it is one among others. And it is as one among others that it is this particular people.⁴⁰

It is not secondary or non-essential to the existence of the church that it should be visible in the world. Its concrete visible existence is a necessary correspondence to the physical, human nature of the incarnate Word. This means that what the church is in its invisibility could never be its own accomplishment. The existence of the church is only by grace. The community's response to the fact that in its human existence it witnesses to what God has done in the world, can only be gratitude, a thankful (eucharistic) obedience.⁴¹

Visibility and Witness

Barth explains that the edification and upbuilding of the church are not, as under the influence of Pietism, primarily about individuals. Edification and upbuilding are for the entire community. Individuals are edified in their work for the good of the community.⁴² The point of sanctification and discipleship of its members is that the church is being shaped into a witness to what Christ has done. The upbuilding of the community is the work of God. At the same time this upbuilding is the work of the community itself. It is not a passive, inert recipient of the Spirit's action, but must work to reform and improve its own life through the Spirit's leading. The community builds itself. It is its own activity and responsibility, "wholly and utterly its own work." Therefore the practices of the church whereby it forms and reforms its members are central to its life as witness.⁴³ The practice of baptism is an eventful witness that proclaims the work of Christ to the participants and the world.

The true being of the church moves from within outwards. God does his invisible work creating and sustaining the church so that the church can exist visibly as a witness to the grace it has received. As Barth explains, the church's "invisible essence must always be made visible in the fact that it is a confessing and missionary Church which leaves

---

40. Barth, *CD* IV/3.2, 726. Emphasis mine. This language speaks of the whole church as sacramental.
41. Barth, *CD* IV/3.2, 725, 732.
42. Barth, *CD* IV/2, 627.
43. Ibid., 634.

those around in no doubt as to whom or what it has to represent among them."[44] Barth insists that because the church is not an end unto itself, its visible nature is absolutely central to its task. As he states in the thesis which heads §67, "The Holy Spirit is . . . fitting it to give a provisional representation of the sanctification of all humanity and human life as it has taken place in Him."[45] The goal of the church is that all would see what was completed for them in Christ. The church is itself a movement toward a goal. As a witness to the sanctification of all in Christ, the church is "savingly necessary."[46] This is the purpose of the time which is given to the church. In the present, the church's witness is immersed in the world of sin and death. Pride, sloth, and falsehood still obscure the church's expression of the divine activity within it. At some points in history, the church has not seemed like the people of God at all.[47] Yet, until the final manifestation of Christ, the visible church remains the bearer of the invisible glory of Jesus Christ and the justification of the sinner in Him.[48]

Salvation was fully accomplished in the life, death, and resurrection of Christ, yet that was not the end but the beginning of the salvation of humanity. Salvation is a movement to a final destination which is present before us. The salvation made reality in Jesus Christ is not somewhere in the past; "it is a living redemptive happening which takes place."[49] In this present movement the church is a representation, however fallible, of what awaits all humanity. God has chosen to make this community of witnesses central to the drama of the world's redemption. Again, as a provisional representation of what is to come, the church must be a visible, concrete community living according to, and in witness to, the new law given in the gospel. This representation constitutes the life of the entire community, not individual saints acting separately.[50]

---

44. Barth, *CD* IV/3.2, 742.

45. Barth, *CD* IV/2, 614.

46. Ibid., 621.

47. Bender notes that Barth even speaks of the human church as a contradiction of the true church. He suggests that a notion of imperfect correspondence would be more useful than asserting a contradiction. Bender, *Karl Barth's Christological Ecclesiology*, 273.

48. Barth, *CD* IV/1, 658.

49. Barth, *CD* IV/2, 621.

50. Ibid., 622.

Baptism and the Visible Church

The place of baptism in Barth's concept of the church has revealed the visible, concrete nature of the church in Barth's ecclesiology. "The Church exists in that it becomes visible to the world . . . as a living community."[51] Baptism is a visible sign marking the existence of the community. The act is an eventful witness to what Christ did in the incarnation, crucifixion, and resurrection. Baptism with water is a necessary practice of the church, yet Barth insisted, it is itself wholly dependant upon the prior baptism of the Holy Spirit. The efficacy of water baptism is not that of the work worked, but that it follows baptism with the Holy Spirit. The communal act of baptism is dependent upon, made possible by, and demanded by the activity of the Holy Spirit. As in baptism by the Spirit, the true being of the church is God's doing. This fact does not negate the importance of the visible church. Indeed, it places serious demands upon it. The concrete church is relativized and made dependent upon another for the ground of its existence, but it is not thereby made anything other than the real church.

As the foundation for life in the church, baptism is a visible, concrete commitment. The goal of baptism is directly related to the visibility of the church. The concreteness of baptism as a human response to grace (itself enabled by grace) gives to the church a particular concreteness which is unavoidable as the church lives in correspondence to Christ. That concreteness is not a purely human phenomenon, as though the real church remains only the hidden work of God, which is other than the gathering congregation. Healy's contention that, for Barth, baptism with water is baptism into merely the *Scheinkirche* and not the true church misses the point of the necessary relation between the visible and invisible.[52]

The relation between the visible and invisible church, like that between water and Spirit baptism are similar. The question that remains is again one of mediation. Does Barth adequately relate the invisible church to the visible church? I answer yes. The true church, constituted by the activity of the Holy Spirit, is not something other than the visible congregation; it happens to the congregation just as the human word of Scripture becomes the Word of God. A close reading of this element of

---

51. Barth, *God Here and Now*, 66.
52. Healy, "Logic of Karl Barth's Ecclesiology," 263.

Barth's ecclesiology shows that the Spirit's work in the being of the church takes place within the visible, human congregation. In chapter three I sought to rethink Barth's distinction between water baptism and Spirit baptism. It was determined that he needed a better mediation between them, so that the visible sign participates in and mediates the spiritual reality. Barth does not succumb to Nestorianism in his Christology, yet his over-emphasis on the distinction between Spirit and water baptism leans in that direction. However, his connection of the visible and invisible in his ecclesiology shows that he did avoid the problem in his view of the church. The church is a visible, gathered congregation, yet this congregation exists by the invisible indwelling of the Holy Spirit. The invisibility of the church makes the visible church possible.

To recall the critique offered in the previous chapter, Barth's discussion of the visible/invisible church offers an explanation of the Spirit's relation to the church that Barth should have continued in his doctrine of baptism. Allowing for sacramental mediation, the human act in baptism would then be understood to participate in the activity of the Spirit, or conversely the Spirit would be seen as acting within the human community. Barth's discussion of the visible and invisible church relates these two aspects of the church in the 'sacramental' manner suggested in the previous chapter for baptism. I noted that Barth's earlier theology provided a means for sacramental mediation; this aspect of Barth's ecclesiology also shows such a relation. I should note here again that the Spirit is closest to the church when the church and its activity are spoken of as witness to Christ. I will now examine the importance of the local, concrete congregation as Barth understands it.

Barth's Congregationalism

The Ekklesia

The most basic form of the church's visibility is the local congregation. Barth clarifies this claim when he uses the term church to means *ekklesia*—the gathered community. Ecclesia means a coming together, a congregation. Barth places this local, gathered church at the center of his ecclesiological reflection. To speak of the church is primarily to speak of the living, concrete congregation.[53] As he says, "the one, holy, universal,

---

53. Barth, *God Here and Now*, 61. This piece is a version of the Amsterdam speech

apostolic Church exists as a *visible congregation*."⁵⁴ Or again Barth says, "The Church is the congregation."⁵⁵ His discussion of the church does not center around an abstract idea, but upon the many individual, local congregations which all belong to the body of Christ in the world. "It is in the concrete event of its gathering that the community has its invisible and also its visible being, that it is the earthly historical *communion sanctorum*, that the Lord Himself is in the midst of it by His Spirit, that it is His own earthly-historical form of existence, that it lives as the body of which He is the Head."⁵⁶ Barth notes positively that in America the "congregation is still a real thing."⁵⁷

Barth's ecclesiology here resembles the baptist view of the church. Baptists have consistently emphasized the reality of the local congregation as the church. According to Franklin Littell the central concern of a free church ecclesiology is the nature of the community of discipleship. The Anabaptists proper "gathered and disciplined a 'true church' upon the apostolic pattern as they understood it."⁵⁸ The emphasis in such an ecclesiology is upon the local, embodied church, not upon the general institutional bodies which seek to serve the churches. As James McClendon describes the baptist view of the church, the church is the local, Spirit-filled, mission-oriented, congregation of the people of God.⁵⁹

In his stress on the church as a congregation, Barth decided to use the term Christian community (*Gemeinde*) rather than the Church (*Kirche*) to underline this emphasis on the gathered congregation in volume four of the *Dogmatics*. The church is not the "ecclesiastical shell" or the "merely nominal church."⁶⁰ The church is "the event which

---

noted in footnote 60. On this idea, see O'Grady, *Church in the Theology of Karl Barth*, 270.

54. Barth, *God Here and Now*, 76. "It belongs to the very essence of the Church . . . that the church is the 'event of a gathering together' and in this sense a 'living congregation.'" Ibid., 67.

55. Barth, *CD* I/2, 217. As Volf states, "the people of God gathering at one place constitute the primary subject of ecclesiality." Volf, *After Our Likeness*, 25.

56. Barth, *CD* IV/1, 671. See Sorge, "Karl Barth's Reception," 90.

57. Barth, *Fragments Grave and Gay*, 49.

58. Littell, *Origins of Sectarian Protestantism*, XVII.

59. McClendon, *Doctrine*, 341–44, 365–71.

60. Barth, "Church," 67. This is an address to the World Council of Churches in Amsterdam in 1948. In it Barth's congregationalism is seen at its clearest.

consists in gathering together (congregatio) those men and women (fidelium) whom the living Lord Jesus Christ chooses and calls to be witnesses to the victory He has already won, and heralds of its future universal manifestation."[61] In this event the sovereignty of God finds a response in the obedience of those whom he has called to service.[62] The congregation is a human fellowship established by divine power.

Every church, as a local congregation, is itself the whole of the church. The one church exists in different geographical locations. The absolute oneness of its head is what keeps the body as one even when separated. The Church is one community separated by distance.[63] Only one church exists, but each congregation is a unified whole in itself.

> Each community has its own locality, its own environment, tradition, language, etc. But in that locality, as established and appointed by the Lord of all the communities, it should be the one complete community.... The one Church does not exist either in an ideal or in an organized or organizing totality to which the individual communities stand in the relationship of participating Churches (like the digits in a figure or the notes in a chord). The one church exists in its totality in each of the individual communities.[64]

Churches should take their local settings seriously. Every community has its own locality in which it has a particular existence and a particular mission, yet each one is itself the one church.[65] As important as locality and particularity are, no one form of the church is absolute. Traditions within Christianity must guard against making their own form and arrangement (worship, experience, life, political involvement) tantamount to being the whole of Christianity or equaling the Word of God.[66]

---

61. Barth, "Church," 68.

62. Note the similarity of this statement to Barth's description of the meaning of baptism.

63. Barth, *CD* IV/1, 671. See Barth, *Church and the Churches*, 29–30.

64. Ibid., 672–73. See Barth, *Dogmatics in Outline*, 142–45, for a succinct statement of the church as the congregation and each congregation as the Church.

65. "Each in its own place can only be the one community beside which there are no others. Each in and for itself and with its local characteristics can only be the whole, as others are in their own locality." Barth, *CD* IV/1, 672.

66. Barth, *God Here and Now*, 70.

Barth does not give much weight to individual church authorities. The Word of God in Scripture is the only authority. The entire congregation is in the service of Scripture. Thus, no absolute distinction needs to be made between classes of clergy and laity. Eberhard Busch notes Barth's critique of "offices" of the church.[67] Congregations should reach a consensus regarding the particular gifts of individual members, including but not limited to, those who are to proclaim the Word to the congregation.[68] Members of the congregation must all mutually guide and aid one another in life and faith. Such guidance is, Barth insists, a matter of service not dominion. Any bodies which are specifically set up as official guidance must be done in an *ad hoc* manner. They are considered another congregation drawn from the various congregations. Such a group should not be a governing body with authority to rule over the congregations.[69] Barth goes further to say that the episcopal form and the synodal forms (Episcopal and Presbyterian) of church leadership hinder the freedom of the congregation for continual renewal and reformation. Such systems of polity give too little responsibility and power to the congregations themselves. As a result of those orders, only the special representatives placed over the churches are entrusted with the life and faith of the churches.[70]

Barth noted that the congregational movement (already seen in 16th and 17th centuries) in England received too little attention. The congregational movements in England were, in his estimate, able to withstand the Enlightenment better than synodal churches with their hierarchies of authority. "It was from these congregations that the 'Pilgrim Fathers' derived. From the free spirit with which they built the Church in America, it can hardly be said that they lacked organizing strength." These Congregationalists needed a greater sense of their "ecumenical validity and significance."[71]

67. Busch, "Karl Barth's Understanding of the Church as Witness," 92.

68. Barth, *God Here and Now*, 79. Compare Yoder's depiction of the universal ministry of the church in *Fullness of Christ*.

69. On the divine authority of the church, see Sykes, "Authority and Openness," 69–84.

70. Barth, *God Here and Now*, 80–83. For an argument that the "marks of the church" need to refer to the congregation not just the clergy or the sacraments, see Yoder, *Royal Priesthood*, 66–101.

71. Barth states that a group of younger theologians have taken up this approach again. Paul van Buren asserts that he may have intended the group which wrote *The Catholicity of Protestantism*, a report given to the Archbishop of Canterbury by a group

Through the power of the Holy Spirit, the many members in the church become a *communio sanctorum*. The saints are saints only by their participation in the community of saints and the relationships, tasks, and gifts which are given therein.[72] The communion of saints is an event. It is the event in which a communion of sinful human beings receives its holiness from God. This event constitutes a history, as the communion treads its way from its original sinful existence to its final participation in the holiness of Christ. This pilgrim community is holy because Jesus Christ is holy. The holiness of church members is an important issue for ecclesiology. Baptists have insisted upon the awakening and regeneration of all members of the church. Indeed, church membership comes through baptism, which is sought and received only by a responsible candidate.[73]

The Order of the Community

According to Barth, the local, gathered community must be marked by form and order. Barth speaks of the form of each community in terms of the order and law (*Ordung und Recht*) which give the community its order and shape as the church. The community's common life takes place in a definite form and under a law to which it is subject.[74] As a witness to Christ the community must correspond to and live in obedience to Christ. According to Barth, only a christologico-ecclesiological conception of the community will be adequate. This conception of the church implies proper order. The Christian community is the relationship between the One who commands and his obedient saints. The church is always secondary to Jesus Christ who is the primary subject of

---

of free church theologians in the English church. Editor's note in *God Here and Now*, 84. See Flew and Davies, *Catholicity of Protestantism*. For their treatment of the church, see 91–114.

72. Barth, *CD* IV/2, 643. The church is a fellowship of thanksgiving, of penitence and joy, of prayer, in relation to the world, of service, of hope, of proclamation of the gospel, and of worship. Ibid., 643.

73. Barth, *CD* IV/1, 695.

74. Barth, *CD* IV/2, 680. *KD* IV/2, 769–70. Barth developed this idea partly in response to Emil Brunner's contention that the church was a fellowship of brothers open to spontaneous forms. It was not an institution with certain order. See Brunner, *Misunderstanding of the Church*.

this conception.[75] Believers' baptism helps enable church order. That the community is made up of people who share a common baptism which is their commitment to, their burial into, Christ means that the entire community is to be held to a certain task and way of life. Life after baptism is then lived as one of the baptized. One could be held accountable because of their submission to baptism. The order of the local church, as formed by its worship, should reflect its task and purpose.

For this reason, the form and life of the Christian community are unique in the world. Because the church is visible, it has a form. Its distinctive, visible form comes from Christ.[76] Scripture is the concrete voice of Christ from which the community receives guidance. Yet the church today does not simply copy or imitate any previous form of the church. We cannot look to scripture to find a blueprint for the community which we merely try to rebuild. Not even the New Testament community, Barth argues, is a model for all churches to strictly follow.[77] We must pay attention to their witness and learn from them, but what the church in each new generation and situation is called to be will be determined only by "the life of the Lord in the community."[78] It is in response and obedience to its head that the church takes on its form in the world. The same Lord who built the communities in the Old and New Testaments builds up the church in the present.

The law which orders this community must be a law of service. As Christ came to serve, so does the church exist for service. The church's service corresponds to the work of Christ as the servant who is Lord.[79] The demand of service is placed upon all members of the church. The entire life of the community is intended to take part in this service in the world. No members and no activities of the community are dedicated to any other type of law. Christian communities must be ordered around service and not domination.[80]

---

75. Barth, *CD* IV/2, 680.
76. Yoder, "Basis of Barth's Social Ethics," 8–9.
77. Barth, *CD* IV/2, 683.
78. Ibid., 686. The phrase is actually a quote of E. Schweizer.
79. Barth, *CD* IV/2, 690–93.
80. Karl Barth, *God in Action*, 33–35.

The law of the community is liturgical law. It is found and made known in the worship of the community.[81] The common work that is at the center of the church, as the true Church, is its worship. Here the church is truly *ekklesia*.[82] The true church is this coming together for worship and baptism. "This is the point where in its totality it becomes a concrete event at a specific time and place."[83] Worship is the act of the congregation's "concrete actuality and visibility." In worship, the church stands out from the secular culture within which it is usually hidden.[84] Weekly worship stands out from the whole of the existence of the community as its center and focal point. In the liturgical law which determines the shape of the community, the event of gathering for weekly worship clarifies and determines the existence of the church as event. This gathering is the "particular happening" which establishes the form of the church. The local congregation exists in prayer, confession, fellowship, proclamation, baptism, and the Lord's Supper. As Barth states, "the word 'Church' denotes the history, the action, the divine giving and the human receiving of baptism and the Lord's Supper."[85] Their lives and work are truly integrated in worship, as the many become one body. This is, again, the action at once of both God and the community building up the church. Individuals who do not participate and invest themselves in the common worship and communion of a given congregation are not truly members of the *ekklesia*.

In worship the community is reminded of what it has received and formed for its task in the world. As Yoder points out, in Barth's view Jesus "must be re-known, re-presented, on through time in a celebratory recounting that ties the particularity of his history to the particularity of ours."[86] The "rest" of the Christian's life should be shaped in this common activity. "Worship and the everyday life of Christians . . . are not two departments which are separate although they belong together." Worship gives everyday life its "content and character."[87] In its praise

---

81. Barth, *CD* IV/2, 695.
82. Ibid., 638.
83. Ibid., 639.
84. Ibid., 698.
85. Barth, *God Here and Now*, 66.
86. Yoder, *Royal Priesthood*, 110.
87. Barth, *CD* IV/2, 640.

of God, the church is to become a sign both of what God has done and who he remains for those who have received his love.[88]

This gathering is a common confession of what is held to be true by the community. In the community, "the human response to the Word of God is the common word of all."[89] This common acknowledgment of one Lord builds a community of brotherhood and mutual trust. Rather than the invisible, true church being hidden within its members, Barth says that the "Christian community is a fellowship of baptism." Here all members trust that those who claim membership have been awakened by the Holy Spirit. Membership is, of course, not simply regional or by virtue of birth, but by a baptism acknowledging that one has been awakened, brought to life, by God.[90]

Worship strengthens and preserves members of the body for eternal life. By eternal life, Barth means human life lived in the new reality brought about in Christ. This point is overlooked by those who argue that Barth gives no place for personal formation in the church.[91] The church gathers for worship to be "prepared for the attainment of their life in this form."[92] Christians are aware of the fact that the world has been redeemed in Christ and work to live accordingly. In worship the community is continually reminded of the truth of things. The church has been shown the truth about the human condition and seeks to offer a provisional representation of what will come to all humanity. Baptism initiates one into this communal representation. The common nourishment of the Lord's Supper strengthens the community for its life as representation of Christ, who they are remembering, and who gives himself to them in the meal. Along with baptism and the supper, the community gathers to pray. "The prayer of Christians, too, demands that it should find its true and proper form in the prayer of the assembled community; in the united calling upon God: 'Our father, which art in heaven.'"[93] The We of the prayer takes a concrete form only in the gathered community praying together.

88. Barth, *CD* I/2, 401.
89. Barth, *CD* IV/2, 700.
90. Ibid., 702.
91. See Hauerwas, *Character and the Christian Life*.
92. Barth, *CD* IV/2, 702. Nigel Biggar has argued that Barth does have a certain place for character formation of Christians. See *Hastening that Waits*, 123-45.
93. Barth, *CD* IV/2, 705. The ethics of reconciliation was to center around the Lord's Supper and the Lord's Prayer in addition the baptism fragment. Church practices

Barth's insistence on an ordered church presupposes a visible, gathered community. Barth emphatically states: "we have to consider all questions of that which is lawful and right in the Church in the light of its assembling for public worship."[94] Of course, Barth will insist that it is the present Christ, active among those gathered, who is the law of the community. Because Christ is living and active, the church which organizes itself according to his law will be living and dynamic.[95] As a living community, it is able to grow and to change. It can be continuously reforming its own life and action. The community should be humble enough to know that it is not its own law.

The church is a society or a fellowship "in which men are freed to exist for the world, and therefore not with certain individuals who exist alone, but with those who are called by the same Lord, who enjoy the same knowledge, who share in the same promise and who stand in the same order. It is in fulfillment of the promise which applies in common to all, and in expressions of obedience to the order which is equally binding on all."[96] The freedom of the church is a freedom to be used in the obedience which is the Christian's only true freedom. It is not a freedom for personal interest or self-satisfaction, nor is it a freedom from the constraints and concerns of the community. Baptism is one's acceptance of the demands of Christian freedom.

Given his emphasis on the gathered ekklesia, Barth's ecclesiology is less transcendental and thus more concrete than some interpreters have suggested.[97] As seen here, the local, gathered community is very important for the church's task as witness to the world. The visible, human dimension of the church is neither unimportant nor unreal for Barth. Admittedly, Barth's ecclesiology is still often rather abstract, but this is not due to a disdain for the visible, concrete church. This abstraction is because every living congregation in it locality and situation will have to determine the concrete shape of its service in that place and time.

---

played largely an ethical role in the life of the community. See Barth, *Christian Life,* for his treatment of part of the Lord's Prayer.

94. Barth, *CD* IV/2, 706.

95. Ibid., 710–11.

96. Barth, *CD* IV/3.2, 780–81.

97. Hütter has argued that Barth's ecclesiology is primarily transcendental and this prevents him from ever giving a concrete account of the church and its practices. Hütter, "Karl Barth's 'Dialectical Catholicity,'" 148–51.

Barth's Actualism

The Church as Event and as History

To describe the being of the church, in both visibility and invisibility, we must meld the distinction between being and act, between essence and existence. As Barth states, the church's "act is its being, its status its dynamic, its essence its existence."[98] The church is an event; it takes place. Its existence is not a divine donation or simply a fixed status. The Christian *communio* "is not the being of a state or institution, but the being of an event in which the assembled and self-assembling community is actively at work: the living community of the living Lord Jesus Christ in the fulfillment of its existence."[99] God's word and work are not simply "deposited and transmitted truths of faith;" they are an event. They take place "in the historical association of the call of Christ and Christian obedience."[100] The church is a work of divine and human activity. The church exists in the action of God and of its members. He says, "the Church *is* when it takes place, and it takes place in the form of a sequence and nexus of definite human activities."[101] It is an ongoing event.

Barth's emphasis on the church as event is a good example of actualism at work in his theology. According to George Hunsinger, Barth's actualism is Barth's tendency to think in terms of activity, events, and relationships in contrast to substances or states.[102] In developing the doctrines of creation and reconciliation, Barth cast his doctrine in terms of a history.[103] Following this way of thinking, Barth emphasizes that the church, as event, is a history. This concept is an important one for Barth's doctrine of reconciliation. Previously, Barth argued that "the atonement

---

98. Barth, *CD* IV/1, 650.
99. Ibid., 652.
100. Barth, *God Here And Now*, 64.
101. Barth, *CD* IV/1, 652.
102. Hunsinger, *How to Read Karl Barth*, 30–32. It is also linked to his conception of God as *actus purus*, not as a Being whose essence stands prior to his existence. God is not potentiality waiting to become actual.
103. Actually the doctrine of election is also described as a history. The encounter between God and man is a history. Barth, *CD* II/2, 175–88. See Ford, *Barth and God's Story*.

is history (Geschichte)."[104] In these narrative terms, it is the history of Jesus Christ, not simply the "person" of Christ which is significant. Who he was and what he did are truly inseparable.[105] In the drama of reconciliation the history which was the incarnation continues to impact and in effect encompass all other histories. Each person's history is enclosed within the larger history of God's reconciliation of the world beginning with Abraham and culminating in the cross and resurrection of Christ. The history of the Christian community is enclosed in the history of Jesus Christ. No single founding of the church occurred in Jesus's life as an event. Rather, Barth states, the whole Gospel narrative is an account of the establishment of the Christian community.[106] The story of the church is set within the one grand drama of reconciliation.

Our own histories make sense only within this larger story concerning the world. Our histories are made *possible* only by this larger history. The church is a history that exists in consequence of the history of Christ. The church plays out, to employ Gadamer's notion, the history of effect (*wirkungsgeschichte*) which Christ had upon the world.[107] What the history of Christ meant and means to the world's history is being made manifest in the community which he called and separated for that task. As Barth states, "the Church exists . . . because Jesus in His resurrection does not shatter the power of death in vain but with immediate effect; because as the witness to eternal life He cannot remain alone but at once awakens, gathers and sends forth recipients, partners and co-witnesses of this life."[108]

The Time of the Church

In his treatment of the Holy Spirit's gathering of the Christian community, Barth states that the Church exists in and as a definite historical time. In God's dealings with the world in creation and redemption, the church has a particular role to play and a stage on which to do so.

---

104. Barth, *CD* IV/1, 157.

105. Frei, *Theology and Narrative*, 169.

106. Barth, *CD* IV/3.2, 683. Yet Barth could only agree with Schleiermacher in saying that Christ's activity "can be seen in its completeness only in the corporate life He founded," in a very carefully qualified sense. Schleiermacher, *Christian Faith*, 377.

107. Gadamer, *Truth and Method*, 300–307.

108. Barth, *CD* II/2, 264.

Barth explains that, "the time of the community is the time between the first *parousia* of Jesus Christ and the second. . . . The community exists between his coming then as the risen One and this final coming. Its time is, therefore, this time between."[109] The church lives in the middle, in the meantime. Its time is between the first direct presence of God in the resurrected Christ and the final direct presence of Christ when he is manifested as Judge. Christianity is "the holy community of the intervening period."[110] The church is this "peculiar history between God and man in the time which is determined and characterized by these two dates, one being its beginning, the other its goal. It is in this history that God allows certain men to live as His friends, as witnesses of the reconciliation of the world with Himself which has already taken place in Jesus Christ."[111]

Between the first and the final parousia stands a second, or middle parousia in the coming of the Spirit at Pentecost. This addition is necessary for the church to exist as it is gathered by this Spirit. The Holy Spirit "is the power of Jesus Christ in which it takes place that there are men who can and must find and see that He is theirs and they are His, that their history is genuinely enclosed in His and His history is equally genuinely enclosed in theirs."[112] Christians find themselves enclosed, enfolded, into the history of Jesus Christ. The work of the Holy Spirit is meant to include us in a narrative relation to the history of Jesus.

This vision of the time of the church is important considering Barth's emphasis on the church as an event. For Barth, the church is not a state which becomes real in history; it *is* a history. Critics of the understanding of church as event take the notion of event to imply an occasionalistic or episodic existence of the church, which is assumed not to exist between events. However, the event that makes the church is the activity of God, the gathering of the Spirit. The existence of the

---

109. Barth, *CD* IV/1, 725. The time of the church is "the time of the parousia of Jesus Christ in its second and middle form, in the time of the power of His Holy Spirit; and therefore it is especially the time of the community. This time is given the community in order that it may be to the world an indication, representation and likeness of its calling in Jesus Christ to the service of God as it proceeds in this time between." Barth, *CD* IV/3.2, 794–95.

110. Barth, *CD* IV/2, 620.

111. Barth, *God Here and Now*, 62.

112. Barth, *CD* IV/1, 648.

church is not within the hands of the community itself but is always the act of God, gathering, ordering and sending this community. The continued existence of the church is guaranteed by the grace of God, not human activity and effort. "Its continuance in time is accomplished in the continuation of its establishment by further demonstrations of the gracious God, in the continuation of the history in which the Holy Scriptures are the active, operating subject. . . . It is God's faithfulness which promises and guarantees this continuance."[113]

That the church is an event does not mean that the church exists only occasionally. Because the church is the work of the Holy Spirit and not only that of human beings it is not therefore unreal or episodic. As Joseph Mangina explains, the language of event is not a denial of the existence of the church. "The point of event-language is not presence or absence along a time line, but the divine mystery of the church's existence at every moment of its life."[114] The church is dynamic living history, an extended, ongoing event. That it is an event does not mean that it is a momentary, punctiliar series of unconnected events without duration. For Barth, the activity of the Spirit in forming the church is neither arbitrary nor sporadic. The church is not merely an occasional appearance, even if its basis is outside itself. As seen above, the local church is the true church, without question, but its existence as such is not self-subsistent. The life of the body is only and always from its Head. As Barth notes, "the church has maintained itself and has to maintain itself in the identity of its essence even in the historical sequence of its forms. It exists in history. It is history. It makes history."[115]

Having its own time, the church constitutes a concrete particular history. The church "not only has a history, but—like man—it exists only as a definite history takes place, that is to say, only as it is gathered and lets itself be gathered and gathers itself by the living Jesus Christ through the Holy Spirit."[116] Barth states, "The word 'Church' denotes the history, the action, the divine giving and the human receiving of baptism and the Lord's Supper. Then and only then is it a meaningful

---

113. Barth, *God Here and Now*, 68.
114. Mangina, *Karl Barth: Theologian*, 154.
115. Barth, *CD* IV/1, 704.
116. Ibid., 650.

word."[117] Barth's exposition of the time of the church lends itself to an interesting narrative interpretation. It has an inherently storied form relating the past of Christ to the continuous history of the church as it has existed since his resurrection.[118]

The Time of Recollection and Expectation

The time of the church is the time of recollection. The Christian community exists primarily to remember and witness to what was done in Jesus Christ. We are called to continue the confession that has constituted the church from its beginning. Revelation occurs within the church, the community that participates in God's revelation in Christ. Becoming a Christian is not a matter of having a private, mystic experience or subjective relationship with God, but becoming a part of the public community that relates to God. God's revelation and grace are experienced personally by each individual, but they are not primarily concerned with individuals. God's love and action are for all of His creation.[119] The church presently exists as a provisional representation of the justification which Jesus Christ has worked for all of the world. It consists of those who have been given a glimpse of God's reconciling work and his lordship over all creation. It then bears witness to this fact to the rest of the world. What the church is now, all creation is intended to be.[120]

The time of the church is also the time of expectation. We hope for the final reconciliation of all things to God based on the church's experience of the resurrection. Our expectation is based on our recollection of Christ; our hope is in him. As Barth states, "the resurrection and ascension reveal that the One who was crucified is the living Lord, present to-day, and coming again one day."[121] The first parousia, the incarnation-death-resurrection of Christ, and the second, the Spirit in the church, are intended to guide us to the final coming of God. As Barth

---

117. Barth, *God Here and Now*, 66.

118. Werpehowski's narrative interpretation of Barth's ethics corrected misreadings that charged Barth's ethics with occasionalism. See "Narrative and Ethics," 334–53.

119. Note Nicholas Lash's important distinction between the "personal" and the "individual." *Theology on the Way to Emmaus*, 141–57.

120. Barth perceptively states that "a world engulfed in a sea of misery is waiting—not for the Church but—to become Church itself." Barth, *God in Action*, 24.

121. Barth, *CD* IV/2, 164.

says, "the one parousia of the one Jesus Christ in its first and second forms is like an arrow pointing to the third. It moves irreversibly in the direction of the final coming."[122] The presence of the Spirit in the church documents the direction of God's economy of salvation.

THE TIME OF PATIENCE

Finally, the time of the church is the time of the patience of God. The community's reason for being "is found only within the extent of this intermediary time when the victory of God has been declared, but has not yet been made manifest in glory. Within the time of God's patience, she announced the grace and judgment accomplished in Jesus Christ, which on his return will be revealed in glory and in public."[123] Its time between the comings exists not for itself. Mission is the core of the church's being. The church is thus teleological in nature; it exists toward a certain end. The community which has Easter behind it has the consummation before it as its goal.[124] When the service of the church is rendered, its time will be at an end and with it all time will end. The church prays for its own end: "thy Kingdom come, thy will be done . . ."

In the time of the church God is still at work in the world. "He still has a goal. . . . He still expects something in the world and humanity created and preserved by Him. He has spoken His final Word, but He has not yet finished speaking it."[125] God is waiting for human response to his Word before he allows it to be fully spoken and the consummation accomplished. Until his grace finds correspondence in a human Yes, God waits and history continues. Just as God's first parousia was not a unilateral decision of force or sovereign overpowering, so now his grace longs for a response, a corresponding gratitude.[126] God wills that the news of his justification in Christ be sounded and met with faith. "In order that this might happen, He still gives to the world space, time, and existence, He allows the end-time to commence and continue."[127] For

---

122. Barth, *CD* IV/3.2, 915.
123. Barth, *Faith of the Church*, 139.
124. Barth, *CD* IV/1, 726.
125. Ibid., 736.
126. Ibid., 737. Mangina's reading of Barth on the crucifixion as the end of history leaving no time for the church misses this. Mangina, "Bearing the Marks of Jesus," 270.
127. Barth, *CD* IV/1, 738.

the sake of what takes place in the world through this community the final parousia is postponed. That humanity might yet respond, "there is still time, even though the last hour has struck: time for the work of the Holy Spirit and for the prayer for Him; time for faith and repentance; time for preaching of the Gospel throughout the world; time for the Christian community, and in this sense the time of grace."[128]

Reading History

Based on its origin and its hope, the church knows its time. This community has Easter immediately behind and the final parousia ever before it. "It knows what time is because it knows that it is this time between, and in this knowledge it is held and impelled and directed both behind and before."[129] This is not to say that the time of the church is anything other than world history. Yet, in Jesus Christ the church sees history "in the form of its new reality. In this form it is manifest to it in Jesus Christ from whom it derives, who is its Lord, and whom it has to attest to all other men."[130] In the midst of human history where the Lordship of Christ and the providence of God are not recognized, the baptized community sees history differently. The church understands the transitory being of world history because it reads history in light of the person and the time of Jesus Christ, the center and norm of history, into whose death and resurrection it has been baptized. In this understanding of time, we can affirm that history is not meaningless flux, the endless passage of time, but is the loving donation of God towards the end for which the church prays Maranatha—Come Lord. The time of the church should be connected with the goal of baptism: the Kingdom of God. The baptized and baptizing community lives in expectation of the coming of Christ.

Barth has an apocalyptic vision of history. Human existence may seem sunk in evil, but Christ has triumphed over it. God is already victorious over evil and death, and so his people are to live accordingly. They are to live lives of humble obedience to grace that was freely given. We live not so that God can win in the eschaton, but because God has

128. Ibid., 739.
129. Barth, *CD* IV/1, 728.
130. Barth, *CD* IV/3.2, 721. "The community would be guilty of lack of faith if it were seriously to regard world history as secular or profane." O'Grady, *Church in the Theology of Karl Barth*, 308.

already won. Christ is the victor.[131] It is not up to us to change the evil world into a good one.[132] It only feeds into the disorder of the world for the church to see itself as bearing the weight of history. As Barth says, the history of the world is completely accomplished, the revelation of the new heaven and earth is what we are awaiting. The consummation will not be our work any more than our salvation has been our doing. In the midst of a world that does not recognize the Lordship of Christ our task is to be witnesses, disciples, servants. "We have plenty for all our hands to do just being that!"[133] The church baptizes because of its eschatological hope. Christians walk in the resurrected life, crucified with Christ that we might live with him (Rom 6:1–11).

Conclusion

The church gathered for baptism and worship is the central meaning of ecclesiology. The proper order of the church is one of service and visible witness. This is learned through liturgical repetition of the life and meaning of Christ. Baptism is a concrete witness in the church's remembrance and the reforming of its common life and its members to Christ. Given the emphasis on the congregation, the church's own concreteness follows this concrete foundation. A properly ordered community is upheld by its common submission to baptism. In baptism each member of the church has renounced their old life for the new way of ecclesial being.

Baptism is initiation into a movement, a transition from the old life to the new. It marks a person's burial with Christ, and resurrection into the living Christ. The goal of baptism and the church it forms is ultimately the kingdom of God. The visible church gathered for worship, including its practice of baptism and Lord's Supper, is a witness to

---

131. "Jesus is Victor" is a section title in *CD* IV/3.2. In this section Barth continues his narrative approach to Christology. See Barth, *CD* IV/3.1, 165–68, 181–83, 191, 211–20.

132. We should compare this to John Howard Yoder, who argues that it is not the task of the church to govern history, especially by the use of force. The church is to be a faithful witness to Christ. It is through the cross and the resurrection that we learn of God's ways of dealing with the world, not through the swords of Christian emperors or presidents. It is not our job to make history turn out "right." Both Yoder and Barth (perhaps Yoder following Barth) affirm that in light of the Kingdom of God Christians must live a certain way, precisely because it is not our task to bring the kingdom about.

133. Barth, "No Christian Marshall Plan," 1332–33. The quote is on 1333.

the world around it. Only the visible church, and only the visible church made possible and reality through the power of the Holy Spirit, can be a provisional representation of the Kingdom. Baptism is one's willing entrance into participation in the event of the church. Of course this is only made possible by the work of the Spirit. The church's visibility points to the Spirit's deeper unseen reality within it.

Baptism as a teleological act looking toward the kingdom corresponds to the teleological nature of the church's existence as history. Baptism is one's initiation into the movement that is taking place between the resurrection and the final coming of Christ. A particular element in Barth's ecclesiology is becoming clearer. Barth's church is at its most concrete and the work of the Spirit becomes most evident when the church is described as a witness.[134] Its mission as provisional representation of the kingdom is the heart of the church. Barth's affirmation of believer's baptism is an attempt to form a church that cannot live in captivity to the interest of any state or culture. It is free from state and culture so that it might provide a healthy witness to them.

---

134. See Buckley, "Field of Living Fire," 89, 97.

5

Baptism and the Free Community

HAVING STUDIED THE BEING OF THE CHURCH AS THE BODY OF CHRIST indwelt by the Spirit and the community's concrete visible existence as the people of God, I will turn in the next two chapters to Barth's view of the baptized community in relation to the world. In this chapter I will examine Barth's understanding of the church's relationship to the state and society in which it finds itself. In the course of the discussion I will deal with Barth's view of the state, pacifism, and political commitment and involvement as they are shaped by his understanding of the church and baptism. Thus I will demonstrate how baptism and ecclesiology are radically interdependent. In this discussion, Barth's rejection of infant baptism in favor of believers' baptism will play a decisive role in shaping his ecclesiology.

John Howard Yoder's Reading of Barth

John Howard Yoder contends that, in the course of Barth's work, Barth gradually developed a free church ecclesiology. He argues that "Karl Barth's social stance was in theory and practice that of a free churchman" and a "radical, i.e., a critic of all authoritarianism."[1] Barth developed his free church understanding over time, so that by *Church Dogmatics* IV/2, "there is no refuting Barth's commitment to the free church vision."[2] Barth was able to see the problems inherent in the Constantinian view of the church and state. According to Yoder, "Barth is a free churchman because of his doctrine of revelation, which demands that he recognize that belief can unite in community only those who respond to the

---

1. Yoder, "Review of *Karl Barth and Radical Politics*," 339.
2. Yoder, "Karl Barth: How His Mind Kept Changing," 171.

word."[3] The civil community should therefore not be addressed as if it had faith in Christ.[4] Yoder argued that the only significant dualism in Barth's ethics is the confession or non-confession of the Lordship of Jesus Christ. Barth "makes this difference the difference that matters."[5]

The Christian community should be identified by its confession of Christ. The civil community is distinct from the church because it does not recognize Christ or promise its allegiance to him as the church does.[6] In his later theology, Barth stepped back from what Yoder calls "the ethos of establishment."[7] The source of this retreat is not simply his experience with the German political situation and the Confessing church, but his theological concentration upon the incarnation, cross and resurrection, i.e., his christocentrism. Barth, Yoder says, was able to do theology in a post-Constantinian mode by thinking in a pre-Constantinian way about the absolute centrality of Christ and his community's allegiance to him as Lord. The Church became important, in Barth's theology, as a visible, counter-cultural community, which witnesses to the new reality of Jesus Christ. Barth increasingly stressed the uniqueness and separateness of the Christian community.

Barth's noted preference for the more concrete term "community," *Gemeinde*, over the more abstract word "church," *Kirche*, was, according to Yoder, a move toward the ecclesiological understanding of German-speaking Baptists and pietists who regarded the church as the assembly or congregation.[8] Barth thought that the term community helped to convey the important truth that the church is not a vague ideal, but a concrete, visible people.[9] As a particular community, the church is to be a community of service rather than a hierarchy of clergy and laity. For Barth, therefore, the church is to be the example for the ordering of

---

3. Yoder, "Basis of Barth's Social Ethics," 8. The doctrine of revelation and the disavowal of natural theology were part of Barth's rejection of culture Christianity. Timothy Gorringe ties Barth's doctrine of revelation to his understanding of the absolute lordship of Christ. Gorringe, *Karl Barth*, 128–47.

4. Yoder, "Karl Barth, Post-Christendom Theologian," 6.

5. Yoder, "Why Ecclesiology is Social Ethics," in *Royal Priesthood*, 109.

6. Yoder, "Basis of Barth's Social Ethics," 7.

7. Yoder, "Karl Barth, Post-Christendom Theologian," 7.

8. Ibid., 9; and "Karl Barth: How His Mind Kept Changing," 170.

9. Yoder also claims that in this later work Barth's Christology also took on a more concrete, narrative form with more attention to the fully human person of Jesus.

civil community, never the other way around. These elements in Barth's ecclesiology, together with Barth's use of Scripture and his view of baptism, led Yoder to argue that Barth was a free church theologian.

George Hunsinger contends, in response to Yoder, that Barth never understood the state and the church's relation to it from the position of sectarian Protestantism. Hunsinger argues that Yoder "mistakes Barth's movement in the direction of a free church ecclesiology with a movement in the direction of a free church self-understanding, as if the two were the same thing."[10] Hunsinger insists that Barth did not understand himself as a free church thinker, i.e., sectarian, even when his own ecclesiology bore a resemblance to that formulated within the free church tradition. He is concerned that the separateness of the church not be pushed too far in explaining Barth's position. For Barth, the church must always participate in the world, and this requires a positive regard for culture and the state. Also, the state is never relegated to the realm of fallen, unredeemed creation. Thus, Hunsinger argues, Barth did not agree with any sectarian desire to sequester the church from the secular realm. In short, Hunsinger argues that Barth held to a free church ecclesiology without the social stance of a sectarian Protestant. Even if his ecclesiology moved to a free church position, Barth retained a fairly positive view of the state generally in line with the Reformed position.[11] Barth did, however, want to free the Church from state sponsorship and control so that it could be free to judge the state in both its positive and negative aspects. Above all, Barth wanted the church to offer a transformative witness to the world, including the state, regarding the activity of the Triune God in both creation and redemption.

Baptism and the Free Community

Central to the ecclesiology seen in this chapter is Barth's critique and rejection of infant baptism. To recall the discussion in chapter two, Barth thought that baptism should be administered to those who were able to respond to God's Word. Baptism is the human response to the grace that one has received. The practice of administering baptism without the desire, commitment or voluntary participation of the candidate was

---

10. Hunsinger, *Disruptive Grace*, 122.

11. Ibid., 126. For Calvin on the state, see Institutes IV, XX; and Lange, "City of God," 140–51.

problematic for Barth. If we understand baptism as "the renunciation and pledge which responds to God's cleansing and renewing work and word in the freedom which God has given for this purpose, and which is made in a free choice and rejection, affirmation and negation," the baptism of infants is a puzzling practice.[12]

In Barth's description, infant baptism became a standard practice after the rise of Christendom associated with Constantine. The so-called Constantinian shift was the merger of state and church into the *Corpus Christianum*.[13] The church was from that point forward identified with the totality of the Christian empire. The baptism of infants arose to include all who are born into the Empire as naturally members of the church by virtue of their birth.[14] Christendom has made "baptism an entrance card into the best European society."[15] By contrast, baptism once expressed the concrete turning in the life of a person.

> It is the perverted ecclesiastical practice of administering a baptism in which the baptised supposedly becomes a Christian unwittingly and unwillingly that has obscured the consciousness of the once-for-allness of this beginning, replacing it by the comfortable notion that there is not needed any such beginning of Christian existence, but rather that we can become and be Christians in our sleep, as though we had no longer to awaken out of sleep. We must not allow infant baptism to induce in us this comfortable notion.[16]

According to Barth, the church clings to infant baptism to keep this relation between church and society.[17] Most major streams of Christian tradition do not want to see the practice of infant baptism done away with for fear of the end of Christendom.[18] Under the watchword of "re-

---

12. Barth, *CD* IV/4, 166.

13. See Harvey, *Another City*, 64–94; and Yoder, *Royal Priesthood*, 54–64, 194–218.

14. Barth, *CD* IV/3.2, 872–73. We should not overlook the importance of the doctrine of original sin in the rise of the baptism of infants.

15. Barth, *CD* IV/3.2, 876. What this does to the relationship between Christians and Jews was particularly troubling to Barth.

16. Barth, *CD* IV/3.2, 517–18.

17. See the discussion of Zwingli's defense of infant baptism as a defense of the national church. Barth, *CD* IV/1, 56–57.

18. As Yoder states, the Anabaptists were not killed for their insistence on a particular form of baptism. They were drowned because the entire Constantinian concubinage was at stake. "Adjusting to the Changing Shape," 206.

sponsibility" the church in Christendom thinks its fate is tied into that of the nation in which it resides.

According to Barth, infant baptism creates a "mass church" which is Christian only in name.[19] As a result, "the Church is watered down, literally watered down with holy water, and then men complain about the dismal state of the churches, which people belong to though they have no faith."[20] Barth describes the result of infant baptism, i.e., whole populations of whole countries automatically made the holy community, as absurd.[21] Yet some Christians still "cannot accustom themselves to the idea that it might be better for the cause and ministry of the Church in or to the world if one day, without being able to rejoice in any acknowledged position or guaranteed continuity, it had to exist again in people, society and state as a small and unassuming group of aliens, though also, freed of much ballast, as a mobile brotherhood."[22] Barth believed that a healthy Christian minority would be of more use to society than an unhealthy, majority Christendom.[23]

It is true that children belong to the covenant of God and that children of believers are said to be holy (1 Cor 7:14). Yet baptism has replaced circumcision in the church, and the church is not to be confused with Christian nations and societies as Israel was a nation.[24] For Israel,

19. "Under these circumstances, one need not be surprised at the stream of indifference and secularism which flows through our church." Barth, *Heidelberg Catechism for Today*, 105.

20. Barth, *Fragments Grave and Gay*, 86. John Colwell shows the similarities in how early Anabaptist Pilgrim Marpeck and Barth argued that infant baptism has disastrous consequences for the life of the church. "Alternative Approaches to Believer's Baptism," 20.

21. Barth, *CD* IV/1, 696. Of course this is a complicated issue, considering the fact that the citizens of a particular country were identified with their king in religious identity. This argument was seen in the Diets at Speyer of 1526 and 1529 and the principle stated in the Peace of Augsburg (1555): "where there is one ruler, there should be only one religion" (*Ubi unus dominus, ibi una sit religio*) or as later restated "whose reign, his religion." See Lindberg, *European Reformations*, 232–47.

22. Barth, *CD* IV/4, 168. Recall Barth's criticism of the Constantinian shift in *Teaching of the Church Regarding Baptism* discussed in chapter one.

23. See Barth, *Teaching of the Church Regarding Baptism*, 53. Brian Spinks points to Soren Kierkegaard's criticism of Christendom and infant baptism as an antecedent to Barth's. Spinks, "Karl Barth's Teaching on Baptism," 280–81. See Kierkegaard, *Concluding Unscientific Postscript*, 325–29, 332–33.

24. On circumcision and baptism see Beasley-Murray, *Baptism in the New Testament*, 334–43.

continuation of the covenant was through physical descent. Physical descent is not the basis for the new covenant.[25] The church, for Barth, is thus not simply a repetition of Israel. The new covenant is not made with a particular nation, but a body drawn from all nations and peoples. One is accepted into this covenant on the basis of faith, not family background or citizenship. No one comes into the church because of family or nationality.[26]

Barth places the individual Christian and the Christian community in a healthy dialectic. On the one hand, individual persons are important. He states that the community exists under the promise of grace. Yet this grace is not fulfilled by merely being a member of the collective. As Barth states: "In baptism a human life comes into the life of the community. It is not submerged therein. It does not lose its individuality. In all its individuality, however, it becomes the life of a member of the community."[27] On the other hand, the church is not formed by individuals who exist in splendid isolation; but it is the fellowship or society of persons who are brought together by the Holy Spirit. Church membership is a personal matter of responsibility and decision in light of one's baptism, but this does not mean individuals seek their own good and enrichment, nor that they exercise their freedom according to their personal judgment.

The concern for individual Christians in the doctrine of baptism, for Barth and for baptists, is not for the sake of the individual but for the sake of a healthy church. Members are freed and empowered for their participation in the community and its work.[28] This concern for the church is also true of the individualism inherent in most baptist theology. Barth repeated his view that the risk of perfectionism in believers' baptism is less dangerous than that of a nominal Christianity in which people can disclaim their responsibility because they were joined to the Church without their own decision.[29]

---

25. Barth, *Heidelberg Catechism for Today*, 104. See also *CD* IV/4, 178.

26. Barth, *CD* III/2, 585.

27. "The union of men with God, as the purpose of their history with Him, has always to be specifically and personally realized by each of them." Barth, *CD* IV/3.2, 781. See also Webster, *Barth's Ethics of Reconciliation*, 169–70.

28. Barth, *CD* IV/3.2, 781.

29. Barth, *CD* IV/4, 193. Colwell states: "the eschatological orientation of baptism undermines any assumption of the Church's present purity or perfectedness—the

Barth's View of the Church's Relation to the World

Barth on the State

Barth's extended discussions of the state are offered in two lectures. "*Rechtfertigung und Recht*," (1938) and "*Christengemeinde und Bürgergemeinde*" (1946). Barth's concern with the church and the state lay not with the respective institutions but the human beings who form these corporate bodies in order to achieve a common goal.[30] The civil community is the "commonality of all the people in one place, region or country in so far as they belong together under a constitutional system of government that is equally valid for and binding on them all, and which is defended and maintained by force." The church, in contrast, is "the common life of these people in one Spirit, the Holy Spirit, that is, in obedience to the Word of God in Jesus Christ, which they have all heard and are all needing and eager to hear again."[31] In another similar definition, Barth states: "Political systems are the attempts undertaken and carried out by men in order to secure the common political life of man by certain co-ordinations of individual freedom and the claims of the community, by the establishing of laws with power to apply and preserve them."[32] Political systems make space for life and history by holding back chaos and preserving a semblance of order and peace.

Barth relies predominantly upon "the Augustinian-Reformed doctrine of the state as an order of preservation."[33] In the patience of God, the state exists to give human beings time. Robert Hood argues that Barth's view of the state is related to his doctrine of providence, "where the content of *conservatio* has to do with being preserved by God against chaos."[34] The state helps stem the tide of chaos so that human beings can survive and in some sense flourish.

> The deepest, ultimate, divine purpose of the civil community consists in creating opportunities for the preaching and hearing

---

perfection of the Church lies in its Christ-enclosed future rather than in its Christ-witnessing present." Colwell, *Promise and Presence*, 73.

30. Barth, "Christian Community and the Civil Community," 15.
31. Ibid., 16.
32. Barth, *Against the Stream*, 80.
33. Herberg, "Social Philosophy of Karl Barth," 36.
34. Hood, "Karl Barth's Christological Basis," 231.

of the Word and, to that extent, for the existence of the Church. But the only way the State can create such opportunities, according to the providence and ordination of God, is the natural, secular and profane way of the establishment of law, the safeguarding of freedom and peace, according to the measure of human insight and capacity.[35]

The purpose of the state is to safeguard the freedom and life of both individuals and the community.[36] "This sinful and perverse government among men is a necessary divine order to restrain its equally sinful and perverse freedom."[37] In his wisdom and patience, God has established the various states to provide room in which his purpose in creation can unfold.[38]

However, Barth does not seek to confuse state with church. He wants to allow the state to perform the function which was given to it by God. The fifth thesis of the Barmen declaration reads thus:

> The Bible tells us that, in accordance with a divine ordinance, the State has the task of providing law and peace in the world that still awaits redemption, in which the Church stands, according to the measure of human insight and human capacity, and upheld by the threat and use of force. The Church acknowledges the benefaction of this divine ordinance with a thankful, reverent heart. It reminds men of God's Kingdom, God's Commandment and justice, and thereby of the responsibility of governors and governed alike. It trusts and obeys the power of the Word by which God sustains all things.[39]

The purpose of the state is to provide stability and freedom for the church to exist and live out its mission. As Rowan Williams declares, "the state exists, not as a thing in itself, but as a means of getting things done."[40] Human law is established with divine providence to provide peace and freedom, in a relative sense, to humanity which still needs time hear the gospel, time to repent and come to faith.[41] This connec-

---

35. Barth, "Christian Community and the Civil Community," 30.
36. Ibid., 16.
37. Barth, *God in Action*, 34.
38. Barth, *Against the Stream*, 94.
39. Barth, "Christian Community and the Civil Community," 50.
40. Williams, "Barth, War, & the State," 187.
41. Barth, "Christian Community and the Civil Community," 21. See also Barth, *Against the Stream*, 80–81.

tion is primarily an indirect one. The state holds back chaos and the impediments to freedom. The state's relation to God's redemption of the world is thus indirect, but this does not imply a negative view of the state.[42]

According to Barth, the state belongs to the order of redemption; it exists in the Christological sphere.[43] Pontius Pilate is mentioned in the second article of the Creed. In a providential way, Pilate both delivered Jesus to his sentence of death and pronounced him innocent beforehand.[44] In this failure on the part of the state, i.e., the capital punishment of an innocent man, what was necessary for our justification took place. Barth thought that without a clear understanding of the connection between church and state, both human justice and divine justice would be misunderstood.[45] "The state as such, belongs originally and ultimately to Jesus Christ; that in its comparatively independent substance, in its dignity, its function, and its purpose, it should serve the Person and Work of Jesus Christ and therefore the justification of the sinner."[46] Without absolutizing the state, Barth insists that the state is a divine ordinance. It is an institution ordained by the will of God (Rom 13:1–7).[47] Barth references the New Testament language regarding the thrones, powers, and principalities.[48]

The Relation Between Church and State

The difficult relationship between church and state in Barth's thought is clarified only if we understand that the state is entirely under the lordship of Jesus Christ. The state is "outside the Church, but not outside the range of Christ's dominion."[49] The civil community is different from the church, yet it is still within the one activity of God in the world. In no sense does the Church wait for the state to become the

42. Williams, "Barth, War, & the State," 181.
43. Barth, "Church and State," 120.
44. Ibid., 112
45. Ibid., 101.
46. Ibid., 118.
47. Ibid., 115–16. Even fallen the powers are still under the Lordship of Christ. See *Christian Life*, 216–18. For Barth's treatment of angels see *CD* III/3, 477–531.
48. On the powers, see Berkhof, *Christ and the Powers*, 19–20; and Yoder, *Politics of Jesus*, 134–61.
49. Barth, "Christian Community and the Civil Community," 21.

Kingdom of God.[50] The church is thankful for what the state provides but does not seek to establish a church-state.[51] Christians should never attempt to create a state "in the likeness of the Kingdom of God."[52] The Church must "be and remain a Christian fellowship and live for its own concerns even in the midst of political changes."[53] The church's own expectation and hopes include the proper ordering of the state, but they are not tied to and identified with the state. That assumption was the particular problem of the Constantinian shift.[54]

But if the State is not to be equated with either the church or the Kingdom of God, neither can church and state be separated as two unrelated kingdoms.[55] The existence of the state in our fallen world is an allegory or an analogue of the Kingdom of God. The church proclaims the kingdom of God and can hope the State will offer a working allegory so that the state and the rule and order that it provides tell us something of God's coming order and rule.[56] Even the worst political system will reveal something of God's wisdom and rule.[57] Though it does the work of the church only indirectly, the civil community can reflect the truth which the Christian community proclaims.[58] According to Barth, this means that Christians must insist that their state keep its responsibility to care for the socially and economically weak members of society. It must look after the poor. In a concrete sense, the church should back

50. Ibid., 31.

51. Ibid., 30 and *Against the Stream*, 99.

52. Barth, "Christian Community and the Civil Community," 31.

53. Barth, *Against the Stream*, 78.

54. By decrying the Constantinian shift the element noted here is what is rejected. I am not implying a "fall" of the church causing doctrine and tradition to be suspect. See Williams, *Retrieving the Tradition*, 101–31, for a description and response to such a view.

55. According to Frank Jehle, Barth had a version of the two kingdoms doctrine of Luther. Christians exist in two kingdoms, the Kingdom of Christ, represented by the church, and the State. The state, is of course still under the rule of Christ, but is allowed to function somewhat autonomously during its time. Jehle, *Ever Against the Stream*, 103–6.

56. Barth, *CD* IV/3.1, 113–50. Such analogies bring some illumination to those who do not have the clear light of Christ. Ibid., 141. See also Wood, *Comedy of Redemption*, 67–72.

57. Barth, *Against the Stream*, 81. See Werpehowski, "Karl Barth and Politics," 232.

58. See Jehle, *Ever Against the Stream*, 74–75, for Barth's view of Switzerland during the war.

the political and social movements that seem to promise the "greatest measure of social justice."[59]

Even with his positive concept of the state in general, Barth was not naïve or blind regarding the shortcomings of historical nation-states, especially in the Germany of his lifetime. He insisted, instead, that judgments regarding states have to be made concretely and from within a given situation.[60] It is important to make sober distinctions between different, historical states. No ideology should hold the church in captivity.[61] Neither obedience nor resistance to a state can be turned into an ideal or absolute position. Christian obedience or resistance to a state must be offered to a specific state and in particular circumstances.[62] The church cannot treat the state as either an infallible god or as an all-devouring demon. As Barth states, "the State can of course become 'demonic,' and the New Testament makes no attempt to conceal the fact that at all times the Church may, and actually does, have to deal with the 'demonic' State. . . . On the other hand, it is not inevitable that the State should become a 'demonic' force."[63] A state will never be the incarnation of evil, because it is under the lordship of Christ. The state is an ordinance of God provided for the fallen world in God's work of redemption. The power wielded by a political system was given to it by God. As such, it is also due a certain honor.[64]

Yet the instability of political systems is a sign of their imperfection and temporality.[65] No perfect civil community exists. The state will never manifest the kingdom. The church does not lend its support to states which are anarchic or tyrannical. In the same way, states which

---

59. Barth, "Christian Community and the Civil Community," 37.

60. Hunsinger states that Barth's politics and view of political praxis is an element of his actualism. We can have a political orientation, but decisions have to be made in the living situation as God and the context demand. "Toward a Radical Barth," 226. For a positive reading of Barth in this regard, see also Osborn, "'Personalistic' Appraisal of Barth's Political Ethics," 313–24.

61. Busch argues that Barth's attempt to do theology "as if nothing has happened," during the political climate of the 1930s, was an avoidance of using our theology to support preconceived political ideas. Busch, "'Doing Theology," 465.

62. Barth, *Against the Stream*, 86, 91.

63. Barth, "Church and State," 118.

64. Ibid., 109–10.

65. Barth, *Against the Stream*, 84. The state, "though a divine institution, is an institution in the human sphere." See Barth, *Fragments Grave and Gay*, 73.

do not serve their purpose, which is to guarantee the freedom of their citizens, are to be opposed. Christians also cannot support a state which establishes and maintains itself with the use of naked force.[66] In any case, neither the opposing or the backing of a political system should be confused with the mission of the church.[67]

The Exemplarity of the Church

When rightly ordered, the Church's life and order should be an example and pattern for the order of other areas of human society, such as political and economic institutions. For Barth, "true Church law is exemplary law."[68] This emphasis characterizes Barth's entire ecclesiology. The church orders itself in distinction from the world, but it does so for the sake of the world. Barth calls this the two-sided responsibility of the church. It has a responsibility to tend to its own internal order and shape so that it may be truly available to the world. Just as Jesus Christ did not do what he did on the cross for himself, so must the church which he sanctified on the cross not exist for itself but the world.[69] The church "as the body of Jesus Christ and therefore the earthly-historical form of His existence, is the provisional representation of the humanity sanctified in Him." The church exists to bear witness to the new reality begun in Christ. James McClendon asserts that "exemplarity" is Barth's primary way of understanding the relationship between church and the state.[70]

Barth's intention is not to "ecclesiasticise the world"; church order is not to be forced upon the rest of the world. Rather, by its existence in the world in a particular form, the church is a witness to civil communities. "In the form in which it exists among them it can and must be to the world of men around it a reminder of the law of the kingdom of God already set up on earth in Jesus Christ, and a promise of its future manifestation. *De facto*, whether they realise it or not, it can and should show them that there is already on earth an order which is based on

---

66. Barth, "Christian Community and the Civil Community," 40.
67. Barth, *Against the Stream*, 85.
68. Barth, *CD* IV/2, 719.
69. Ibid.
70. McClendon, *Ethics*, 231. The church models service, trust, mutuality, and flexibility to the world.

that great alteration of the human situation and directed towards its manifestation." The church witnesses to the state about the kingdom of God and instructs the state of its true purpose.[71] The church is meant to be a community in the world which orders and maintains itself differently from others. In particular the church exemplifies, or should do so, the order of service, mutual trust, common responsibility, and brother and sisterhood among all members.[72] The Christian community seeks a better order, a better peace, and a better freedom than that of the world in rebellion against God.

The state establishes its power with the sword and all those within its boundaries are compelled to abide by its authority:

> The Church has found its calling to consist in something else than in the establishment and maintenance of such a rule. It will give to Caesar what is Caesar's, but it can never give its unconditional sanction to any such form of mastery, to any form of the state or trend of culture. It cannot join hands with any of them for better or worse.... For the sake of God and man, it will keep its hands free for its own peculiar task. The sign which it is called to erect is a sign other than the sign of dominion.[73]

The church's law is a law of service. It exists as it serves its Lord, and by its nature and purpose it serves the world in which it lives. The church exists not to dominate but to serve, just as Christ its head came not to be served but to serve. The Jesus of the Gospels consistently states that servanthood is the way in which his followers must live in the world.[74] The demand is placed upon the church that, with the totality of its being and in all its activity, the church is to serve; individuals and the community are all to be servants. The new freedom which is given to the church is the freedom to serve.[75] By being a community of service and not dominion, love and not force, the church is to exist as a witness to the political structures within which it lives.

It is not the church's responsibility to set up the kingdom of God on earth through human progress and amelioration. That belief in in-

---

71. Barth, *CD* IV/2, 721. See *Fragments Grave and Gay*, 74.
72. Barth, *CD* IV/2, 723–24.
73. Barth, *God in Action*, 34.
74. See Mark 9:35–37 (Matt 18:1–5) and Mark 10:42–45 (Matt 20:25–28).
75. Barth, *CD* IV/2, 698–99.

evitable progress was the mistake of nineteenth century Protestantism. Barth states, in contrast, that the Kingdom already exists. The Kingdom was made a reality by Christ; it is, thus, not the work of the church or the state.[76] Yet, the order and form of the church are of central significance as it witnesses to Christ and his new reality. The church does not work to usher in the Kingdom, but lives according to what we know of it, as seen in Christ.[77] With the elements which characterize its own order, the church should serve as a model for other institutions to learn from and imitate. The church's influence on the world's law should be corrective. The church must model for the state how a community should be ordered so that it can be a source for renewal and correct use of power by the state.[78]

Yoder drew out this element in Barth's theology in "Why Ecclesiology Is Social Ethics," as one of his Stone Lectures given in 1980. According to Yoder, Barth made the essential distinction in ethics and politics to consist in the difference between the confession or non-confession of Jesus Christ. This is what distinguishes civil community and Christian community. Following this distinction, "social ethics should consist in the exemplarity of the church as foretaste/model/herald of the kingdom."[79] The demarcations of church and world denote two different political and social identifications. "Barth is affirming for the first time in mainstream Protestant theology since Constantine the theological legitimacy of admitting, about a set of social structures, that those who participate in them cannot be presumed to be addressable from the perspective of Christian confession."[80]

In the standard, even if inadequate, terms provided by Ernst Troeltsch, Barth takes a sectarian approach, in that the church real-

---

76. Ibid., 725.

77. Yoder has a helpful way of putting the matter. The church is not responsible for the outcome of history, "but the church is responsible for the congruence between its ministry and that new world that is the church's way because it is on the way." Yoder, *Royal Priesthood*, 126.

78. Barth, "Christian Community and the Civil Community," 48.

79. Yoder, *Royal Priesthood*, 106.

80. Ibid., 108. "To celebrate, and to celebrate repeatedly in memory of Jesus, the glory of God as righteous and as sovereign means to cultivate explicitly an alternative consciousness, to maintain a sense of reality running against the stream of the unquestioningly accepted commonplaces of the age." Ibid., 123.

izes that it is not in control of the society in which it finds itself.[81] This approach goes against the common assumption of Christian "responsibility," in which Christian ethics seeks to serve the needs of secular society.[82] While Barth rejects this conception of the church's responsibility to the state, he also insists that the church can never withdraw from the world. Barth's ecclesiology offers a free church vision that does not become "sectarian." Philip Kenneson considerably clarifies Barth's ecclesiology by rejecting any simplistic understanding of distinct spheres. Kenneson states:

> "Church" and "world" are in no straight forward way two distinct places, as if one could retreat or withdraw from the world (in either sense).... A proper understanding of the church's service and mission to the world requires being in contact with the world. What makes the church different from the world is not that it occupies some different spatial location. The church is different from the world because its life is animated by a different Spirit—a difference manifested in its material practices and institutions, as well as in the narratives and convictions that give them shape and intelligibility. Christians should regard the world not as a separate place, but as a way of life ordered by a set of narratives, practices, and convictions that is at odds with those narratives, practices, and convictions the church is called to embody as a condition of its discipleship to Jesus Christ.[83]

While the state needs the church because it is the only source of true knowledge regarding its legitimation and necessity, the church also honors and expects the best from the earthly state because it is waiting for the eternal state. In relation to the state the church must remain the church. Even though "the State is in the Kingdom of Christ, this does not mean that God is revealed, believed, and perceived in any political community as such."[84] No political system, not even democracy, exists as the one authorized bearer of Christianity as opposed to other systems or forms of government. The Christian community has as its task the proclamation of the gospel, which is the good news of the rule of Christ

---

81. Ibid., 108. For Troeltsch's categories of church, sect, and mysticism, see Troeltsch, *Social Teaching of the Christian Church*, 993.

82. Yoder, *Royal Priesthood*, 111.

83. Kenneson, *Beyond Sectarianism*, 86–87.

84. Barth, "Christian Community and the Civil Community," 25.

and the coming Kingdom of God. This task can never be relinquished to the civil community.[85] The church should not look to the state for any guarantee of the effectiveness of its preaching. The only "guarantee" the church looks to the state to provide is a limited guarantee of its freedom.[86]

The Free Church and the State Churches

Contemporary theologians have begun to see the danger of the inherited state-church arrangements, due in large part to Barth's free church ecclesiology. As James McClendon states: "if the developing free-church ecclesiology of the latest volumes of Barth's *Church Dogmatics* is a guide (as I am convinced it is), then there appeared at mid-century an ecclesial standpoint, a theology of culture, willing to allow the world to be world, to be no longer simply the Holy European Church (including its overseas, American branch) attending to its customary civil tasks."[87] Jürgen Moltmann argues in a similar way that the church reform he envisioned in *The Church in the Power of the Spirit,*

> can be followed only if we are prepared to break away from passive church membership and to make a new beginning by entering into active participation in the life of the congregation. In our society, affiliations that are imposed are losing their power to shape people's lives and lend them significance. Forms of community that are accepted personally and entered into voluntarily are becoming more important. . . . The old established "national" or regional churches, which were supposed to care for all the people, are losing members. . . . Free decision in faith, voluntary sociality, mutual recognition and acceptance of one another and a common effort for justice and peace in this

---

85. Ibid., 22. Barth was opposed to all "Christian" political parties and thus withdrew from the Christian Socialists with which he was associated earlier in his career.

86. Hunsinger cautions: "I think it is exceedingly Constantinian to hold . . . that the decisive test for any social order is the freedom it grants to the Church. Nothing could be more Constantinian that for the Church to expect special privileges from the State. The State finds its decisive test, in my opinion, not in the privileges enjoyed by the Church, but in how well justice and peace are actually secured in practice (cf. Romans 13:3-4)." Hunsinger, "To Hauerwas," 255.

87. McClendon, *Witness*, 322. McClendon states that to read Barth in this way is to invoke Yoder's reading of Barth.

violent society of ours: these are the guidelines for the future of the church.[88]

After Barth, theologians such as Hauerwas, Yoder, McClendon and others have recognized the importance of letting the church be church and the world be the world.[89] By rejecting infant baptism, Barth attacked the marriage of convenience between church and state in which the church is reduced to something of a chaplain for society. These arrangements have resulted in the church's irrelevance since we are all "Christians" anyway.

In line with his rejection of infant baptism, Barth rejected the state or national churches tied to the interests of a particular nation. As Barth states, "Christianity exists in Germany and Switzerland and Africa, but there is no such thing as a German or Swiss or African Christianity. There is a Church in England, but in the strict sense there is no Church of England."[90] Since Christianity merged with the Roman Empire, the church has usually assumed a continuity between civilization and culture and the Church. Yet a person can no longer be a Christian according to their birth. "There is therefore no such thing as a Christian State corresponding to the Christian Church."[91] Craig Carter argues that Barth's ecclesiology is a completion of the work of the Reformation. The Reformers failed to reform the church's relation to the state and its coercive power.[92] Particularly troubling to Barth during the 1930s and 40s were the religious claims of National Socialism.[93]

---

88. Moltmann, *Church in the Power of the Spirit*, xiii–xiv.

89. Yoder states: "The church's responsibility to and for the world is first and always to be the church." Yoder, *Royal Priesthood*, 61.

90. Barth, *CD* IV/1, 703.

91. Barth, "Christian Community and the Civil Community," 25. As a result of his experiences in the world wars and the politics which surrounded them, Barth was able to say "there is no doubt that in recent years the whole conception of a Christian civilization in the West has been pitilessly exposed as an illusion." Karl Barth, *Against the Stream*, 57.

92. Carter, "Karl Barth's Revision of Protestant Ecclesiology," 36.

93. "It [protest] must be directed fundamentally against the fact (which is the source of all individual errors) that, beside the Holy Scriptures as the unique norm of revelation, the German-Christians affirm the German nationhood, its history and its contemporary political situation as a second source of revelation, and thereby betray themselves to be believers in 'another God.'" Barth, *German Church Conflict*, 16.

One should also remember Barth's disavowal of any other gods in his 1933 piece "The First Commandment as an Axiom of Theology," 63–78. Barth notes, "The com-

When the church becomes a national church the true interests of the church and its mission are lost to the interests of the nation which it supports and undergirds.[94] Rather than looking to the interests of one nation, the church is a truly international commonwealth which is made up of all peoples and tribes. The wonderful freedom of the church lies in the ability "to recruit across the frontiers of nations, states, and other natural or historical unions and societies, not removing the distinctions or boundaries but transcending them, not identifying itself with any but being one and the same *ecclesia una catholica* in all, existing within them as a universal people, indeed as *the* universal people."[95]

The ministry of the church that Barth labels "evangelisation" is the conversion of "Christendom" to Christianity. Numerous nominal Christians are present in the Christian west who have no knowledge of or participation in Christ and his community. They are Christian only in name. Barth implicates the practice of infant baptism for leading to this non-Christian Christendom, the *corpus christianum*. Christians are called to present the gospel to these baptized but nominal Christians who are in truth ignorant of and strangers to the Gospel.[96] Insofar as the state is nominally Christian it encourages a nominal Christianity. If, however, the church calls it to be a just and charitable secular state, it will fulfill its proper role, which includes upholding a stability in which the church has the freedom to make its witness—even to the state.

The Voluntary Community

The church must realize that no state decision or compulsion makes people Christians. Church membership, as Anabaptists and Baptists have insisted, needs to be voluntary in nature. "The Christian commu-

---

mandment lays its hand on the Israelites. It isolates all of Israel from those people who have other gods." Ibid., 70. We must also note Barth's insightful warning regarding the word "and," such as revelation and ethos of culture or revelation and human existence. Ibid., 72–73.

94. In the depiction of Aaron in Exod 32, the episode with the golden calf, Aaron gives in to the grumblings of the Israelites and fashions them an image of God as they demand. According to Barth, Aaron "is the man of the national Church, the established Church. He listens to the voice of the soul of the people and obeys it. He is the direct executor of its wishes and demands." Barth *CD* IV/1, 429.

95. Barth, *CD* IV/3.2, 741.

96. Ibid., 872–73.

nity does not embrace all men, but only those who profess themselves Christians and would like, more or less seriously, to be Christians" even though it reaches out to all.[97] No Christian societies or Christian governments can exist. "The idea of a Christianity which is automatically given and received with the rest of our inheritance has now become historically impossible, no matter how tenaciously it may linger on and even renew itself in various attempts at restoration by the Church and the world. The Christian West ... no longer exists either in the city or in the peace of the remotest hamlet."[98] As far as the mission of the church is concerned, the state serves the church best by being a secular state.

Simply stating that church membership is voluntary—in the sense that no state or church power should force someone to join an ecclesial body or confess a particular creed—does not end the matter. On a sociological level Barth's understanding of the church is indeed voluntary. No one should be coerced or forced into the church. Such practices have done nothing but harm the church's life and witness. On a stronger, theological level the church is not voluntary, however, if by voluntary we mean that people form and join the church solely of their own decision and for their own purposes.[99] This type of voluntarism can quickly become an insidious individualism and Pelagianism. The church "can never be understood as a society which men join of themselves and in which they are active in the pursuit of their own ends, however religious."[100]

To understand the voluntary nature of the church, the role of grace in human commitment must be considered. Barth insists that grace

97. Barth, "Christian Community and the Civil Community," 19.

98. Barth, *CD* IV/3.2, 524–25.

99. See Reimer, "Adequacy of a Voluntaristic Theology," 135–48; and Stanley Hauerwas's recent argument for the church as a non-voluntary community in *Sanctify Them in the Truth*, 164–67.

100. Barth, *CD*, IV/2, 654. Members of the church "have not met by accident, or gathered together arbitrarily, but have been brought together by the revelation of His name," thus "they are not left to their own devices in their common action, but their King and Lord Himself gives them direction and orders and commands, and consolation and promises." Barth *CD* IV/2, 699. "The Church is not a chance, i.e., an arbitrary construction. It is not created, formed and introduced by individual men on their own initiative, authority and insight. It is not the outcome of a free undertaking to analyse and come to terms with the self-revealing God by gathering together a community which confesses Him, by setting up a doctrine which expounds and proclaims His truth in the way that seems most appropriate to these men." Barth, *CD*, I/2, 213.

does not override human freedom. Grace enables human conversion and fidelity. As Barth says, "the Church gathers its members through free individual decisions, behind which stands the quite different free choice of God."[101] It is possible, and indeed necessary, for Barth to speak of the church as both voluntary in membership and as called and ordered by God. In fact, the reception of grace and baptism into the church are not to be separated. Church membership is a gift. We are called and brought into the church by the Holy Spirit. In other words, membership in the community of Christ is not simply one's "choice" because being brought to the church is the work of the Holy Spirit. Yet, this decision is voluntary because the Spirit enables free human decision and commitment. Thus the church is voluntary in two senses. The church is a voluntary community because it should be free from state or social coercion and because the Holy Spirit enables real human commitment rather than rendering it unnecessary. The community consists of the new humanity who have heard the Word and responded to it. They are, by the work of the Spirit, reconciled to God in Christ and thus are baptized as their initiation into the body of Christ. The activity of the Spirit in the formation of the church is not the theological equivalent of a state forcing people into its church.

We must allow for a God-given secularity in regards to the necessity of church membership, which we understand does not equate a theological secularity.[102] To be faithful to its mission, the church can no longer make use of the force of the state, or the pressure of culture, to coerce the reception of its message. According to Barth, the Spirit is already at work in human life, apart from the church and its witness. But

---

101. Barth, "Church and State," 131.

102. A theological secularity would assert a sphere or domain of the "secular" within which God is not present or atleast not active. No such "secular" sphere is possible. However, the church must allow the state its own autonomy, a "political secularity" free from the control of (or over) religious interests. God is not removed from the world, including the state, for that would be an impossibility. Yet the state is not God's vehicle for representing the kingdom of God and thus is not the object of a Christian's allegiance. This issue was also present in the previous distinction between a sociological and a theological understanding of voluntarism.

John Milbank has argued that the concept of the secular is a modern invention. Not until modernity was the world conceived of as a pure entity existing by and for itself. Milbank has argued, following Henri de Lubac, that pure nature, or ungraced nature, does not exist. Milbank, *Theology and Social Theory*, 9–12. See also Milbank, *Suspended Middle*.

in the proclaimed Word, the Spirit speaks specifically and powerfully, enabling those "who have ears to hear." This claim does not eliminate the possibility of rejection and the refusal to heed the Word. To be good news, this terrible possibility must be acknowledged.[103] But the positive reception of the Word is not the product of some allegedly independent will or autonomous reason either, but rather of the Spirit's action on and with the consent of all believers.

While no secular world exists in the sense of freedom from the lordship and dominion of Christ, because of sin we must allow for a relative secularity in regards to the state. In the present age, a secular state is necessary for the church to be the church. When the church associates itself and its goals with the state, its free gospel is lost to the will of the state. While the state is an ordinance of God for the good of a fallen creation and thus related to the gospel, it is not the bearer of the gospel or Christ's reconciling work in the world.

Barth has taken both Creation and Fall with utmost seriousness. According to Barth, the world exists only because of the creative and redemptive work of God in Christ. Sin, however, has marred that creation. Nevertheless, Christ is Lord of the world whether the world recognizes it or not. History is not a secular process, but operates as if it were. Thus, history is itself God's rule over a free creation. The Christian community reads history differently than the rest of the world. In fact, the church would be "guilty of a lack of faith and discernment if it were seriously to see and understand world history as secular or profane history."[104]

Church and Culture

For Barth the relationship between Church and world is not only the issue of church and state, but also the church and culture or society. The church should not be equated with Western culture any more than with political systems. Barth insists that the church remember both its distinction and its unity with the world in which it lives. The church is to be different from the world, but only so that it can witness to the world. As Colin Gunton states, "Christendom presupposed a consensus

---

103. Yoder argues that Christian accommodation to philosophical foundationalism is an intellectual form of Constantinianism. It is an attempt to avoid vulnerability so that people will have to believe. "On Not Being Ashamed of the Gospel," 285–300.

104. Barth, *CD* IV/3.2, 687.

between theology and culture. When the consensus is lost, theology must find its basis in the church, because it must take shape in the place where God's reality is acknowledged." This is not an evasion of responsibility for culture. "It is, rather, the quest for a place from which culture may be addressed."[105] The key to the relation of the church to culture is again its witness. The community of Jesus Christ must practice solidarity with the world. Precisely because of his willingness to let the church be the church and the world be the world, Barth is able to view culture favorably.[106] The church is not conformed to the world, but it is committed to it. "Solidarity with the world means full commitment to it, unreserved participation in its situation, in the promise given it by creation, in its responsibility for the arrogance, sloth and falsehood which reign within it, in its suffering under the resultant distress, but primarily and supremely in the free grace of God demonstrated and addressed to it in Jesus Christ, and therefore in its hope."[107]

In its human weakness, the church is a part of the world. "The world, therefore, is not just around it, but—in all its members—within it."[108] As James McClendon states it, the line between the church and the world passes through the heart of each Christian and the center of each church.[109] As a human institution the church is sinful. The saints who participate in the *communio sanctorum* are still *peccatores*. The Christian community is different from other communities primarily in its confession and proclamation of the lordship of Jesus Christ.[110] Baptism as a confession of the lordship of Christ separates Christians from their society. The fact that Christians are baptized should mean that their allegiances and commitments are different from those around them. As a result their lives and their conduct, even at times their politics, will often be different. As Kenneson notes, the church tells a different story about the world and this is embodied in different practices and convictions. As such, this community will encounter resistance in the world. Resistance has at points in history elicited active persecution, yet more

---

105. Gunton, "Karl Barth and the Western Intellectual Tradition," 299.
106. Wood, *Comedy of Redemption*, 60, 69.
107. Barth, *CD* IV/3.2, 773.
108. Barth, *CD* IV/2, 666.
109. McClendon, *Ethics*, 17 and *Doctrine*, 362.
110. See Healy, *Church, World and the Christian Life*, 6–7, on "Paul's Rule."

often the church is met with either pressure to be more reserved and more positive toward culture, or else it is met with sheer indifference.

Two dangers lie before the path of the church. The church can succumb to either alienation or to self-glorification, or, in other terms, secularization or sacralization. In secularization, non-Christian, secular ideas are baptized as Christian concerns. If the church is completely secularized it will become merely one more institution in society, losing its true existence. The church is an "alien and disruptive body."[111] The community cannot forget this without losing touch with its task and its purpose as Christ's body, the baptized who are dead to the world and thus alive to Christ. The church should remember its status as a minority, marginal group in the society in which it lives. "However great may be the solidarity which Christians feel and practice in relation to the world, their way can never be that of the world—and least of all that of the supposedly Christianized world."[112]

The church's task is the "witness which it has to make by its paradigmatic existence."[113] When the church allows itself to be determined from outside and controlled by the voice of a stranger it is alienated from its own origin and goal. "When the Church becomes secular, it is the greatest conceivable misfortune both for the Church and the world. And this is what takes place when it wants to be a Church only for the world, the nation, culture, or the state—a world Church, a national Church, a cultural Church, or a state Church."[114] The other danger which threatens those sinful human beings who constitute the church is to glorify themselves rather than God. When the church takes glory in itself and its own institutions and structures, rather than in Jesus Christ, it again loses touch with its own being. When the church assumes the lordship of Christ for itself it makes of itself a dead idol.[115] Ultimately the church walks this fine line between complete solidarity with the

---

111. Barth, *CD* IV/3.2, 744.

112. Barth, *CD* IV/2, 610.

113. Barth, *CD* IV/3.2, 747.

114. Barth, *CD* IV/2, 668. "It is necessary that a sanctuary be built in the midst of our world. And this sanctuary must not be a hybrid of Church and world, it must be truly Church, a Church which will remind men of the eternal kingdom of God." Barth, *God in Action*, 143.

115. Barth, *CD* IV/2, 670.

world and isolated ecclesiasticism, while attempting to avoid any pressures to change its message or its pattern of living in the world.

The Church's Responsibility and Allegiance

Political Involvement

The church created by baptizing believers is by nature a political entity. The term *ekklesia* is a borrowed political term referring to the assembly of people who constitute the church. The description which the New Testament gives of the new order, the world to come, is a political one. It employs the language of kingdom and city. The goal of the Christian community is the "*polis* built by God" which will come from heaven to earth and guide the other nations; it is a "heavenly *politeuma*" and the "*basileia* of God." In Barth's theology, the church is thus of central political significance.[116] Using New Testament language, Barth labels the church a "commonwealth," gathered and ordered by the word of God.[117] The church exists for the world and seeks the good of the state, yet their allegiance is ultimately to Christ as Lord. The fundamental confession that Jesus Christ is Lord, makes baptism a political act. The confession of loyalty to Christ bears political and ethical implications.[118] Baptism, rightly understood as one's transfer into a new culture, can be profoundly subversive.[119]

Christians belong to the state in which they find themselves, yet they "have their home elsewhere."[120] Barth's conception is reminicent of the description of Christians in society given in the Epistle to Diognetus. Christians "live in their own countries, but only as aliens.... Every foreign country is their Fatherland, and every Fatherland is foreign.... They live on earth, but their citizenship is in heaven." Christians are to the world what the soul is to the body. The soul is dispersed through the body; it is in the body, but not identical with it.[121] The true city or state

---

116. Barth, "Christian Community and the Civil Community," 19.
117. Barth, *Evangelical Theology*, 37.
118. Haymes, "Baptism as a Political Act," 76–77.
119. See Rodney Clapp on baptism as civil disobedience, *Peculiar People*, 99–102.
120. Barth, "Christian Community and the Civil Community," 24.
121. Epistle to Diognetus, 5–6. Quotes are from 5.5 and 5.9 in Holmes, *Apostolic Fathers*, 299.

of Christian is not of the "present age" but of the "age to come." As Barth explains:

> In this future city in which Christians have their citizenship here and now (without yet being able to inhabit it), we are concerned not with an ideal but with a real State—yes, with the only real State; not with an imaginary one but with the only one that truly exists. And it is the fact that Christians have their citizenship in this, the real State, that makes them strangers and sojourners within the State, or within the States of this age and this world."[122]

This hope for a new age is what actually separates the church from the state. In this age the church is a stranger.[123] Barth points out that writers of the Epistle to the Hebrews and of First Peter did not encourage their persecuted readers by telling them that they had a home in the present age. Rather, Christians have no abiding, permanent city. They are sojourners. The church is "nowhere at home on the earth"; "it can only lodge and camp here and there as the pilgrim people of God . . . at best it can only be permitted to stay but not granted any rights of settled citizenship."[124] This people of God share in the homelessness of Christ; they have no permanent place in the world.

As it sojourns, the church has a responsibility to the state. Christians are required to work for the good of the state. They must bear the responsibility and the work of the state in which they live.[125] Christians cannot withdraw from the functioning of the state and its law. The deep involvement and outspoken nature of Barth's political stance is highlighted by Frank Jehle. According to Jehle, one of Barth's statements could stand as a fitting motto for Barth's politics throughout his life: "A silent community, merely observing the events of the time, would not be a Christian community."[126] It is the particular duty of the church to pray for the leaders of the State in which they find themselves. They are to pray for their leaders so that in their governance these

---

122. Barth, "Church and State," 122–23.
123. Ibid., 125.
124. Barth, *CD* IV/3.2, 743.
125. Compare Jer 29:5–7. See also Yoder, *For the Nations*, 66–70.
126. Jehle, *Ever Against the Stream*, 80. See the sampling of Barth's political activism in Deschner, "Karl Barth as Political Activist," 56–60.

leaders will provide a quiet and peaceable life for the nation or state.[127] This intercession is the primary service which the church owes to the State.[128] Of course, Barth conceived of prayer as action. Thus, political involvement or opposition, done for the overall good of the state, can be understood as prayer. Barth's refusal to take the oath of allegiance to Hitler can be conceived of as prayer for the good of the German government. Barth refused to swear allegiance to Hitler at the University of Bonn in 1934, unless it was clearly understood that his allegiance to the government was secondary to his allegiance to God. This qualification reflected his belief that Christians "must always see themselves and act first decisively as Christians, and only then as members of this or that nation, citizens of this or that state, participants in the work of this or that cultural society."[129] After consideration, Barth was dismissed from the university in 1935.[130]

Civil power is binding on Christians, yet the Christian community does not submit in blind obedience to the state. Christians are to obey the laws of their state and seek its good, unless that state oversteps its bounds and demands of the church that it act against its beliefs and practices. The community does what is required for the establishment and functioning of the state so that it can carry out its proper tasks. However, the ultimate allegiance of the church is given to no one but Christ. The Church waits for the city whose builder and maker is God.[131]

Because the state bears the sword and is established and maintained by force, it "participates in the murderous nature of the pres-

---

127. Barth, "Church and State," 128 and *Fragments Grave and Gay*, 79.

128. Jehle, *Ever Against the Stream*, 107.

129. Barth, *CD* IV/3.2, 741. "Christians will always be Christians first, and only then members of a specific culture or state or class or the like. Similarly in all these different spheres the Church must always be the Church first, and only then, in the first instance in the advocacy of its own cause and to that extent always with a certain alienation, can it enter into positive relationships with these other spheres." Barth *CD* IV/2, 703.

130. Herberg, "Social Philosophy of Karl Barth," 41 and Busch, *Karl Barth*, 255–62. See Glenthoj, "Karl Barth and the German Salute," 309–24.

131. Barth, "Christian Community and the Civil Community," 26. In a sermon Barth stated: "The disciples of Jesus are men who are responsible to Jesus, and for that reason are responsible to no one else; they are wholly committed, and for that reason are free men in their commitment." Quoted in Busch, *Karl Barth*, 255.

ent age."[132] Yet because of human sin, force is required to uphold law. Barth agrees with the Reformers that Christians need to participate in military service to the State. He states: "the work of Christians in the world may include responsible involvement in using or threatening force. Whether it is right or wrong in particular cases is of course open to discussion."[133] Similarly, Christians can and should participate in the business of governance. Barth does think that certain duties are not binding upon the church. Christians do not have to swear an oath to a totalitarian state, nor do they have to adopt a particular philosophy of life (*Weltanschauung*). In both instances the secular realities would be overstepping their place in God's ordinance.[134]

Practical Pacifism

One of the key elements of Swiss Anabaptism was pacifism. Except for Balthasar Hubmaier, the Anabaptists proper felt that the sword was to be employed by the state, but not by Christians faithful to Christ's new way in the world. To relate Barth to the free church ecclesiology created by believer's baptism, a brief look at Barth's view of pacifism and war should prove helpful. Pacifism was an element of the socialism in which Barth participated early in his career. In separating himself from the religious socialists, Barth did not allow himself to be a pacifist as an absolute commitment. He was opposed to any such absolutism in his ethics. As his theology developed however, Barth came to appreciate pacifism as it relates to the work of the church. In *Church Dogmatics* III/4, Barth could say that "the inflexible negative of pacifism has almost infinite arguments in its favour and is almost overpoweringly strong." Discussions of war must at least take pacifism seriously in the majority of cases.[135] Barth's discussion of war falls within a larger section on "The Protection of Life." In regard to the state Barth says that "war should not on any account be recognized as a normal, fixed and in some sense necessary part of what on the Christian view constitutes the just state,

---

132. Barth, "Church and State," 142.
133. Barth, *Fragments Grave and Gay*, 79–80.
134. Barth, "Church and State," 142–43.

135. Barth, *CD* III/4, 455. A complete discussion of Barth's view of war and the extremes which make it justified cannot be included here. See Barth, *CD* III/4, 61–70; and Yoder, *Karl Barth and the Problem of War*.

or the political order demanded by God."¹³⁶ War is not a proper work of the state, but is an *opus alienum*. Christians do not have to be pacifists to say that war is not of the essence of the state and it work. "It is no part of the normal task of the state to wage war; its normal task is to fashion peace in such a way that life is served and war kept at bay."¹³⁷ Yet peace must at times, in extreme cases, be protected by force. In such instances, soldiers are not murderers, but doing the will of God through this alien work of the state.¹³⁸

Christian concern should first be for peaceful solutions among states in the face of war. In a powerful statement, Barth declares of the church:

> it is not commissioned to proclaim that war is absolutely avoidable. But it is certainly commissioned to oppose the satanic doctrine that war is inevitable and therefore justified, that it is unavoidable and therefore right when it occurs, so that Christians have to participate in it. . . . The Church must not preach pacifism, but it must see to it that this sane intelligence is voiced and heard so long as this is possible.¹³⁹

Barth insisted that he was not a war theologian. He stated that ninety-nine percent of what he wrote was anti-war.¹⁴⁰ He strove for peace and worked for peace during the Second World War.¹⁴¹ On the other hand, Barth approved of Switzerland's defense of its borders, and he himself enlisted in the military in his fifties. Barth also approved of Czechoslovakia's self-defense against German forces. Yet from that time Barth moved further toward the pacifist position. Barth came to

---

136. Barth, *CD* III/4, 456.

137. Ibid., 458.

138. Ibid., 464. Given the state's role to guarantee order, war is justified only when it can be understood as a large scale police action. Okholm, "Defending the Cause," 159.

139. Barth, *CD* III/4, 460. Barth exclaimed, "May the Church show her inventiveness in the search for other solutions before she joins in the call for violence!" Barth, "Christian Community and the Civil Community," 41.

140. Barth, *Fragments Grave and Gay*, 81–83. No nuclear war could ever be a just war. See Yoder, *Karl Barth and the Problem of War*, 51–52.

141. Aboagye-Mensah, "Karl Barth's Attitude to War," 44. See also Rosato, "Karl Barth as Spokesman and Practitioner," 112–32. As Werpehowski states, "Strategically the Christian community refuses to rule out war in principle, yet incessantly poses critical questions supporting genuine peace and opposing the ideology of war." Werpehowski, "Karl Barth and Politics," 239.

question the "fixed idea of the necessity and beneficial value of force."[142] Hunsinger thinks that by the time Barth reached volume four of the *Dogmatics* his view of the use of force had changed and he may not have viewed war and police action so enthusiastically.[143]

Yoder argues that "Karl Barth is far nearer to Christian pacifism than he is to any kind of systematic apology for Christian participation in war. For him it is theologically not possible to construct a justification of war. There is no Christian argument for participating in war. There is only the possibility of 'limiting cases,' whose sole ground is God's sovereign and (exceptional) command to man."[144] Yet, even in this late material, in which Barth came quite close to holding a pacifistic position, he was unable to become a pacifist in principle. This hesitancy was primarily because God may demand of his people amidst a difficult future circumstance that they use force. Barth was opposed to the absolutist principle of pacifism as a categorical statement which in effect limited God's freedom. Pacifism catches something very central to the gospel, yet we cannot close ourselves off from the freedom of God to command something other than "thou shall not kill" in a contemporary situation.[145] This possibility was not simply a way of stating that there is an exception to every rule. It is rather a statement about the sovereignty of God and the limits of human beings in the interpretation of God's Word.[146] This notion of the *Grenzfall* is of a piece with Barth's emphasis on the freedom of God, yet it does create significant problems. Most

---

142. Barth, *CD* IV/2, 549.

143. Hunsinger, *Disruptive Grace*, 127. Oliver O'Donovan has noted the tension between Barth's assertion of the rightness of the state having force to back up its law and his insistence that the state's use of force is an abnormality. O'Donovan has argued that around World War II Barth argued for the appropriateness of the state's power and in later writings Barth stressed the state's use of power as inappropriate. He wonders if Barth doesn't have some ideal picture of the state which does not exist in reality. O'Donovan, "Karl Barth and Ramsey's 'Uses of Power,'" 1–30. Yoder also notes this shift. Yoder, *Karl Barth and the Problem of War*, 97–98.

144. Yoder, *Karl Barth and the Problem of War*, 52.

145. The command of God is always specific and particular. See Barth's discussion of the definiteness of the divine command in the Bible in *CD* II/2, 672–76. Biblical commands are not to be taken out of their context and applied as general ethical principles.

146. Yoder, *Karl Barth and the Problem of War*, 35.

noteably it allows for the possible contradiction of the concrete revelation already given in Christ.[147]

Even if he could not be a pacifist, Barth could state: "According to the sense of the New Testament we cannot be pacifists in principle, only in practice. But we have to consider very closely whether, if we are called to discipleship, we can avoid being practical pacifists, or fail to be so."[148] Pacifism is an option only as a following after Jesus. Barth stated in an earlier volume that Jesus's "identity becomes normative for what is demanded of us."[149] Those who belong to the kingdom of God find their entire existence to be changed. Yoder notes that Barth's practical pacifism is rooted in the discipleship of a baptized community.[150] Baptized Christians stand under a different law. In particular, Christians are to love all, even their enemies. "The decisive contradiction of the kingdom of God against all concealed or blatant kingdoms of force is to be seen quite simply in the fact that it invalidates the whole friend-foe relationship between man and man.... What the disciples are enjoined is that they should love their enemies (Matt 5:44). This destroys the whole friend-foe relationship, for when we love our enemy he ceases to be our enemy."[151] By being practical pacifists we thus live in a way which should be the usual stance for the disciple of Christ.

Conclusion

While Yoder is correct in his reading of Barth's ecclesiology, Hunsinger is correct that Barth held a positive, Reformed view of the state as an

---

147. Yoder raises important questions regarding the concept of the *Grenzfall*. He questions the nature of God's freedom that the idea suggests. Is God free to contradict the revelation of himself in Jesus Christ? Yoder's particular concern is the possibility for exceptions to the commandment not to kill during war or other such exceptional cases. Ultimately, Yoder thinks the *Grenzfall* is inadequate as an ethical tool. It functions, he argues, as a form of casuistry even though Barth sought to avoid such ethical reasoning. One could also ask whether the concept of the *Grenzfall* is a lapse into a voluntaristic understanding God's freedom and power. See Yoder, *Karl Barth and the Problem of War*, 64–81. See also Clough, "Fighting at the Command of God," 214–26. Clough argues that it does not make sense for a state to continually prepare for war when war is not the proper work of the state, nor even permissible except as an exception.

148. Barth, *CD* IV/2, 550.

149. Barth, *CD* II/2, 606.

150. Yoder, "Karl Barth, Post-Christendom Theologian," 8.

151. Barth, *CD* IV/2, 550.

ordinance given by God. Barth's decision for believers' baptism is an important link between these two elements in his theology. Barth's affirmation of believers' baptism is based on his belief that the one coming for baptism must be responding to the word of God and the baptism of the Holy Spirit. In turn, this emphasis upon the candidate's commitment makes for the health of the church. The Christian community is a fellowship of the baptized. The Christian life is a fellow-humanity among all those whom Jesus has awakened. The church is a communion of saints. Their life together is a witness to the world.[152]

Barth shares the free church distinction between church and world (or state). Yet the relationship between them is not one of separation or withdrawal, but one of witness. The church keeps itself distinct from the state so that it will have a place from which to speak to the State. The church is distinct for the sake of its witness to the world. The church must be the church and the state must be the state. Both have unique tasks in the furthering of Christ's work in the world. The state's task is to provide order, justice, and freedom for institutions such as the church. The church's task is to witness to Christ. Believer's baptism, Barth argues, better avoids the Constantinian link between culture and church. The baptism of those who are able to make a response and commitment to Christ and his community helps the church to avoid blurring the lines of church and world. As initiation into the church, baptism should be a matter of commitment and covenant.[153] Baptism upon confession of faith best signifies what baptism represents.[154] A responsible church, faithful to its Lord and living in healthy witness, is Barth's first concern, not the control of society.

---

152. Barth, *CD* IV/4, 37.

153. McClendon, *Doctrine*, 391.

154. Yoder, "Karl Barth, Post-Christendom Theologian," 5. Affirming the sacramental nature of believers' baptism, I would say that baptism *as* a confession of faith best signifies what baptism *effects* (or more accurately stated: what God effects through baptism). With a number of Baptists, I would not say that infant baptism is invalid, but that baptism's sacramental nature and, following Barth, its political import are best signified by believer's baptism.

6

Baptism and the Witnessing Community

THIS FINAL CHAPTER IS A STUDY OF THE CHRISTIAN COMMUNITY AS it is called to be a holy community witnessing to the world. In light of baptism, understood as an active witness, I will examine the church as it is sent into the world as witness. The two main sections of this chapter will treat Barth's doctrine of sanctification and Barth's ethics. Both, I will show, are integral to Barth's ecclesiology and both are intricately related to Barth's view of baptism as initiation into a new community that seeks to achieve the goal of baptism, the Kingdom of God. The purpose of sanctification is for the church to be a provisional representation of the Kingdom. Baptism is a pledge that Christians are on their way from the old to the new. It is an initiation into a movement. Barth's ethics center on the concept of witness and are situated in the church that hears God's voice. Those who have been baptized are responsible for their ethical lives as a witness to the world, again so that the church may offer a provisional representation of the Kingdom in this time between the times.

The Community for the World

The God met in Jesus Christ is not a self-absorbed, solitary monad. The God named by the Christian tradition is self-giving love. God is the triune relations of mutual love, unity, and participation. God created the world from the overflow of this love, and thus not out of need or lack. As Barth insists, the creation of humanity was for the purpose of the covenant which God made with Israel.[1] The God who is not depen-

---

1. See the sections, "Creation as the External Basis of the Covenant," and "The Covenant as the Internal Basis of Creation," in Barth, *CD* III/1, 94–329. Barth states: "The covenant is the goal of creation and creation the way to the covenant." Barth, *CD* III/1, 97.

dent upon anything else for his being is never for himself alone, but always for his world. God is triune love so that love can be extended and shared. This identification of the loving God is the very heart of Barth's doctrine of election. In his Trinitarian being, apart from the creation of the world, God is love. Also in his relation to the world, the Triune God is love.

Barth draws upon the Trinitarian nature of God in asserting that, as the Father sends the Son, he also sends the church through the Son. In John 17:18, Jesus utters his high-priestly prayer and again in 20:21 he tells the disciples that the Father sent him, and he, in turn, is sending the church. Both sendings have the same purpose; both are directed to the world.[2] For Barth, the divine reality defines the reality of the human situation.[3] Thus, like the God who calls it into existence and whom it serves, the church's existence is for others. "As God exists for it [the world] in His divine way, and Jesus Christ in His divine-human, so the Christian community exists for it in its own purely human."[4]

Barth states that the church is called to active service of God in the world. God's active work for humanity makes any human inactivity or sloth impossible for his community.[5] Precisely because of the fact that the community exists for God, it exists actively for the world. "The community is the people which is called out of the nations by the Word of God, which is separated from the world, which is separately constituted within it and which is thus set over against it. . . . Called out of the world, the community is genuinely called into it."[6] The church cannot be its own meaning and telos. It is sent on the same mission as Christ—to the world.[7]

> The peace of God experienced in the community and by its members could only be a false peace if limited to this circle and

---

2. Barth, *CD* IV/3.2, 768.

3. See Hunsinger on the theme of "objectivism" in *How to Read Karl Barth*, 35–39.

4. Barth, *CD* IV/3.2, 786. Thus, "the community of Jesus Christ is the human creature whose existence as existence for God has the meaning and purpose of being, on behalf of God and in the service and discipleship of His existence, an existence for the world and men." Ibid., 762.

5. Ibid., 776–77.

6. Ibid., 763–64. We need to keep in mind Barth's view of the relationship between the church and society discussed in the previous chapter.

7. Barth, *CD* IV/3.2, 791.

enjoyed only within it. For the justification and sanctification of man accomplished in Jesus Christ did not take place in order that so many Christians should be its privileged beneficiaries and should mutually strengthen, comfort and admonish one another as such.[8]

The church does not side with God over against the world. The church is that portion of the world that is called to exist within the world as God's representation and witness. This is an important point for Barth: the church is on the same level as the world. The church does not have a privileged status.

The church actually loses its own identity and mission as witness when it seeks to shut itself off in concern for its own purity and reputation.[9] As Hunsinger argues, "in Barth nonconformity is always instrumental and subordinate to solidarity; the church separates itself from the world only in order to participate in it."[10] In fact, sectarian withdrawal is actually a form of conformity to a world which is self-absorbed and concerned only with itself. If the community is going to stand out in separation from the world, its existence for the world should be a visible marker of its life. "The world exists in self-orientation; the Church in visible contrast cannot do so."[11] Eberhard Busch notes that, for Barth, the church's existence to give active worldly witness could be included as one of the *notae ecclesiae*.[12]

Barth offered three statements in regard to the church's relation to the world: "1. the world would be lost without Jesus Christ and His Word and work; 2. the world would not necessarily be lost if there were no Church; and 3. the Church would be lost if it had no counter-part in the world."[13] These statements have given interpreters trouble.[14] Barth's point is not that the church is somehow unimportant and unnecessary. Nor is it a statement of the priority of the nation-state, as "world," over

---

8. Ibid., 764. The church must resist a "holy egoism" that leads the church to think that it exists as an end unto itself. Ibid., 767.

9. Ibid., 775.

10. Hunsinger, *Disruptive Grace*, 122.

11. Barth, *CD* IV/3.2, 780.

12. Busch, "Karl Barth's Understanding of the Church as Witness," 96.

13. Barth, *CD* IV/3.2, 826.

14. Hauerwas, *With the Grain of the Universe*, 193, and Healy, "Logic of Karl Barth's Ecclesiology," 265.

the church. He is urging the church to remember its solidarity with and mission to the world. God could do what he does through the church by some other means. In his radical freedom, God could order the economy of salvation differently.[15] If that were the case, the rest of humanity and the Christian community would still live together in the world. Their existence is a co-existence. The church, on the other hand, would be lost without its mission to the world. The mission and ministry of the church are its basis and its existence. The church is actually "in peril" when it neglects its mission.[16] The church is a servant to a world "which needs service and not dominion, liberation and not enslavement, elevation and not suppression."[17] The ministry of the community is "active subordination to God from whom it derives and therefore to man to whom it turns and whom it is to serve if it serves God."[18]

The Christian community's solidarity with the world does not mean that it is conformed to the ways of the world. The church is the community that is able to know the world as it is. In knowing Jesus Christ, the church is given knowledge of the world. The church can rightly name the world as the world. The world itself does not know the reality of its own existence, either its sin or its salvation. This knowledge is not a hidden *gnosis*, but the truth that the community shares with the world in its activity and speech. The church must be open and free in its naming of the world. In fact, this generosity should be something visible to the world.

The church is a "likeness," a provisional representation of the kingdom of God. The community is changed "not into an *alter Christus*, but necessarily into an image of the unrepeatably one Christ."[19] The purpose of the church's existence is

---

15. The real problem with these statements is that Barth seems to be going against his actualism. He seems to suggest a nominalist picture of the will of God that he seeks to avoid otherwise. In the voluntarism seen in nominalist understanding, God could will whatever God wanted regardless of the order of creation and revelation. On nominalism and its influence on modernity, see Gillespie, "Theological Origins of Modernity," 1–30.

16. Barth, *CD* IV/3.2, 827.

17. Ibid., 830.

18. Ibid., 833.

19. Ibid., 793.

> the subsequent and provisional representation of the calling of all humanity and all creatures to the service of God as it has gone forth in Jesus Christ. The origin and goal of the ways of God, which took place initially but perfectly in the resurrection of Jesus Christ, and which will take place definitively and no less perfectly in His final appearing, is the calling of every man and indeed of all creation to the service of God. The function of the community is to follow and yet at the same time to precede His universal call.[20]

The task of the community of Christ is the proclamation of the gospel, the good news of what was done for us in Jesus Christ.[21]

The community attests to the world at once the true situation of humanity, its ignorance and alienation, and what God has done for it in Christ—that the world has been rescued from this alienation, that the grace of God has broken into our present situation. "Taking man to Himself, God reveals to him beyond his present state a very different future, and impels and conducts him to his future."[22] The baptized community thus lives in "anticipatory joy" awaiting the fulfillment of the world's reconciliation with God.[23] Barth states that "within this teleology of the will of the God who loves the world, the Church is also specifically a baptismal community." Every baptism points to God's will for the world's salvation. Each time the church baptizes a new member, it "declares that it does not exist for itself alone, nor for particular individuals, but for all men."[24]

The work of the community in the world is a work of witness. In its service to God and humanity, the church's role is to attest what was completed by Christ. As seen before, the concept of witness should not be taken too lightly. The positive mission of witness is not an inconsequential role in the economy of salvation. The church witnesses by word and deed, by its existence, to the reality accomplished in Jesus Christ.[25]

---

20. Ibid.

21. "To proclaim Jesus Christ is to attest the goodness of God, no more, no less, no other.... If in Jesus Christ our main concern is absolutely with the goodness of God, this implies that man is the content of the task committed to the community." Ibid., 798–99.

22. Ibid., 809.

23. Ibid., 812.

24. Barth, *CD* IV/4, 200.

25. Busch, "Karl Barth's Understanding of the Church as Witness," 91.

"At every point and in all the functions of its life the Church is concerned to offer that great likeness of the kingdom of God."[26] It cannot reconcile the world to God, nor usher in the kingdom. The community is called to perform the task that is expected of it, rather than assuming too much of itself.[27]

In this ministry of witness, the church has a promise that it will not be abandoned to its own weakness. The promise of the kingdom and the new reality inaugurated by Christ give the community the strength to carry out its task. This hope reassures the church that "its mission to the world is not the absurdity which it might often seem to be."[28] The promise to the church is seen in its fulfillment in the person of Jesus Christ. The promise that sustains the community is the very content and theme of its witness. What it proclaims to the world, i.e., the world's reconciliation and redemption in Jesus Christ, is also what sustains and renews the community. The church can proclaim to the world that it has been baptized into Christ.

Baptism establishes the community for its task as witness to Jesus Christ. It is the sign which marks a person for this task. "In baptism we have the once-for-all and conscious entry and reception, manifested in the sign of purification, of the individual man into membership of the people of those who are called by God in free grace to be His witnesses, to participate in the work of His witness."[29] Baptism is the entrance into this community which exists for the world. Barth's views of sanctification and ethics explicate this thesis even further.

---

26. Barth, *CD* IV/3.2, 854.

27. Ibid., 834–36. Barth describes the nature of witness as declaration, exposition, and application of the Word of God. Whatever the church does it must correspond to the Word of God in its life and in its proclamation point to the content of the Gospel. This is its first task. With this it must explicate or exposit the gospel to make it intelligible to the world. The community is to narrate the history of God's doings in the world into which humanity is invited to participate. Thirdly, the witness of the church is the proclamation of the gospel as evangelical address. It is proclaimed so that it is a concrete reality that applies to its hearers. Ibid., 843–54.

28. Ibid., 841.

29. Ibid., 901.

Sanctification and Discipleship

In the intricate development of volume four of the *Dogmatics*, Christ's person and work shed light on the sin of humanity. Humanity's sin is met by God's dealings with sin in Christ himself. In light of the sins of pride, sloth, and falsehood that are identified by Jesus Christ in the simultaneous humiliation of the Son of God and the exaltation of the Son of Man, the work of Christ is given in answer to the human condition. In response to the sin of humanity, God was in Christ reconciling the world to Himself.[30] In response to the *pride* of humanity stands God's justification of sinners. Through Christ, and not our own works or merit, human beings are justified, i.e. set in right relation to God. In response to our *sloth*, Christ draws us out of our downward spiral and places us in the teleological life oriented toward the kingdom of God. Our refusal to live up to what was intended for us is met with our sanctification. Our failure to make use of our freedom is challenged by the Holy Spirit calling us to be holy as God is holy. In sanctification (*Heiligung*), God claims human life and activity for the fulfilment of his will.[31] In response to the *falsehood* of humanity, we are made a part of the prophetic work of Christ witnessing to God's work in the world.

Justification, sanctification, conversion, and transformation have taken place for all (objectively) in Jesus Christ. Yet, many do not know their new situation or even the truth about their old situation. God has set aside the Christian community in order for the world to know its standing and reality. God is fashioning these people into a holy people who will witness to the fact of the world's redemption. All are invited to join God's people, but, obviously, not all people have yet come. Those who have been awakened to faith belong to the community of God. They are a special people called aside from all others, but not as an end unto themselves. Christians exist as those who can attest to their sanctification as proclaiming the universal action of God in anticipation of the redemption of the entire world by God.[32]

---

30. Daniel Spross claims this is the central theme of Barth's doctrine of sanctification. Spross, "Doctrine of Sanctification," 54–55.

31. Barth, *CD* IV/1, 101.

32. Barth, *CD* IV/2, 511.

Communio Sanctorum

We must first note that sanctification is ecclesial in nature for Barth. Barth states, "the reconciliation of the world with God in its form as sanctification takes place as God fashions a people of holy men, i.e., those who in spite of their sin have the freedom, which they have received from Him to live in it, to represent Him among all other men and to serve Him in what they are and do and suffer."[33] The process of sanctification is a common life together in community.[34] Barth highlights the fact that in the New Testament the saints are referenced only in the plural. "Sanctity belongs to them, but only in their common life, not as individuals.... The holiness of the community, as of its individual constituents, is to be sought in that which happens to these men in common.... We may hazard the provisional definition that the ἅγιοι are the men to whom ἁγιότης comes in a common history which constitutes them an ἔθνος ἅγιον."[35] In their common sanctification, these people are unified as a community. The existence of this community is to be a foretaste, a provisional representation of what all will come to know.

The world should behold a correspondence and copy of God's holiness in the existence of this people.[36] The holiness of Christ comes as an instruction to live holy lives. In Barth's theology, the indicative bears with it an imperative.[37] The holiness of Christ becomes an imperative to the church. The body is told by its head: "Be holy as I am holy." Barth follows Calvin in saying that, "the righteousness of God calls for a *sym-*

---

33. Ibid.

34. L. Gregory Jones argues for the importance of friendship for the Christian life. "People are incorporated into the friendships and practices of particular communities which shape people's discipleship, thereby recognizing that the patterning of life in Christ is only completed by the rich diversity which comprises Christian community." Jones, *Transformed Judgment*, 119.

35. Barth, *CD* IV/2, 513. Cf. John Zizioulas's discussion of ecclesial existence as authentic human existence in *Being as Communion*, 53–65. He states that baptism is one's new birth into a new mode of existence.

36. Barth, *CD* IV/2, 501. In the present this representation is at best provisional and flawed. In its likeness to other societies, the distinctness of the church is not always seen. The confession that the church is holy is one that can only be made in the power of the Holy Spirit. Members of the church hold a "twofold citizenship." Christians are usually members of several communities as well as the Church. Barth, *CD* IV/1, 686.

37. Barth, *CD* IV/1, 701.

metria, a *consensus*, which must be actualised in the obedience of the believer."[38]

The community is holy only because it is the body of Jesus Christ. Only the presence of the Holy Spirit makes the church holy. In itself, the church shares in the sin and guilt of all humanity. Individual members are holy only because the calling of God makes them members of his body. The *communio sanctorum*, not individual Christians, exists in separation from the world. The invisible presence of the Holy Spirit is what makes the visible church holy and separate. Its holiness is not its own doing. Barth affirms with Luther that holiness is passive.[39] Yet this does not mean that

> the Church, with its activity and members, is only as it were covered by a holiness which Jesus Christ places over it from without, so that although its human and visible existence is certainly protected by its invisible holiness it is also blurred by it as by a shade, so that it is not affected or disturbed by it, but is left to go its own way in independence of it.... It does not mean that its holiness has only—in the deepest sense of the world—a theoretical and not a practical and concrete significance for its human and visible existence.[40]

The holiness of Christ which is given to the community in a free act of grace places that community in a relationship of obligation to the Holy One. In all of its activity the church is confronted by Christ. "It is continually asked whether and to what extent it corresponds in its visible existence to the fact that it is His body, His earthly-historical form of existence."[41] Baptism is entrance into the body of Christ which as the *communio sanctorum* is a teleological community. We have already seen that believers' baptism encourages a responsibility for one's life after baptism.

---

38. Barth, *CD* IV/2, 506.

39. Jesse Couenhoven unconvincingly argues that Barth is closer to Luther on the issues of justification and sanctification that he is to Calvin. He asserts that Barth emphasizes justification over sanctification. Below it is shown that Barth's view is more complex than that. Couenhoven, "Grace as Pardon and Power," 81.

40. Barth, *CD* IV/1, 700.

41. Ibid., 700–701.

Sanctification and Justification

Barth follows Calvin in emphasizing the inseparable connection between justification and sanctification. Justification and sanctification are not, for Barth, two different works or actions of God. They are two elements of the one activity of God in salvation.[42] Thus, no temporal *ordo salutis* is implied by the distinction between these two aspects. Justification cannot be separated from sanctification; neither can the two be identified or confused. The telos of justification and atonement is sanctification. The grace that is given to humanity in Jesus Christ is both justifying and sanctifying grace. As Calvin taught, we receive a *duplex gratia* by our participation in Christ.[43] Grace is two-fold: we receive new life based upon justification in conjunction our old being is given its limit. Justification consists of the destruction of the sinful life and the establishing of a new life; a new person who is righteous is brought to life. In the classic terms, this corresponds to mortification and vivification. Sanctification is entirely inseparable from this justification. They are both elements of the unified action of God on humanity.[44]

Barth's develops the doctrine of justification in order to stress the transition from death to life. It is a transition from sinful existence to faithfulness and right relation to God. This transition took place in the person of Christ. In the particular history of Christ, the co-existence of God and humanity, which has been the subject of all history in its broken form, is fulfilled.[45] Justification is an event, not a static state. It is not simply a legal fiction, but an ontological alteration of human existence. In Christ, human beings are made just. Again we see Barth's actualism in effect. Justification takes the form of a movement, a narrative; it is a drama.[46] "We are dealing with the history in which man is both rejected and elected, both under the wrath of God and accepted by Him in grace, both put to death and alive: existing in a state of transition, not here only but from here to *there*; not there only but from *here* to there."[47]

---

42. Calvin, *Institutes*, III, XI, 6 and XVI, 1.
43. See Calvin, *Institutes*, III, XI, 1.
44. For this paragraph see Barth, *CD* IV/2, 501–9.
45. Barth, *CD* IV/1, 544.
46. Ibid., 546.
47. Barth, *CD* IV/1, 516.

Barth notes Jesus' description of himself as the way. A way, or a path, has a beginning and an end, which is somewhere else. A way traverses from one place to another, different place.[48] Jesus Christ is our justification. In him we are on the way. Humanity must learn that as strange as it seems to us now the history of Jesus Christ is our history. Jesus Christ took the place of sinful human beings. Christ represents all humanity; his righteousness is ours. We are, as a result, taken from one place, our sinful existence as enemies of God and one another, and moved to another, our redeemed life of joy, love, and service in the community which anticipates the kingdom of God.

Just as the condescension of God and exaltation in humanity in Christ are one unitary work, so justification and sanctification are accomplished together. Together they are the one event of salvation. "The one grace of the one Jesus Christ is at work, and it is both justifying and sanctifying grace, and both to the glory of God and the salvation of man."[49] We are justified that we can be sanctified and we are sanctified in light of our justification. To merge them or to separate them would have negative results.[50] Barth's understanding of baptism embodies this insistence on the unity of justification and sanctification. Baptism is the human response to divine grace. The prevenient grace of God makes baptism a possibility. This grace recognized in baptism also makes possible and demands the new life of the baptized.

The Nature and Purpose of Sanctification

In his salvation of the world, God creates his own witnesses. God is creating, by sanctifying the church, a people who can be witness to and a provisional representation of the kingdom. The goal of sanctification is "the creation of a new form of existence for man in which he can live as the loyal covenant partner (*Bundesgenosse*) of God who is well-pleasing to and blessed by Him."[51] As a faithful covenant partner with God, the community of Christ can now exist in correspondence to Christ. "His

48. Ibid., 558. One should also remember the early name for the Christian community mentioned in Acts 9:2.

49. Barth, *CD* IV/2, 508–9.

50. Ibid., 502–11.

51. Barth, *CD* IV/2, 514. *KD* IV/2, 581. The covenantal formula of Exodus 19 is important to Barth: "'I will be your God' is the justification of man. 'Ye shall be my people' is his sanctification." Barth, *CD* IV/2, 499.

own divine confrontation of the world and all men should find a human (and as such very inadequate, but for all its inadequacy very real) correspondence and copy in the mode of existence of this people."[52] God expects holiness and righteousness from those who worship Him. At the same time, God makes possible and enables faithfulness and righteousness.

According to Barth, all of humanity has already been sanctified in Christ. The sanctification of all has taken place in One in a once-for-all, objective manner.[53] The sanctification of Christ, as our representative, is the sanctification of all human beings. As Hunsinger explains the basis for salvation is the objective work of Christ, not our existential participation by faith.[54] Barth's understanding of sanctification, he argues, is not that of a gradual development in time as Calvin taught. Rather humanity was sanctified once and for all in Christ. This sanctification comes to us, not as a development, but continually new. We receive sanctification "not more and more, by a process of gradual growth, but again and again, continually from without and ever anew."[55]

Reflection on sanctification, Barth insists, must be centered upon Christ, not upon individuals. While holding on to the centrality of Christ in our sanctification, Barth's notion of objective sanctification needs to be reconsidered. Barth's assertion that we have been sanctified in Christ leaves little room for growth. This is an ambiguous element of Barth's discussion of sanctification. Anthony Hoekema offers a critique of Barth's view of objective sanctification.[56] His primary concern is with the notion of all of humanity being sanctified objectively in Christ's sanctification. He argues that the objective sanctification of all humanity in Christ is unbiblical and meaningless. He thinks that arguing that all people have been objectively set aside and made holy in Christ is meaningless because not all people have been transformed in the present. Yocum asked similarly whether the New Testament even teaches that all people are sanctified in Christ. It is not clear if there is such a thing as *de iure* sanctification. Such a view may even undermine the

---

52. Barth, *CD* IV/2, 501.

53. Ibid., 514–15.

54. Hunsinger, "Tale of Two Simultaneities," 78.

55. Ibid., 84.

56. Hoekema, *Karl Barth's Doctrine of Sanctification*, 20–21. Hoekema, whose further criticisms miss their marks, put his finger on an important point here.

efficacy of baptism.[57] I would agree that it does not help to conceive of all humanity as set apart and consecrated but not realizing it. Ultimately of what significance is this objective sanctification?

Barth's notion of objective sanctification may be in part a rejection of the idea of a limited atonement (See CD IV/2, 520). But, it would make more sense to say that the sanctification of all people is possible because of the sanctification of Christ. Our justification was completed by Christ and our transformation and sanctification is made possible. These are of course, inseparable. The identification of the church as those set aside to bear witness to the work of Christ would, seen in this light, be more meaningful as well as more Trinitarian in nature as the Holy Spirit sanctifies those in Christ. James Leo Garrett reminds us that, "like justification, sanctification is by the grace of God through faith."[58] God is the Sanctifier, but human beings are not made holy without their active participation with the work of the Holy Spirit upon their lives.

From this perspective, our sanctification is not left up to ourselves. We would still assert with Barth that "our sanctification consists in our participation in His sanctification."[59] The sanctification of Israel before and the church after Christ are derivative from the original divine act of sanctification which took place in the exaltation of humanity in the person of Jesus Christ. The sanctification of the saints is only a reality in the holiness of the One who is holy, but the church's sanctification is still truly important for its life and witness.

The cross of Christ is, accordingly, the central element of the doctrine of sanctification. It was in the offering and losing of his life that Jesus showed himself as the true royal man. In response to Christ's fulfilled work on the cross, the people of God in the world are to bear the cross as it is given to them. "The special fellowship of the Christian with Christ involves participation in the passion of His cross."[60] Our obedience and suffering, our bearing of the cross, are always in response to and made meaningful by Christ's prior obedience and suffering.[61] The dignity of the Christian comes in bearing his or her cross in correspon-

57. Yocum, *Ecclesial Mediation*, 112–14.

58. Garrett, *Systematic Theology*, 367–68. This seems to fit better with Barth's view of Baptism with the Holy Spirit seen before.

59. Barth, *CD* IV/2, 517.

60. Ibid., 604.

61. Ibid., 600.

dence to the exaltation of Christ and His cross. It is not the case that Christ's own cross still needs to be carried. The life of the Christian is not a repetition or supplementation of the cross of Christ. As important as our task is, we do nothing to add to the reconciliation of the world with God. Christians carry their crosses as servants following their Master. Our participation is that of an "echo of His sentence" as we witness to his cross.[62]

The Christian may have to face struggles and hardships in faithfulness to Christ. Suffering and adversity for Christ's sake are a part of sanctification as the Christian is taken through the transition from the old to the new. The bearing of the cross is the outworking and fulfillment of sanctification.[63] Barth elaborates this in four points. One, bearing the cross helps to keep the Christian humble. Our suffering and adversity keep us conscious of frailty and of our limit as creatures. Two, the cross that one bears comes as a certain form of punishment. This punishment is discipline by fatherly love. Third, bearing the cross will be a discipline and strengthening of the Christian's faith, obedience, and love. Fourth, in bearing the cross a Christian may receive verification. The Christian can do good works which are pleasing to God by this correspondence to Christ.[64]

In the New Testament, according to Barth, bearing the cross refers fundamentally to persecution. Because of the historical developments since the time of the New Testament and the early Church, Christians in the "Christian West" will not have to face persecution for allegiance to Christ. Yet they will still face the struggle that comes from being set apart within the world. As Barth states, "however great may be the solidarity which Christians feel and practice in relation to the world, their way can never be that of the world – and least of all that of the supposedly Christianised world."[65] This will often cause offence to the society in which Christians find themselves. Yet, fidelity must be the first goal, even when threatened. According to Barth, not only persecution but

---

62. Ibid., 604. The Christian can face rejection by society as Christ did, but never by the whole of humanity or by God as Christ did for them. Thus the relationship of the cross of Christ to that of His disciple is one "of similarity in great dissimilarity." Ibid., 605.

63. Ibid., 607.

64. Ibid., 607–9.

65. Ibid., 610.

all affliction and hardship can be a bearing of one's cross when faced in Christ or with Christ.[66] The Christian does not seek suffering, but faces it when it comes because we can suffer with Jesus. Through our sanctification, the Holy Spirit makes a community whose members are able to bear their cross in the world.

Properly speaking, sanctification is the work of the Holy Spirit.[67] The work of the Holy Spirit allows for the *participatio Christi* by God's people. The Holy Spirit brings it about that people can participate in Christ and receive his sanctification.

> The Holy Spirit is He Himself [Christ] in the action in which He reveals and makes Himself known to other men as the One He is, placing them under His direction, claiming them as His own, as the witnesses of His holiness. The Holy Spirit is the living Lord Jesus Christ Himself in the work of the sanctification of His particular people in the world, of His community and all its members.[68]

The Holy Spirit acts in us to form us into Christ-likeness. The saints are called to obedience. The recipients of direction from the Holy Spirit are called and given a new determination. They are pointed to their new situation and given correction and instruction for participating in that new reality.[69]

Those who are awakened to realize their sanctification are in reality "disturbed sinners." They have been awakened from their slothful slumber, but they are still sinners.[70] When they receive direction from God they understand themselves as sinful. Only the confrontation with the incarnate Son of God reveals this fact to humanity. Yet, this disturbing of one's existence is the restoration of freedom, the freedom necessary to be obedient to the covenant with God, and in sanctification a

---

66. Ibid., 611.

67. Cochrane, "Doctrine of Sanctification," 383.

68. Barth, *CD* IV/2, 522. This quote raises Jenson's question whether Barth treats the Holy Spirit as a person or as a capacity. Jenson, "You Wonder Where the Spirit Went," 304.

69. Barth, *CD* IV/2, 523.

70. Barth can affirm Luther's phrase *simil justus et peccator* as long as we truly emphasize both facts: being justified and being a sinner. He would object to using the notion to defend a resignation to the inevitability of sin.

limit is set to the sinful being of the sinner.[71] The new life of the saints marks the limit as well as the eventual aim of their lives as sinners. The disturbance of the sinner becomes a new positive determination. This community is set in motion to become conformed to the being of Jesus Christ. Christ liberates the sinner from the domination and slavery of sin and gives them the sanctifying grace to lift themselves up from the downward drag of sloth and look to Jesus Christ.[72] As Christians are baptized into this teleological movement they are baptized into a communal life of discipleship.[73]

Following Jesus—The Life of Discipleship

To work out the implications of *de facto* sanctification, Barth turns to the category of discipleship.[74] This discussion of discipleship coheres with Barth's latter description of believers' baptism better than an overemphasis on his notion of objective sanctification. The call to sinful people to become Christians and to look to Christ takes a "definite form and direction." Christians are called to follow Christ. "The call issued by Jesus is a call to discipleship."[75] Barth repeats a theme common to his theology and ethics: grace comes to us as a command. The faith which Jesus expects of his people takes the form of obedience. Obedience to Jesus Christ is central to discipleship. We are disciples of Christ only in this obedient faith. We are disciples because we have been called and demanded to be obedient by the Lord.[76]

This obedience requires a denial of oneself. Obedience to Christ requires an about-face, a new opportunity. To follow Christ people must turn from their own direction which they were following previously. Embarking on the path of discipleship is a renunciation of one's prior

---

71. Barth, *CD* IV/2, 524–25.
72. Ibid., 530–31.
73. Compare this to the view of Balthasar Hubmaier offered in the introduction.
74. Bromiley, *Introduction to the Theology of Karl Barth*, 209.
75. Barth, *CD* IV/2, 533. Barth tells us that in this section of IV/2 he is indebted to Bonhoeffer's *Discipleship*. In fact, he admits that he is in such agreement with the book that he is tempted to simply offer an extended quotation from it for his treatment of discipleship. Ibid., 533–34.
76. Ibid., 537. Barth's discussion of the vocation of the Christian could be included here as well. The primary role of the Christian is witness to Christ.

loyalties and allegiances.[77] The life of discipleship begins with a break. The call of Jesus to follow him in discipleship severs our new life from what came before. In this call the kingdom of God confronts and contradicts the person called. Though no one can break the control of the orders and forces which keep all of humanity under their rule, this call breaks the power of our current "gods." When we are freed from the gods that we served before, we are liberated to become a witness to Jesus Christ. Through the work of Christ our lives can be a vindication of the new day that has dawned. Our baptism is this transfer of our loyalties and our allegiances.

The call to discipleship relativizes the given attachments between people, such as family, and questions our attachment to possessions or honor among men. Many of the sayings of Jesus "assume the existence of men who are freed by the concretely given command of Jesus from the universal dominion and constraint of ordinary conceptions of what constitutes social status and dignity and importance."[78] Our task as witness involves the liberation of others.[79]

This new action and attitude will, naturally, be offensive to the powers and principalities, and to those who still worship the gods and are thus trapped under their control. Discipleship, like the baptism which initiates this life of sanctification, is not a matter of a mystical tranquility or of a turn inward. Our task as disciples is to give "practical indication" of the fact that the authorities and powers which govern human existence, the gods, have been defeated by Christ. Barth states that a person "loses his soul, and hazards his eternal salvation, if he will not accept the public responsibility which he assumes when he becomes a disciple of Jesus. It is more than doubtful whether he is doing this if his existence does not force those around him to take notice—with all the painful consequences this may involve for him."[80] The centrality of the concrete baptismal life of the church for the doctrine of sanctification cannot be denied. It is in baptism that one publicly assumes the life of

---

77. Ibid., 538–40. Remember Barth's description of baptism as a renunciation of the old and a pledge to live the new life. Believers' baptism is a good symbol of this turn.

78. Ibid., 549.

79. Ibid., 546. Barth discusses as discipleship the love of one's enemies and the question of pacifism raised in chapter five.

80. Ibid., 545. For this paragraph see 543–46.

discipleship. Barth's affirmation of believers' baptism is consistent with this development of the life of the church as a life of discipleship.

The Praise of Works

In contrast to a familiar wrong-headed reading of Barth, human works are truly important within his theology.[81] In his discussion of sanctification, Barth speaks of the praise of works. With the ambiguity of this genitive phrase, Barth intends both possible meanings. Barth asserts that human works can be worthy of God's affirmation and approval. In addition, human works can be a form of praising God whereby our works affirm and acknowledge God. The lives of those called and awakened by God will necessarily reflect their calling. Christians should do good works. In this, Barth is in the biblical tradition which emphasizes that saving faith will result in works of love.[82] Barth insists, of course, that human works can never justify the person who does them. Yet for Christians, their works can be considered good "on the presupposition of justification by faith alone."[83]

Human works must be considered good in the context of the work of God. It is the activity of God which makes human works good works. As witnesses, human beings share in the work of God.[84] The good works of Christians are in correspondence with the history of the covenant, i.e., of God's activity. We become "co-workers" with God. The work of Christ on our behalf makes the works done by human beings useful for the service of God. Our works are truly ours, but that these works

---

81. See Webster, *Barth's Moral Theology*.

82. Anabaptist theologian Balthasar Hubmaier sought to combat distortions of Luther's emphasis on grace and human inability to do good works. He wrote: "As soon as one says to them it is written (Ps. 37:27): Depart from evil, and do good–immediately they answer: 'We cannot do anything good; all things occur by the determination of God and of necessity'—meaning thereby that it is allowed them to sin. If one says further: It is written (John 5:29; 15:6; Matt 25:41) that they who do evil go into eternal fire, immediately they find a girdle of fig leaves to cover their crimes and say: 'Faith alone saves us and not of our works.' Indeed, I have heard from many people that for a long time they have not prayed, nor fasted, nor given alms because their priests tell them how their works are of no avail before God and therefore they at once let them go." Hubmaier, "On Free Will," 115. This was obviously a distortion of Luther for whom true faith resulted in works of love. See Luther in Lull, *Martin Luther's Basic Theological Writings*, 613, 624–25.

83. Barth, *CD* IV/2, 587.

84. Ibid., 592.

witness to Christ is His doing. "It is God's free gift."[85] Our work as witnesses is done in spite of sin, not without sin. Our work witnesses to the good works of God on our behalf.[86] In doing good works, the Christian belongs to the communion of saints, to the people of God in his or her own particular situation. One should listen to the others in the fellowship of the baptized because they are working for a common good.[87]

Conversion

Another important element in Barth's treatment of sanctification is conversion (*Umkehr*). The basis and origin of conversion is the Christ-event. It is in Jesus Christ that it is truly revealed that God is for humanity and humanity is for God. "The dynamic principle of this movement is the truth, revealing itself to man, that God is for him, and that—in virtue of the fact that God is for him—he is for God."[88] In the power of the Holy Spirit, the Christ-event is "effective and valid for many."[89] Jesus fulfilled the movement from the old to the new. We live in response to the fact that he first loved us.

Christians are those who have been awakened to the reality of their situation and their identity before God. The awakening is solely the work of the Holy Spirit. However, this does not exclude the reality and decision of the human person. The awakening takes place according to the "law of divine action." This includes human action. To be the real sanctification of a real person, conversion cannot take place without the will of the person. "It takes place to and in him. It involves the total and most intensive conscription and co-operation of all his inner and outer forces, of his whole heart and soul and mind, which in the biblical sense in which these terms are used includes his whole physical being. Otherwise it would not be his awakening."[90]

Conversion is a historical event, i.e., on earth and in time. It thus does not take place without human action, nor does it negate human

---

85. Ibid., 594.
86. Ibid., 591.
87. Ibid., 596.
88. Ibid., 579.
89. Ibid., 582.
90. Ibid., 556.

existence, even while it is primarily the work of God.[91] Conversion is not a magical or mechanical event or process. As seen before, the omnipotence of God is not a brute force which acts upon a human being as a mere object, "like a spar of wood carried relentlessly downstream by a great river." The omnipotence of God is God's omnipotent mercy.[92] Conversion is the work of the Holy Spirit liberating the human being. The awakening of persons to conversion is an important element in the biblical witness and is part of believing in a living God who acts in our present as the God of the covenant. It is the power of God which liberates human beings to be obedient covenant partners with God. This liberation is also a compulsion, something one must do.

> But the compulsion is not a mere compulsion. It is not abstract. It is not blind or deaf. We have to realise that a mere compulsion is basically evil and demonic. The compulsion obeyed in conversion is not of this type. It is the compulsion of a permission and ability which have been granted. It is that of the free man who as such can only exercise his freedom.[93]

We have seen before that for Barth, true freedom is not mere choice or decision, but the exercise of freedom in obedience to God. We are freed in order that we may press forward to the new in conversion.[94]

Conversion, Barth explains, is a movement. This movement is not a gradual improvement, but a radical alteration and renewal of the person. Conversion is "nothing less than *regeneration*. New birth!"[95] This movement extends over a person's entire life. It is the "totality of the whole life movement of man."[96] The movement is from the old to the new person. Conversion is an alteration of the entire person, in relation

---

91. "Being qualified and claimed by God for co-operation (*Mitwirkung*), it [the creaturely] co-operates (*wirkt mit*) in such a way that the whole is still an action which is specifically divine." Ibid., 557. KD IV/2, 630.

92. Barth, *CD* IV/2, 578.

93. Ibid., 578.

94. Cochrane, "Doctrine of Sanctification," 387.

95. Barth, *CD* IV/2, 563. "What is meant by sanctification (*sanctificatio*) might just as well be described by the less common biblical term regeneration (*regeneratio*) or renewal (*renovatio*), or by that of conversion (*conversio*), or by that of penitence (*poenitentia*) which plays so important a role in both the Old and New Testaments, or comprehensively by that of discipleship which is so outstanding especially in the Synoptic Gospels." Ibid., 500.

96. Ibid., 566.

of other people, both in disposition and in action. No element of the person is left unaffected by the movement of conversion. We can equate conversion in this treatment of sanctification with the baptism of the Holy Spirit as the divine-change that makes us Christians. As baptism with the Spirit leads to water baptism, so is conversion not an end in itself. It involves a public responsibility. The assumption that conversion is for one's own sake alone is a "far too egocentric Christianity."[97]

In conversion the person is put at odds with him or herself. A person must cease the current movement and leave the old way. The awakening to conversion sets the person on a new path, in a new movement. In this way, the person is both wholly a sinner and wholly reconciled to God. The person is both old and already the new person. Conversion is the transition from the old person to the new. In the present we are always *homo peccator* and *homo sanctus*. Because of the new, what a person already is, the Christian can no longer remain the old person that he or she still is. Barth agrees with Calvin, in opposition to "the Anabaptists and their companions the Jesuits," that conversion takes place in the whole life of believers and not in a once-for-all event or in penitential works.[98] Christians need to be re-awakened continuously through the course of their lives. One could speak of the life of conversion. Conversion is the awakening of the whole person.[99] In the typical understanding of an *ordo salutis* conversion would be closely related to justification which begins the Christian life. In Barth's development of conversion, conversion is related to, or even equated with, sanctification. In describing conversion as a movement and transition from the old to the new which spans the whole of one's life, conversion sounds much like a traditional understanding of sanctification, and this conversion is the meaning of baptism.

Baptism and the Doctrine of Sanctification

Stanley Hauerwas has raised a concern regarding Barth's seeming lack of concern for the elements of Christian community and practice which shape Christian character. In Hauerwas's early writing he argued that Barth's ethics led to an inadequate understanding of character and

---

97. Ibid., 565.
98. Ibid., 569.
99. Cochrane, "Doctrine of Sanctification," 387.

sanctification. Barth, he concluded, had no way to include the growth and development of sanctification.[100] Obviously Barth's doctrine of sanctification, as seen above, does not intend to neglect the concrete, visible church as a representation for the world to behold. Barth's insistence on the human action of the church should make us question the interpretation of the objective reality of our sanctification in Christ which says that it "does not need to be further realized in the Christian life."[101] Barth's hesitancy regarding the work of the Spirit in the practices of the church and the confusing notion of objective sanctification lead to this understanding.

As the sections on discipleship and works have shown, Barth's emphasis is upon the objective work of Christ, but in a manner that leads to the *de facto*, subjective sanctification of the Christian life, not in a way which excludes it. The objective sanctification of humanity, if it is to have any real meaning, issues in personal Christian obedience empowered by the Holy Spirit. Sanctification seeks to create loyal covenant partners. As Barth himself says, "in the Christian there is an appropriation of the grace of God ascribed to all men in Jesus Christ, a subjective apprehension of what has been done for the whole world in the happening of atonement." Our sanctification in Christ takes place in a life of discipleship, for Barth is clear that the subjective appropriation of the atonement takes place primarily in the sphere of the church.[102] Of course, the power of this appropriation is derived only from the grace of God seen in the person of the Holy Spirit.[103] Barth goes to lengths to avoid making atonement a matter of personal experience (thus his insistence on our objective sanctification), but this should not lead us to think that Barth never emphasizes human responsibility adequately grounded in the person and work of Christ. The human appropriation of grace as enabled by the Spirit is secondary, but it is nonetheless essential.[104]

---

100. Hauerwas, *Character and the Christian Life*, 129–77. More recently he has also argued that Barth's ethics are excessively abstract and do not account for the community and its practices in which ethical lives function. See *Dispatches from the Front*, 58–79, and *With the Grain of the Universe*, 192–95.

101. Mangina, *Karl Barth on the Christian Life*, 193.

102. Barth, *CD* IV/1, 150.

103. Ibid., 147.

104. Barth, *CD* IV/3.1, 220.

Hauerwas's critique still shows us the need to connect this discussion with the revision of Barth needed in chapter three. An emphasis on sanctification and discipleship is essential for the church, yet a still tighter connection between sanctification and the life of discipleship in community begun at baptism is needed. To reflect on the doctrine of sanctification after Barth, we need to include an understanding of the Spirit forming the community to be his witness through the concrete practices of the church.[105]

Incorporating the church's practices, such as baptism, into his view of sanctification would have been helpful. Along with communion, baptism is a formative practice which recreates and continually shapes the Christian community under the Spirit's guidance.[106] Baptism is the beginning of the Christian life. It is the beginning of the subjective process of the sanctification of the Christian community, initiation into the *communio sanctorum*. The church, as the fellowship of the baptized, continues to baptize new members into this community. Thus the practice of baptizing new members also continues to challenge Christians to remember their own baptism. In witnessing the baptism of another we are repeatedly reminded of our own death and burial into Christ as well as our being raised to walk in new life. Baptism is a powerful practice which incorporates new Christians into the movement which baptism initiates and which shapes and instructs those who are already baptized. Being witness to a baptism, even as a member of the congregation, reminds a person that the Christian life is based on grace, that

---

105. Such a view of the moral significance of the practices of the church, i.e., baptism and eucharist, is offered by L. Gregory Jones, *Transformed Judgment*, 137–58. Thomas Aquinas asserted that "the sacraments . . . are employed as signs for man's sanctification." *Summa Theologica*, III,60,6. The sacraments signify our sanctification: the cause, which is Christ's passion (past); the form, which is the grace given to us and the virtues formed within us(present); and their end, which is eternal life (future). III,60,3. It is the work of God to sanctify us and God has chosen the sacraments as a means to do so. III,60,5.

106. Barth was heading in this direction with his plan to include baptism and communion as the heart of his ethics of reconciliation. Gunton says that a virtue ethic needs to be grounded in a theology of baptism. However he goes on to state the matter differently: "Joining the Church is not an ethical act but one whose stress is on that which is received: the turning round of the old Adam symbolized by the water which drowns. The strengths of the traditions of infant baptism are that they stress that the path of virtue is one on which we have to be set by others, as they place us in a community oriented to the death of Christ." Gunton, "Church as a School of Virtue," 224.

it is a life of gratitude, that it is a life of fellow-humanity, and that it is a life of forward movement.[107] The church is the company which has gone before the candidate and now welcomes the new pilgrim into the traveling company. Part of one's own sanctification is the instruction and formation of new members of the community.

Specifically tied to sanctification, we need to remember the meaning of baptism seen in chapter two—namely, that baptism is an act of obedience to Christ. The life of obedience that follows baptism is a life of discipleship. Baptism is an act of hope. The church baptizes with a view to the future consummation of all things. Baptism is a renunciation of the old and pledge of the new. This is the same language Barth uses in his treatment of sanctification. This connection is most clearly seen in Barth's assertion that baptism is the mark of one's conversion.[108] Baptism is the confirmation of a person's conversion. It is a sign that one is "leaving an old path and entering upon a new."[109] In baptism, the old person is buried with Christ so that the new person can be united with him in his resurrection. All of these elements of baptism have corresponding elements in Barth's doctrine of sanctification. In addition, his insistence upon believer's baptism is an insistence upon a responsible community that can bear witness to Christ. As such baptism should play a role in sanctification.

The Life of the Baptized Community as Christian Ethics

Barth's Divine Command Ethics Revisited

Barth's ethics are frustrating to some readers because they are not simply an attempt to grapple with contemporary problems. Something else precedes the ethical problem, or the decision; something is prior even to the character of the ethical agent. According to Nigel Biggar, "the crucial and most distinguishing feature of the legitimate form of ethics, as Barth presents it, is that it conceives human apprehension of the good in terms of hearing a command of God."[110] Barth begins his ethics with

---

107. Barth, *CD* IV/4, 31–40. All of which are dependent upon the prior work of the Spirit.

108. Ibid., 138.

109. Ibid., 135.

110. Biggar, *Hastening that Waits*, 14.

the command of God, rather than human deliberation, because to value or choose the things that *I will* is to act as "an Atlas bearing and holding together the great building of the universe" and thus to make a "foolish over-estimation" of myself.[111] Ethics begins with a proper understanding of our place in relation to God, our place under the Command of God.[112] The command of God precedes the ethical problem. A positive Christian life exists before one tackles issues of the day.[113] Barth states that sanctification is "the basic presupposition of all Christian ethics."[114] Barth's ethics are specifically ecclesial ethics. They are for the sanctified, baptized community.

When the grace of God confronts us, when our sins are revealed, we are obligated to become faithful to God. Grace "sanctifies man. It claims him for God. It puts him under God's command."[115] No neutral stance exists from which Christians exist and act. Barth reversed the usual Protestant understanding by proclaiming that the Gospel precedes the Law. The grace of God places an obligation, a demand upon its recipient. Barth states: "Who can possibly see what is meant by the knowledge of God, His divine being, His divine perfections, the election of His grace, without an awareness at every point of the demand which is put to man by the fact that this God is his God, the God of man?"[116] The gospel immediately lays claim to humanity as law.[117] This is similar

---

111. Barth, *CD* IV/1, 450. Barth avoids what Gabriel Marcel calls the "illusion of moral egocentricity." Marcel, *Homo Viator*, 19.

112. According to John Webster, Barth's ethics constitutes his attempt to offer a moral ontology, i.e., to offer a description of the moral reality of human beings. Webster, *Barth's Ethics of Reconciliation*, 214–30.

113. See John Milbank's interesting contrast between "morality" and Christianity in *Word Made Strange*, 219–32.

114. Barth, *CD* IV/1, 101. Barth stated in his early lectures that Ethics is a "special elucidation of the doctrine of sanctification" and ethics "is reflection on how far the Word of God proclaimed and accepted in Christian preaching effects a definite claiming of man." Barth, *Ethics*, 3.

115. Barth, *CD* II/2, 516.

116. Ibid., 512. "A reality which is conceived and presented in such a way that it does not affect or claim men or awaken them to responsibility or redeem them, i.e., a theoretical reality, cannot possibly be the reality of the Word of God, no matter how great may be the richness of its content or the profundity of its conception. Dogmatics has no option; it has to be ethics as well." Barth, *CD* I/2, 793.

117. See Jüngel, *Karl Barth*, 105–26.

to Calvin's third use of the law. A new, proper function is given to the law in the life of believers.[118]

The context for all ethical action and understanding is the history of God in covenant with humanity. Each particular event in which one finds oneself commanded by God is understood by its place within the history of the triune God's encounter with creation. Therefore, no ethical events occur in "empty space." The command of God is not ahistorical, but always concrete and situated. The task of special ethics is to narrate "this history of God and man from creation to reconciliation and redemption." This history provides the field in which a particular point takes place, and it is in this field that we can make sense of events and commands.[119] The history of God and humanity in covenant gives the context, the story, in which events and commands take place and have meaning.[120] Christian ethics are incomprehensible without this history. As Barth explains, "it is to this history that Christian ethics is related. Christian ethics is the fruit that grows on this tree. Christian ethics cannot be understood if this story is omitted or misunderstood."[121] The Bible is not a code book or magic box that we turn to in order to find our answers.[122] Yet the Bible reveals to us God and His works and, as such, it can become the Word of command to its readers. Barth states, "in practice . . . this God and the Bible, His commanding and its commanding, are not to be separated."[123] We read the Scripture to obey what is commanded, and in so doing we learn to hear what we may be commanded to do. Scripture prepares us to hear the command of God by enabling us to recognize it in relation to God's previous commands.[124]

We cannot overlook the specificity and particularity of the divine command which Barth insists upon. The divine command is always

---

118. Calvin, *Institutes*, II, VII, 12. The law teaches believers the nature of the Lord's will to which they aspire. The law rouses Christians to obedience and strengthens them rather than simply showing their depravity.

119. Barth, *CD* III/4, 27.

120. For a good treatment of the history of relationship between God and persons see Werpehowski, "Narrative and Ethics in Barth," 334–53.

121. Barth, *God Here and Now*, 88.

122. Barth, II/2, 705.

123. Barth *CD* II/2, 706.

124. See Hays, *Moral Vision of the New Testament*, 233 and Biggar, *Hastening that Waits*, 117. It is this contextuality and specificity which situates Barth's allowance for the problematic *Grenzfall*, which I dealt with earlier.

contextual, always historical. The divine command approach to ethics raises fears of an external, artibrary form of ethics.[125] Barth would insist that while the command is never our own to make or to validate, it is not the command of an absolute, almost capricious, despot as it is made out to be. On the contrary, "God calls us and orders us and claims us by being gracious to us in Jesus Christ."[126] The commands of God are meaningful only within the story of God's covenant with the world. The basis for God's claim upon human beings is not the divine power or even the eternal goodness of God, but rather his own self-offering.

Barth insists that for us to make sense of human existence and ethical agency, we must first pay attention to the revelation given to us in the person of Christ. In Christ we learn the shape of human existence. The divine commands are unified in the person of Jesus Christ. Christ is the command of God. The biblical accounts of Jesus Christ provide the standard for Christian existence. Because Jesus Christ is "not only the ground and content but also the form of the divine claim. . . . This identity becomes normative for what is demanded of us."[127] The story of Christ reveals God's decision for humanity. What is good and what is evil has been decided in the cross and resurrection of Christ.[128] Barth explains, "We must seek it [the command of God] only in what happened in Bethlehem, at Capernaum and Tiberius, in Gethsemane and on Golgotha, and in the garden of Joseph of Arimathea. In this event God uttered his command."[129] God's determination of right conduct is made for us in Jesus Christ. In Christ, "we have both the Gospel which reconciles us with God and illumines us and consoles us, and the Law which . . . binds us and obligates us."[130] God's finished action for humanity places a claim upon us.

---

125. On this question, see Huebner, "Can a Gift be Commanded?," 474–81. I am at a loss to see how the concept of gift is less abstract than the commands of God as narrated in Scripture.

126. Barth, *CD* II/2, 560. Barth states: "God has given us Himself. He is not only mighty over us. He is not only the essentially good. He is not only our complete satisfaction. He has given Himself to us. He has graciously turned to us. He has made Himself ours." Ibid., 557.

127. Ibid., 606.

128. Ibid., 536.

129. Ibid., 559.

130. Ibid., 539.

In their ethical life, Christians become "co-operative in the course of the history of the covenant of grace."[131] Jesus Christ offers the only true service to God. Yet, human beings can participate in His faithfulness. We do not submit to God's law in order to win God's favor, but we find ourselves claimed by God precisely because we have received God's grace. The foundation of the Christian life is the awakening of a human faithfulness corresponding to God's faithfulness. And, as Barth states, the foundation of the Christian life is baptism which corresponds to the baptism of the Spirit. Baptism is the pledge of fidelity to Christ, the Christian's thankful obedience to the grace he or she has received.

Human action does not complete or even extend the work of God in Christ, but the action of the church corresponds to the activity of God. Christians are to reflect and copy the grace of God in our lives.[132] We can participate in his activity. Barth states:

> To participate in it is only for those who believe in Jesus Christ, i.e., who confess Him as their Lord, who put their trust in His person and work, *who are baptised in His name*, who share in His Holy Spirit, and are therefore ready and able, in their own sphere, to have a part in His office and mission. Because believers in Jesus Christ know and accept the truth that His righteousness avails for their unrighteousness, His holiness for their sin, His life for their death . . . they are the ones to whom this demand applies, to whom its fulfilment is vital, and from whom it can be expected. Their nobility obliges them . . . to a life which, because it is binding on all men, must at all costs be lived out among all men as a token of its universal obligatoriness.[133]

The atoning work of God creates the possibility for good human action. Only under the gracious command of God is a human being free to become and do what he or she would not do or become before, be faithful to God.[134]

Criticisms that Barth's ethics do not provide an adequate account of moral character raise a real concern.[135] Barth's deontological ethic involves the character of the recipient of God's command within the

---

131. Ibid., 678.
132. Ibid., 576.
133. Ibid., 715. Emphasis mine.
134. Barth, *CD* IV/4, 5–6.
135. See the discussion in Biggar, *Hastening that Waits*, 127–45.

concept of vocation, rather than the formation of dispositions.[136] While a command of God could be universally valid, only the community of God recognizes its responsibility as the recipients of grace. Thus duty is character-dependent or, one could say, dependent upon one's baptism.

To be obedient to the command of God is to live as a person to whom grace has come in Jesus Christ. Barth asserts that a theological ethics must be an ethics of grace.[137] For this reason, Christian ethics involves the baptized community. Baptism constitutes the first step in the life of those who belong to God and who stand in fellowship with the One judged in our place. Because we have received God's grace, we are obedient to the command of God. This first step is followed by many others all "modelled on the first."[138] The only proper response to the grace of God is therefore gratitude. This gratitude takes the form of humble obedience or obedient humility.[139] Baptism is the beginning of a life of obedience, not based on fear or compulsion, but gratitude. Living in gratitude is the witness of the people of God; a testimony to grace by its recipients.

Ecclesiology as Ethics

The ethics I have been examining are an essential part of Barth's dogmatics and cannot be separated as an independent subject. The Word of God never has to do solely with God, but also involves God's relation to humanity.[140] The Word speaks to the totality of the human being,

---

136. Biggar, *Hastening that Waits*, 43–45, 133–36. Biggar deals with the limited role of character in Barth's ethics.

137. "A Christian is one who knows that God has accepted him in Jesus Christ, that a decision has been made concerning him in Jesus Christ as the eternal Word of God, and that he has been called into covenant with Him by Jesus Christ as the Word of God spoken in time." Barth, *CD* II/2, 547.

138. Barth, *CD* IV/4, 201–3. Quote is on 202.

139. Barth, *CD* IV/1, 620.

140. Barth boldly stated that "Dogmatics itself and as such is ethics as well." Barth, *CD* I/2, 783. Previously Barth had stated because theology deals with the problem of the Christian man, "without ceasing to be dogmatics, reflection upon the Word of God, it is itself ethics." Ibid., 371. Webster has convincingly demonstrated that the entirety of Barth's theology is ethics. Barth assumed the "coinherence of dogmatic and ethics." Webster, *Barth's Moral Theology*, 7. See also Stanley Hauerwas, *Sanctify Them in the Truth*, 32–34.

and therefore the human being as active, ethical agent.[141] If the entirety of Barth's theology is ethics, Barth's ethics, as the rest of his theology, are meant from beginning to end for the life of the church. The gospel, his subject matter, is not a theory, or 'impossible ideal,' which is later applied to life. The gospel is the very form and content of our lives.[142] In the Church we learn how to live as creatures of a loving God, the recipients of God's commanding grace and this requires learning to love one another. Timothy Gorringe refers to the church as the "School of Love."[143] For the baptized, the task of ethics is attending to the life of the community that is being sanctified, the ethics of discipleship.

Barth was not primarily concerned with the "knowledge, faith, sanctification, and blessedness of the individual."[144] Barth did not struggle to provide meaning to Cartesian knowers or Schleiermacherian feelers, but with the historic, situated body of Christ as it seeks to make known the reconciliation of the world with God. Though the Command of God comes to every person in his or her concreteness, Barth's ethics are not individualistic. "The individual with his actions is not an atom in empty space, but a man among his fellows, not left to himself in his cases of conscience nor in a position to leave others to themselves."[145] "Moral fellowship" arises between people who are under the decision of God together.[146] Barth states, in fact, that "the desire to be for ourselves is not salvation but perdition, and it is from this that the command frees us."[147] The Command of God prompts us to act with others, on behalf of others, and even at time interfering with the path of others. Human beings are often the vehicle for God's commands. The Holy Spirit uses human beings to give the command in concrete form to one another.[148]

---

141. Barth, *CD* I/2, 788.

142. For Barth, "the purpose of theological endeavor is not to describe the world in terms that make sense, but rather to change lives, to be reformed in light of the stunning assertions of the gospel." Hauerwas and Willimon, *Resident Aliens*, 28.

143. Gorringe, *Karl Barth*, 256–58.

144. Barth, *CD* I/1, 124.

145. Barth, *CD* III/4, 9. "The Word of God addresses itself in different places to different men at different times, it summons them out of their isolation, calls, brings and binds them together, and unites them both invisibly with God and visibly with one another." Barth, CD, IV/3.2, 740.

146. Barth, *CD* II/2, 716.

147. Ibid., 599.

148. Barth, *CD* III/4, 9.

Christian should hold one another accountable on the basis of their baptism. As Barth states, "they may now be addressed on the basis of the decision which they then made."[149]

Thus, the church is the "medium" and framework through which the Command of God is given.[150] Christians are committed to living according to the election of God as a follower in the footsteps of many, not as the first disciple to do so.[151] "The Word of God is not spoken to individuals, but to the Church of God and to individuals only in the Church. . . . The Word of God, therefore demands this community of hearing and receiving."[152] This moral fellowship and community of hearing is, of course, the church as the community of those who have been awakened by God—the community of the baptized.

Barth's theological emphasis upon the grace of God contains with it an emphasis upon the recipients of that grace. In his sovereignty and aseity, God freely elects not to exist alone, but remains in eternity God-for-us. Barth insisted that "Jesus never exists alone and for Himself, but always as the first-born among many brethren. . . . Those who belong to Him are bearers of the grace of God for all men."[153] The grace of God gathers and sends this community into the world. As seen before, Barth's conception of grace is teleological. "Grace is the movement and direction of man in accordance with his determination."[154] The existence of the people of God is the concrete form of this teleological power of grace. The church is the community which bears the weight of grace for the world.[155] The teleological power of grace in ethics should be linked again to the doctrine of sanctification. And of course, the doctrine of sanctification has to do with the community which is inaugurated into this movement by baptism.

Christians are summoned, Barth says, to freedom for an "active life," "a life lived by man as his own act in obedience to his Creator and

---

149. Barth, *CD* IV/4, 196.

150. Biggar, *Hastening that Waits*, 144. Barth actually commends Schleiermacher and Herrmann for their attention to the church as a prominent element of ethical reflection. *CD* III/4, 516.

151. Barth, *Humanity of God*, 79.

152. Barth, *CD* I/2, 588.

153. Barth, *CD* II/2, 571.

154. Ibid., 567.

155. Ibid., 571.

Lord."[156] In our place and within our limits Christians follow Jesus Christ and thus are made witnesses to Christ. The command of God becomes concrete in the particular communities of God. "The basic form of the active life of obedience understood and affirmed as service of the cause of God is man's direct or indirect co-operation in the fulfilment of the task of the Christian Community."[157] Members of the Christian community are aware of the coming of the kingdom and in their active life they are ambassadors and heralds of the comprehensive and radical alteration of the human and cosmic situation. They do not contribute to this alteration, but they announce it and live within it.[158]

The responsibility of the individual is to co-operate in the work of the church, especially, Barth says, in its prophetic service. The whole community is to bear the light into the darkness. The prophetic ministry of the church is no one person's private task. "The supreme and proper form of the active life required of man, the given step to freedom, the ministry for which he is needed and to which he is called, is thus his co-operation in the inward and outward service of the Christian community."[159] The prophetic service of the community is its service in a particular place and time attesting to the Word of God. In its timely way, the community's prophetic work is to proclaim the Kingdom come and coming. As Hauerwas argues "Barth rightly saw that the truthfulness of Christian speech about God is a matter of truthful witness."[160] A wicked, quarrelsome community can falsify its prophetic word. The community of witness must be one of grace and hope. Its voice can be powerful or it can be weak and confused. It depends upon the Christians within it who can be either wise and loyal or foolish and lazy.[161] Hauerwas is correct in asserting the importance of the church as witness in this respect.[162] In its life it should imitate and represent the love with which God loved the world. The love which sustains this com-

---

156. Barth, *CD* III/4, 470.

157. Ibid., 483.

158. Ibid., 487.

159. Barth, *CD* III/4, 515.

160. Hauerwas, *With the Grain of the Universe*, 194. See also Webster, *Barth's Ethics of Reconciliation*, 218–20.

161. Barth, *CD* III/4, 513.

162. See *With the Grain of the Universe*, 193–204.

munity should also mark its service in the world.[163] The word "Church" must point to the conduct of the community.[164]

As stated above, the church exists as those who by grace have come to participate in what God has done in the world. It is the provisional representation of what all people are meant to realize. In the entirety of its being and action the baptized Christian community is "a provisional representation of the sanctification of man as it has taken place in Jesus Christ."[165] The order of the community should bear the marks of the Kingdom of God. The church should show the world that "there is already on earth an order which is based on that great alteration of the human situation and directed towards its manifestation."[166] As the provisional representation, the church calls to all humanity to serve God.[167] The church lives in the time between Easter and the final Parousia of Christ. Christ will make his Lordship of the universe known but in the meantime, the church proclaims that contested Lordship.

The Christian community shares an understanding of the world and its history; it sees now what all will one day understand: the all sufficient, sovereign grace of God. Its baptism is performed in light of that vision. Martin Buber once remarked: "to the Jew the Christian is the incomprehensibly daring man, who affirms in an unredeemed world that its redemption has been accomplished."[168] In believing that this redemption, or in Barth's terms this reconciliation, has been accomplished, the community of God now views and lives in history in a different way. It lives in the time after Easter. "As the new reality of world history is made known to the people of God in Jesus Christ, it is enabled, permitted and commanded to see things differently in practice, to participate in world history very differently in its own attitude and action, than is the case with those who do not yet have knowledge of this new reality."[169] Barth asserts that the church can identify the world

163. Barth, *CD* III/4, 500–502.

164. Barth, *God Here and Now*, 66.

165. Barth, *CD* IV/2, 677.

166. Ibid., 721. "For Barth, to be a Christian, to anticipate here and now the future, universal praise of God, is to be a member of a limited and prophetic minority." Hauerwas, *With the Grain of the Universe*, 198.

167. Barth, *CD* IV/3.2, 793.

168. Buber, *Israel and the World*, 40.

169. Barth, *CD* IV/3.2, 716.

for what it truly is.[170] This means we can identify our reality as fallen, yet redeemed, while living, alas, as though it is not. According to its new reading of history, this community is to live according to the decision and judgment made in Jesus Christ for humanity so that it may witness to that decision. Disciples of Jesus Christ do not exist for themselves. The church's entire existence is its mission, its service to the world. For Barth, ecclesiology is ethics.[171]

Conclusion

Baptism sets the standard for the Christian life. I have noted that the Christian life is "a being from baptism."[172] It is not inconsequential that Barth's treatment of baptism was offered in the ethics of reconciliation. Barth recognized the "interconnectedness of baptism and the life of responsible discipleship."[173] Baptism is initiation into the life of obedience to the divine command. It is indeed the first such command which the believer must respond to in obedience. For this reason, baptism should be administered to those who are capable of responding to the Word of God. Submitting to baptism places oneself under the demands of the life of discipleship and witness to Christ. Barth forged a closer relationship between baptism and ethics than he did between baptism and sanctification, but the implications for sanctification are important. And yet the hesitation noted before needs to be raised again: Barth's ethics of command still need an understanding of the Spirit in the practices of the church as it forms the character of Christian disciples. Grace in this understanding would still never be the possession of the Christian or the church. Grace is the Spirit working in the community through these concrete practices, sanctifying the community for its life in the world.[174]

The primary function of both ethics and the sanctification of the Christian community is to participate in and bear witness to the grace of God. Barth's ethics of the command of God requires an ecclesial (baptismal) context in which the command is received and given, a community of hearing. Barth's theological ethics focuses upon the community

---

170. Ibid., 769.
171. See Yoder, "Why Ecclesiology is Social Ethics" in *Royal Priesthood*, 103–26.
172. Barth *CD* IV/4, 202.
173. Webster, *Barth's Ethics of Reconciliation*, 152.
174. Mangina, "Stranger as Sacrament," 322–40.

as dwelling under the command of God, as having received grace and love which it did not merit, yet which claim it for a purpose and a task. Christian ethics are concerned with the baptized community. The command of God takes an ecclesial form. It is made concrete in the life of the community living according to the grace it has received. Witness is what ties together Barth's doctrine of sanctification, his ethics, and his ecclesiology. In Barth's ethics of sanctification, the baptized community is being formed to offer a provisional representation of the kingdom before the world.

Christian ethics that do not rely on the community in which they function become individualistic and self-reflexive, or they are primarily concerned with another community besides the church, such as the nation-state. Either way, the Christian life loses its *telos*. The locus of theological and ethical reflection is the body of Christ, the baptized community being sanctified by the Spirit. Only the inclusion of ethical reflection within an ecclesiastical framework, i.e. an ecclesial context and an ecclesial form, can adequately deal with the human ethical situation. To make sense of our lives together as fallen yet redeemed humanity, requires the post-Easter hermeneutic of the church. It requires the incomprehensibly daring community which remembers, retells, and relives the story of Christ's redemption of the world.

Conclusion

THIS STUDY HAS OFFERED A CRITICAL REAPPRAISAL OF KARL BARTH'S eccesiology. The guiding principle has been the material content of his doctrine of baptism. My primary goal has been to explicate Barth's ecclesiology in light of his view of baptism. To conclude, I will review the course of the study and attempt to show the importance of the issue raised here for contemporary theology.

This study has demonstrated that Barth's doctrine of baptism and his ecclesiology are intricately related. To understand one we need to understand its relation to the other. Eddie Mabry argued concerning Balthasar Hubmaier that the doctrine of the church and the doctrine of baptism "are very closely related, and his doctrine of the baptism endorses his doctrine of the church. One might even say that Hubmaier's doctrine of the church is worked out in his attempt to develop his doctrine of baptism."[1] This statement is also true of Barth. Barth's view of baptism is the direct product of his ecclesiology and looking backwards through the lens of baptism, his ecclesiology becomes clearer. His description of the practice and theology of baptism is a concrete embodiment of his understanding of the church, including his notorious rejection of pedobaptism for believer's baptism.

Attending to Barth's doctrine of baptism provides us with the best approach to reading Barth's ecclesiology. To demonstrate this, I have detailed the elements of Barth's ecclesiology that are seen clearest through his doctrine of baptism. In a few places I have had to draw this connection a little tighter than Barth himself made it, but in those places I think it strengthens Barth's ecclesiology to do so. Baptism provides us with a lens through which to see the church, which that baptism creates.[2] This approach helped us to see Barth's ecclesiology in the area

---

1. Mabry, *Balthasar Hubmaier's Doctrine of the Church*, 154.

2. Once again, the statement that baptism creates the church must be taken sacramentally. The Holy Spirit calls and gathers the church. The Spirit does so through the freely ordained means of baptism.

of his strongest contributions, the understanding of "church" in terms of the kingdom-oriented, concretely embodied, local congregation; and also in the area which most needed a corrective, Barth's view of the relation of the Spirit to the practices of the church. Both of these elements of his ecclesiology became clearer in light of Barth's doctrine of baptism. Overall, Barth's understanding of baptism and his view of the church lean toward the believers' church tradition. As I have shown, due to his insistence upon the absolute uniqueness of Christ and the sufficiency of Christ's work, Barth came to the best insights of the believers' church tradition by his own difficult path. He is able thus to maintain a high Christology and a free church ecclesiology.

In the one divine movement, the objective work of Christ and the Spirit's work function not as two acts, but as two foci of God's one act in creating the Christian life. Water baptism, in Barth's theology, is the human response to the change which the Spirit works in the person. Human faithfulness thus corresponds to and responds to God's faithfulness, but it is only possible because of the prevenient work of God. The human endeavor with which the Christian life begins is genuine and necessary, but one cannot forget the fact that it is secondary to the work of the Holy Spirit. Barth overly stressed the separation of these two elements, but baptism serves as the foundation of the Christian life, only when both of these elements are in place.

Christians are baptized into the community that lives in expectation of the Kingdom of God. The Christian life is directed toward its fulfillment. The meaning of baptism is found, according to Barth, in its nature as a human act. Water baptism is a human decision that corresponds to God's work. Thus baptism is not a sacrament, but the obedient response to the one true mystery or sacrament, which is Jesus Christ. The meaning of baptism lies in the relation between the human action and the divine action from which it originates. Baptism is an act of obedience to Christ, its basis. It is also an act of hope in regard to the Kingdom of God, its goal.

The four particular aspects of the church I have examined in Barth's work are not chosen arbitrarily but are thrown into relief by his doctrine of baptism. They have, indeed, turned out to be the central elements of Barth's ecclesiology. First, the church is Christ's presence in the world, the earthy historical form of his existence in the present. Christ exists as the *totus Christus*. The being of the church is a dimension of the being of Christ. Baptism is initiation into this body. Related to this discussion is the role of the Holy Spirit in the church. The Holy Spirit makes the objective work of Christ a subjective reality. The doctrine of baptism enables us to see the place of the Spirit with greater clarity. It was determined in the course of the discussion of baptism that Barth needs a better conception of sacramental mediation. Within the Baptist tradition is an understanding of believers' baptism as a sacrament which stresses both the necessity of human commitment and action as well as God's grace, i.e. God acting in baptism. This sacramental view corrects the lack in Barth and in the dominant Baptist position. Baptism entails an initiation into the vocation of the church, both enabled by the Spirit and requiring the faith-commitment of the person who is baptized.

Second, in light of the nature of baptism as a visible witness, the concrete, visible nature of the church becomes clearer. Barth taught that the church consists of the local, gathered congregation. The church is visible, like baptism, so that it might be a witness to those who discern it. Of course, for Barth the church is also invisible. The unseen work of the Holy Spirit who creates the church makes the visible human construct the true church. This discussion enabled us to continue the corrective to Barth's non-sacramental view. The relationship that Barth describes between the invisible and the visible aspects of the church can be used to better describe the Spirit's presence in the practices of the church such as baptism, and thus the unbreakable relationship between water baptism and action of the Holy Spirit is made clear.

Barth's congregationalism and Barth's actualism were both found to contain a concern for the concrete, visible community. In his congregationalism, Barth was concerned for the life of the local community as it gathers for worship and baptism. The order of the community is essential to the witness it offers the world. Through his actualistic motif Barth describes the church as a history. The church exists in the time between the comings of Christ. The church is a history; it is as it takes place. Baptism is entrance into that historical movement. The central point of all ecclesiology is the community gathered for worship, baptism, and eucharist.

The third aspect of Barth's doctrine of baptism that clarified his ecclesiology was Barth's acceptance of believers' baptism rather than infant baptism. The result of believers' baptism should be a community that is free from cultural and political control, so that it can serve the world and witness to it. John Howard Yoder's interpretation of Barth as free church theologian opened up a way to think of the interconnectedness of baptism and the church in Barth. I thus detailed how Barth's recognition of the importance of believer's baptism is essential to his view of the church's relation to society. Barth demonstrated the central notion that believers' baptism calls us to embody—namely the church as a community of disciples distinct from the world, so that it can be for the world. While the church exists for the world, Barth requires a distinction between church and the state or culture. The church's interests are inevitably lost in Constantinian arrangements, but seldom, if ever, are those of the state similarly lost.

Finally, in light of baptism's being as a visible witness to the world, the church is understood as a community created to witness to the world. Baptism as Christian commitment helps shape a community that takes up its responsibility to live as a witness. The people of God are being shaped for this witness; this is their sanctification. Corresponding to his view of baptism, Barth holds that the purpose of sanctification is to shape this community into a provisional representation of what awaits all people. Indeed, his discussion of conversion in his treatment of baptism clearly seconds the discussion of conversion in his doctrine of sanctification. I sought, however, to critique Barth for not utilizing baptism, as a practice of the church, for the work of sanctification. The life of this sanctified community is, Barth said, Christian ethics. Barth conceives of ethics only within an ecclesial context. Baptism is a central part of the ethics of reconciliation. Baptism is initiation into the responsibilities of Christian witness.

One can discern that the unifying theme resounding throughout this study is the church as witness to Jesus Christ. Baptism is itself a witness. It is also the entrance into the community who embody Christ in the world. This community is a visible, concrete community who gather for worship, including baptism. The Holy Spirit is working within this community to create a provisional representation of the Kingdom of God. In all that it does, the baptized community seeks to witness to the world's newly-constituted reality after Easter. It lives in that time between the two comings of Christ. The Spirit is in the church making it a witness to the watching world.

In the introduction I noted the ecclesiocentric focus of some contemporary theology. Barth wrote that all past theology becomes the fluid material for future theology. What is important is that the church keep striving for adequate doctrine.[3] As the church continues to reflect on its own being and mission we should take heed of a few points in Barth's ecclesiology, all of which were emphasized in his doctrine of baptism. First the overall relationship between baptism and the church which were seen in this study should not be forgotten. Baptism is the practice through which God shapes the church. Baptism is initiation, by burial with Christ, into the eschatological community that anticipates the rule of God. Something of a hermeneutical circle is at work in this relationship. One's ecclesiology shapes one's doctrine of baptism, which in turn creates and forms the community that lives according to its baptism. The church must consider what kind of church it is shaping in its baptismal practice and theology.

Thus, to refuse baptism as a sacrament is to make the foundations of the church simply human practice or the work of God unrelated to the practice itself, which makes baptism superfluous. Too often, I am afraid, Baptists unwittingly make one of these mistakes despite all of their focus on believers' baptism.

We also need to remember Barth's insistence upon the primacy of Christ in ecclesiology. The church exists only as the body of Christ. As I have shown, this understanding of the place of Christ also needs to be cast in Trinitarian terms. The work of the Holy Spirit in the church cannot be totally eclipsed by Christology. Here Barth needed the most correction. We should, however, listen to Barth's concerns regarding the Spirit's relation to the Church. Even if we think that Barth is too cautious about the Spirit's presence in the practices of the church, including baptism, we should take seriously his reasoning for being so concerned.

After Barth, contemporary believers' church (baptist) ecclesiology must continue to conceive of the church as the visible, embodied community which is the presence of Christ in the world. A description of the church as the local, concrete, gathered people, such as Barth's, should be central to ecclesiological reflection today. This theology is in line with traditional baptist theology. Along with this emphasis many in the believers' church tradition need to remember that it is only the mystery of the Holy Spirit that makes the human community the church of God. Even in our contemporary culture, in some respects especially in

---

3. Barth, *CD* I/2, 769.

our culture, we need to continue to assert the validity of the free church vision. The church cannot lose sight of its identity and its mission, even as it exists for the sake of the world. To best serve the world, the church needs to be a healthy community whose interests are not subservient to the state or the culture in which it lives. This community is being formed and sanctified by the Spirit to offer a provisional representation of the Kingdom. Again, the Spirit's presence and work within the formative practices of the church, such as baptism, must be stressed. Christians must constantly remember their baptism.

It is appropriate to conclude this project on a particularly Barthian note. If the church's practice of baptism creates a community of responsibility of which much is seriously demanded, we must end by remembering that baptism should also engender a deep, abiding joy within the community. We have been crucified with Christ; Christ now lives within us. Baptism marks the Christian's conversion. This turn is liberation from the bondage of sin and death. Baptism is the recognition of Christ's victory. The Spirit makes possible the true freedom of obedience to God. Through baptism and the Supper the church remembers what Christ has done for the world and that the Holy Spirit allows us to participate in his finished work. It is entrance into the teleological movement, the life of discipleship, the goal of which is the kingdom of God inaugurated in Christ. Even in a world of violence and suffering, and even under the weight of the church's mission to that world, participation in the Triune God's redemption of the world is cause for joy.

Bibliography

Aboagye-Mensah, Robert. "Karl Barth's Attitude to War in the Context of World War II." *Evangelical Quarterly* 60 (1988) 43–59.

Aquinas, Thomas. *Summa Theologica*. Translated by Fathers of the English Dominican Province. Allen, TX: Christian Classics, 1948.

Balke, Willem. *Calvin and the Anabaptist Radicals*. Translated by William J. Heynen. Grand Rapids: Eerdmans, 1981.

Balthasar, Hans Urs von. "Christology and Ecclesial Existence." In *Explorations in Theology*. Vol. 4, *Spirit and Institution*, translated by Edward T. Oakes, 139–67. San Francisco: Ignatius, 1995.

———. *The Theology of Karl Barth: Exposition and Interpretation*. Translated by Edward T. Oakes. San Francisco: Ignatius, 1992.

Barth, Karl. *Against the Stream: Shorter Post-War Writings 1946–52*. Translated by E. M. Delacour and Stanley Godman. London: SCM, 1954.

———. "The Christian Community and the Civil Community." In *Against the Stream: Shorter Post-War Writings 1946–52*, translated by E. M. Delacour and Stanley Godman, 15–50. London: SCM, 1954.

———. *The Christian Life*. Translated by Geoffrey W. Bromiley. Grand Rapids: Eerdmans, 1981.

———. "Church and State." In *Community, State, and Church*, translated by G. Ronald Howe, 101–48. Garden City, NY: Anchor, 1960.

———. *The Church and the Churches*. Grand Rapids: Eerdmans, 1936.

———. *The Church and the Political Problem of our Day*. New York: Scribners, 1939.

———. *Church Dogmatics*. Edited by G. W. Bromiley and T. F. Torrance. Edinburgh: T. & T. Clark, 1956–1977.

———. "The Church—The Living Congregation of the Living Lord Jesus Christ." In *Man's Disorder and God's Design*, 67–76. New York: Harper, 1949

———. *Dogmatics in Outline*. Translated by G. T. Thomson. New York: Harper & Row, 1959.

———. *Ethics*. Translated by Geoffrey W. Bromiley. New York: Seabury, 1981.

———. *Evangelical Theology: An Introduction*. Translated by Grover Foley. Grand Rapids: Eerdmans, 1963.

———. *The Faith of the Church: A Commentary on the Apostle's Creed According to Calvin's Catechism*. Translated by Gabriel Vahanian. New York: Living Age, 1958.

———. "The First Commandment as an Axiom of Theology." In *The Way of Theology in Karl Barth: Essays and Comments*, edited by H. Martin Rumscheidt, 63–78. Translated by George Hunsinger et al. Princeton Theological Monograph Series 8. Allison, PA: Pickwick, 1986.

———. *Fragments Grave and Gay*. Translated by Eric Mosbacher. London: Collins, 1971.

———. *The German Church Conflict*. Translated by P. T. A. Parker. Richmond: John Knox, 1965.

———. *God Here and Now*. Translated by Paul M. van Buren. New York: Harper & Row, 1964.

———. *God in Action*. Translated by E. G. Homrighausen and Karl J. Ernst. Manhasset, NY: Round Table, 1936.

———. *The Heidelberg Catechism for Today*. Translated by Shirley C. Guthrie Jr. Richmond: John Knox, 1964.

———. *The Humanity of God*. Translated by John Newton Thomas and Thomas Wieser. Atlanta: John Knox, 1960.

———. "No Christian Marshall Plan." *The Christian Century* (December 8, 1948) 1330–33.

———. *The Teaching of the Church Regarding Baptism*. Translated by Ernest Payne. London: SCM, 1948. *Die Kirchliche Lehre von der Taufe*. Zollikon-Zurich: Evangelischer,1947.

Barth, Markus. *Die Taufe ein Sakrament? Ein exegetischer Beitrag zum Gespräch über die kirchliche Taufe*. Zollikon-Zürich: Evangelischer, 1951.

Beasley-Murray, G. R. *Baptism in the New Testament*. New York: Macmillan, 1963.

Bender, Kimlyn. *Karl Barth's Christological Ecclesiology*. Burlington, VT: Ashgate, 2005.

Berkhof, Hendrik. *Christ and the Powers*. Translated by John Howard Yoder. Scottdale, PA: Herald, 1977.

Berkouwer, G. C. *The Triumph of Grace in the Theology of Karl Barth*. Translated by Harry Boer. Grand Rapids: Eerdmans, 1956.

Biggar, Nigel. *The Hastening that Waits: Karl Barth's Ethics*. Oxford: Clarendon, 1993.

Blond, Philip, editor. *Post-Secular Philosophy: Between Philosophy and Theology*. New York: Routledge, 1998.

Bornkamm, Gunther. "μυστήριον, μυέω." In *Theological Dictionary of the New Testament*, edited by Gerhard Kittel, 4:802–28. Translated by Geoffrey W. Bromiley. Grand Rapids: Eerdmans, 1964.

Boyce, James Petigru. *Abstract of Systematic Theology*. Philadelphia: American Baptist Publication Society, 1887.

Bromiley, Geoffrey W. *Introduction to the Theology of Karl Barth*. Grand Rapids: Eerdmans, 1979.

Brunner, Emil. *The Misunderstanding of the Church*. Translated by Harold Knight. Philadelphia: Westminster, 1953.

Buber, Martin. *Israel and the World: Essays in a Time of Crisis*. Syracuse, NY: Syracuse University Press, 1976.

Buckley, James J. "A Field of Living Fire: Karl Barth on the Spirit and the Church." *Modern Theology* 10 (1994) 81–102.

———. "Christian Community, Baptism, and Lord's Supper." In *The Cambridge Companion to Karl Barth*, edited by John Webster, 195–211. New York: Cambridge University Press, 2000.

Busch, Eberhard. "'Doing Theology as If Nothing Had Happened'—The Freedom of Theology and the Question of Its Involvement in Politics." Translated by Martin Rumscheidt. *Studies in Religion* 16 (1987) 459–71.

———. *Karl Barth: His Life from Letters and Autobiographical Texts*. Translated by John Bowden. Grand Rapids: Eerdmans, 1975.

———. "Karl Barth's Understanding of the Church as Witness." *Saint Luke's Journal of Theology* 33:2 (1990) 87–101.

Calvin, John. *Institutes of the Christian Religion*. 2 vols. Edited by John McNeill. Translated by Ford Lewis Battles. Philadelphia: Westminster, 1960.

———. *Treatises against Anabaptists and against the Libertines*. Translated by Benjamin Wirt Farley. Grand Rapids: Baker, 1992.

Carson, Alexander. *Baptism: Its Mode and Its Subjects*. Grand Rapids: Baker, 1957.

Carter, Craig A. "Karl Barth's Revision of Protestant Ecclesiology." *Perspectives in Religious Studies* 22 (1995) 35–44.

Clapp, Rodney. *A Peculiar People: The Church as Culture in a Post-Christian Society*. Downer's Grove, IL: InterVarsity, 1996.

Clark, Neville. *An Approach to the Theology of the Sacraments*. Chicago: Allenson, 1956.

Clough, David. "Fighting at the Command of God: Reassessing the Borderline Case in Karl Barth's Account of War in the *Church Dogmatics*." In *Conversing with Barth*, edited by John C. McDowell and Mike Higton, 214–26. Burlington, VT: Ashgate, 2004.

Cochrane, Arthur C. "Doctrine of Sanctification: Review of Barth's *Kirchliche Dogmatik*, IV/2." *Theology Today* 13 (1956) 376–88.

———. "Markus Barth—An Un-Barthian Barthian: The Place of the Doctrine of Baptism in the Church Dogmatics." In *Intergerini Parietis Septum: Essays Presented to Markus Barth on his 65th Birthday*, edited by Dikran Y. Hadidian, 39–49. Princeton Theological Monograph Series 33. Pittsburgh: Pickwick, 1980.

Colwell, John. "Alternative Approaches to Believer's Baptism (From The Anabaptists to Barth)." *The Scottish Bulletin of Evangelical Theology* 7 (1989) 3–20.

———. *Promise and Presence: An Exploration of Sacramental Theology*. Waynesboro, GA: Paternoster, 2005.

Conner, W. T. *The Gospel of Redemption*. Nashville: Broadman, 1945.

Couenhoven, Jesse. "Grace as Pardon and Power: Pictures of the Christian Life in Luther, Calvin, and Barth." *Journal of Religious Ethics* 28 (2000) 63–88.

Courvoisier, Jaques. "Zwingli et Karl Barth." In *Antwort: Karl Barth Zum Siebzigten Geburtstag Am 10. Mai 1956*, edited by Ernst Wolff et al., 369–87. Zollikon-Zürich: Evangelischer, 1956.

Cross, Anthony R. *Baptism and the Baptists: Theology and Practice in Twentieth-Century Britain*. Carlisle, Cumbria: Paternoster, 2000.

———. "Dispelling the Myth of English Baptist Baptismal Sacramentalism." *The Baptist Quarterly* 38 (2000) 367–91.

Cross, Anthony R., and Philip E. Thompson, editors. *Baptist Sacramentalism*. Carlisle, Cumbria: Paternoster, 2003.

———. *Baptist Sacramentalism 2*. Carlisle, Cumbria: Paternoster, 2008.

Cullmann, Oscar. *Baptism in the New Testament*. Translated by J. K. S. Reid. Studies in Biblical Theology 1. Chicago: Regnery, 1950.

Cyprian. "On the Unity of the Church." In *Ante-Nicene Fathers*, edited by Alexander Roberts and James Donaldson, 4:421–29. Translated by Ernest Wallis. Peabody, MA: Hendrickson, 1994.

Dagg, John L. *Manual of Church Order*. Harrisonburg, VA: Gano, 1990.

Demura, Akira. "Zwingli in the Writings of Karl Barth—with Special Emphasis on the Doctrine of the Sacraments." In *Probing the Reformed Tradition: Historical Studies in Honor of Edward A. Dowey, Jr.*, edited by Elsie Anne McKee and Brian G. Armstrong, 197–219. Louisville: Westminster John Knox, 1989.

Deschner, John. "Karl Barth as Political Activist." *Union Seminary Quarterly Review* 28 (1972) 55–66.

Dinkler, E. "Die Taufaussagen des Neuen Testaments. Neu untersucht im Hinblick auf Karl Barths Tauflehre." In *Zu Karl Barths Lehre von der Taufe*, edited by F. Viering, 60–153. Gutersloh: Gerd Mohn, 1971.

Durnbaugh, Donald. *The Believer's Church: The History and Character of Radical Protestantism*. New York: Macmillan, 1968.

Ellis, Christopher. "Baptism and the Sacramental Freedom of God." In *Reflections on the Water: Understanding God and the World through the Baptism of Believers*, edited by Paul S. Fiddes, 23–45. Macon, GA: Smyth & Helwys, 1996.

Fiddes, Paul S., editor. *Reflections on the Water: Understanding God and the World through the Baptism of Believers*. Macon, GA: Smyth & Helwys, 1996.

Flew, R. Newton, and Rupert E. Davies, editors. *The Catholicity of Protestantism*. London: Lutterworth, 1950.

Ford, David. *Barth and God's Story: Biblical Narrative and the Theological Method of Karl Barth in the Church Dogmatics*. New York: Lang, 1985.

Fowler, Stanley K. *More Than a Symbol: The British Baptist Recovery of Baptismal Sacramentalism*. Carlisle, UK: Paternoster, 2002.

Frei, Hans. *Theology and Narrative: Selected Essays*. Edited by George Hunsinger and William Placher. New York: Oxford University Press, 1993.

Friedman, Robert. *The Theology of Anabaptism*. Scottdale, PA: Herald, 1973.

Fuller, Andrew. "The Practical Uses of Christian Baptism." In *The Complete Works of the Rev. Andrew Fuller*, 3:339–45. Harrisonburg, VA: Sprinkle, 1988.

Gadamer, Hans-Georg. *Truth and Method*. 2nd ed. Translated by Joel Weinsheimer and Donald G. Marshall. New York: Continuum, 1994.

Garrett, James Leo. *Systematic Theology: Biblical, Historical, and Evangelical*. Vol. 1. Grand Rapids: Eerdmans, 1995.

Gill, John. *A Body of Doctrinal and Practical Divinity; or, A System of Practical Truths Deduced from The Sacred Scriptures*. Streamwood, IL: Primitive Baptist Library, 1977.

Gillespie, Michael Allen. "The Theological Origins of Modernity." *Critical Review* 13 (1999) 1–30.

Gilmore, Alec. *Baptism and Christian Unity*. Valley Forge, PA: Judson, 1966.

———, editor. *Christian Baptism*. London: Lutterworth, 1959.

Glenthoj, Jorgen. "Karl Barth and the German Salute." *Journal of Church and State* 32 (1990) 309–24.

Grantham, Thomas. *Christianismus Primitivus or, The Ancient Christian Religion*. London: Francis Smith, 1678.

―――. *A Sigh for Peace: Or The Cause of Division Discovered*. London: Printed for the Author, 1671.

Gorringe, Timothy. *Karl Barth: Against Hegemony*. New York: Oxford University Press, 1999.

Gunton, Colin, "Baptism: Baptism and the Christian Community." In *Father, Son and Holy Spirit: Essays Toward a Fully Trinitarian Theology*, 201–15. New York: T. & T. Clark, 2003.

―――. "The Church as a School of Virtue? Human Formation in Trinitarian Framework." In *Faithfulness and Fortitude: In Conversation with the Theological Ethics of Stanley Hauerwas*, edited by Mark Thiessen Nation and Samuel Wells, 211–31. Edinburgh: T. & T. Clark, 2000.

―――. "Barth, The Trinity, and Human Freedom." *Theology Today* 43 (1986) 316–30.

―――. "Karl Barth and the Western Intellectual Tradition. Towards a Theology After Christendom." In *Theology beyond Christendom: Essays on the Centenary of the Birth of Karl Barth May 10, 1886*, edited by John Thompson, 285–301. Princeton Theological Monograph Series 6. Allison, PA: Pickwick, 1986.

Hall, Robert. "Terms of Communion, with a Particular View to the Case of the Baptists and Paedobaptists." In *The Works of Robert Hall, A.M.*, edited by Olinthus Gregory, vol. 1. London: Bohn, 1843.

Hartwell, H. "Karl Barth on Baptism." *Scottish Journal of Theology* 22 (1969) 10–29.

Harvey, Barry A. *Another City: An Ecclesiological Primer for a Post-Christian World*. Harrisburg, PA: Trinity, 1999.

Hauerwas, Stanley. *Character and the Christian Life*. San Antonio: Trinity University Press, 1975.

―――. *Dispatches from the Front: Theological Engagements with the Secular*. Durham, NC: Duke University Press, 1994.

―――. *Sanctify Them in the Truth: Holiness Exemplified*. Nashville: Abingdon, 1998.

―――. *With the Grain of the Universe: The Church's Witness and Natural Theology*. Grand Rapids: Brazos, 2001.

Hauerwas, Stanley, and William H. Willimon. *Resident Aliens: Life in the Christian Colony*. Nashville: Abingdon, 1989.

Haymes, Brian. "Baptism as a Political Act." In *Reflections on the Water: Understanding God and the World through the Baptism of Believers*, edited by Paul S. Fiddes, 69–83. Macon, GA: Smyth & Helwys, 1996.

Hays, Richard. *The Moral Vision of the New Testament: A Contemporary Introduction to New Testament Ethics*. San Francisco: HarperSanFrancisco, 1996.

Healy, Nicholas M. *Church, World and the Christian Life: Practical-Prophetic Ecclesiology*. New York: Cambridge University Press, 2000.

―――. "Karl Barth's Ecclesiology Reconsidered." *Scottish Journal of Theology* 57 (2004) 287–99.

―――. "The Logic of Karl Barth's Ecclesiology: Analysis, Assessment and Proposed Modifications." *Modern Theology* 10 (1994) 253–70.

Hector, Kevin. "God's Triunity and Self-Determination: A Conversation with Karl Barth, Bruce McCormack and Paul Molnar." *International Journal of Systematic Theology* 7 (2005) 246–61.

Helwys, Thomas. *A Short Declaration of the Mystery of Iniquity*. Edited by Richard Groves. Macon, GA: Mercer University Press, 1998.

Herberg, Will. "The Social Philosophy of Karl Barth." In *Community, State and Church: Three Essays*, 11–67. Anchor Books. Garden City, NY: Doubleday, 1960.

Hoekema, Anthony. *Karl Barth's Doctrine of Sanctification*. Grand Rapids: Calvin Theological Seminary, 1965.

Holmes, Michael W., editor. *The Apostolic Fathers*. 2nd ed. Translated by J. B. Lightfoot and J. R. Harmer. Grand Rapids: Baker, 1989.

Hood, Robert E. "Karl Barth's Christological Basis for the State and Political Praxis." *Scottish Journal of Theology* 33 (1980) 223–38.

Hubmaier, Balthasar. "On Free Will." In *Spiritual and Anabaptist Writers*, edited by George H. Williams and Angel M. Mergal, 114–35. Philadelphia: Westminster, 1957.

———. "On the Christian Baptism of Believers." In *Balthasar Hubmaier: Theologian of Anabaptism*, edited and translated by H. Wayne Pipkin and John H. Yoder. Scottdale, PA: Herald, 1989.

Huebner, Chris. "Can a Gift be Commanded? Theological Ethics without Theory by way of Barth, Milbank, and Yoder." *Scottish Journal of Theology* 53 (2000) 472–89.

Hunsinger, George. "Baptism and the Soteriology of Forgiveness." *International Journal of Systematic Theology* 2.3 (2000) 247–69.

———. *Disruptive Grace: Studies in the Theology of Karl Barth*. Grand Rapids: Eerdmans, 2000.

———. *How to Read Karl Barth: The Shape of His Theology*. New York: Oxford University Press, 1981.

———. "Robert Jenson's Systematic Theology: A Review Essay." *Scottish Journal of Theology* 55 (2002) 161–200.

———. "A Tale of Two Simultaneities: Justification and Sanctification in Calvin and Barth." In *Conversing with Barth*, edited by John C. McDowell and Mike Higton, 68–89. Burlington, VT: Ashgate, 2004.

———. "To Hauerwas: On Learning Faithfulness in a Fallen World." In *Barth, Barmen and the Confessing Church Today*, edited by James Y. Holiday, 252–56. Katallagete Symposium Series 28. Lewiston, NY: Mellin, 1992.

———. "Toward a Radical Barth." In *Karl Barth and Radical Politics*, translated and edited by George Hunsinger, 181–233. Philadelphia: Westminster, 1976.

Hütter, Reinhard. "The Church." In *Knowing the Triune God: The Work of the Spirit in the Practices of the Church*, edited by James J. Buckley and David S. Yeago, 23–47. Grand Rapids: Eerdmans, 2001.

———. "Karl Barth's 'Dialectical Catholicity': Sic et Non." *Modern Theology* 16 (2000) 137–57.

———. *Suffering Divine Things: Theology as Church Practice*. Translated by Doug Stott. Grand Rapids: Eerdmans, 2000.

Jehle, Frank. *Ever Against the Stream: The Politics of Karl Barth 1906–1968*. Translated by Richard Burnett and Martha Burnett. Grand Rapids: Eerdmans, 2002.

Jennings, Willie James. "Grace Without Remainder: Why Baptists Should Baptize Their Babies." In *Grace Upon Grace: Essays in Honor of Thomas Langford*, edited by Robert Johnston, L. Gregory Jones, and Jonathan Wilson, 201–16. Nashville: Abingdon, 1999.

Jenson, Robert. "Response to Watson and Hunsinger." *Scottish Journal of Theology* 55 (2002) 225–32.

———. *Systematic Theology.* Vol. 1, *The Triune God.* New York: Oxford University Press, 1997.

———. "You Wonder Where the Spirit Went." *Pro Ecclesia* 2 (1993) 296–304.

Johnson, William Stacy. *The Mystery of God: Karl Barth and the Postmodern Foundations of Theology.* Louisville: Westminster John Knox, 1997.

Jones, L. Gregory. *Transformed Judgment: Toward a Trinitarian Account of the Moral Life.* Notre Dame: University of Notre Dame Press, 1990.

Jüngel, Eberhard. "Invocation of God as the Ethical Ground of Christian Action." In *Theological Essays*, 154–72. Translated by John B. Webster. Edinburgh: T. & T. Clark, 1989.

———. *Karl Barth: A Theological Legacy.* Translated by Garrett Paul. Philadelphia: Westminster, 1986.

———. "Karl Barths Lehre Von Der Taufe." In *Barth-Studien*, 246–88. Zürich: Benziger, 1982.

———. "Zum Verhältniz von Kirche und Staat nach Karl Barth." *Zeitschrift für Theologie und Kirche* Beiheft 6 (1986) 76–135.

Keach, Benjamin. *Gold Refin'd; or Baptism in its Primitive Purity.* London: Nathaniel Crouch, 1689.

Kenneson, Philip D. *Beyond Sectarianism: Re-Imagining Church and World.* Harrisburg, PA: Trinity, 1999.

Kierkegaard, Søren. *Concluding Unscientific Postscript.* Translated by David F. Swenson. Princeton, NJ: Princeton University Press, 1941.

Lange, A. N. S. "The City of God: Church and State in Geneva." In *Articles on Calvin and Calvinism*, vol. 10: *Calvin's Ecclesiology: Sacraments and Deacons*, edited by Richard C. Gamble, 140–51. New York: Garland, 1992.

Lash, Nicholas. *Theology on the Way to Emmaus.* Reprinted, Eugene, OR: Wipf & Stock, 2005.

Lindberg, Carter. *The European Reformations.* Malden, MA: Blackwell, 1996.

Littell, Franklin H. *The Origins of Sectarian Protestantism: A Study of the Anabaptist View of the Church.* New York: Macmillan, 1964.

Long, D. Stephen. *The Goodness of God: Theology, The Church, and Social Order.* Grand Rapids: Brazos, 2001.

Lossky, Vladimir. *The Mystical Theology of the Eastern Church.* Crestwood, NY: St. Vladimir's Seminary Press, 1957.

Lubac, Henri de. *The Splendor of the Church.* Translated by Michael Mason. San Francisco: Ignatius, 1986.

Lull, Timothy, editor. *Martin Luther's Basic Theological Writings.* Minneapolis: Fortress, 1989.

Mabry, Eddie. *Balthasar Hubmaier's Doctrine of the Church.* Lanham, MD: University Press of America, 1994.

Mangina, Joseph. "Bearing the Marks of Jesus: The Church in the Economy of Salvation in Barth and Hauerwas." *Scottish Journal of Theology* 52 (1999) 269–305.

———. *Karl Barth on the Christian Life: The Practical Knowledge of God.* Issues in Systematic Theology 8. New York: Lang, 2001.

———. *Karl Barth: Theologian of Christian Witness*. Louisville: Westminster John Knox, 2004.

———. "The Stranger as Sacrament: Karl Barth and the Ethics of Ecclesial Practice." *International Journal of Systematic Theology* 1 (1999) 322–39.

Marcel, Gabriel. *Homo Viator*. Translated by Emma Craufurd. New York: Harper, 1962.

McCabe, Herbert. *God Matters*. Springfield, IL: Templegate, 1987.

McClendon, James Wm. Jr. "Baptism as a Performative Sign." *Theology Today* 23 (1966) 403–16.

———. "A Conversionist Spirituality." In *Ties that Bind: Life Together in the Baptist Vision*, edited by Gary Furr and Curtis Freeman, 23–32. Macon, GA: Smith & Helwys, 1994.

———. *Doctrine: Systematic Theology*. Vol. 2. Nashville: Abingdon, 1994.

———. *Ethics: Systematic Theology*. Vol. 1. Nashville: Abingdon, 1986.

———. *Witness: Systematic Theology*. Vol. 3. Nashville: Abingdon, 2000.

McCormack, Bruce. L. "Grace and Being: The Role of God's Gracious Election in Karl Barth's Theological Ontology." In *The Cambridge Companion to Karl Barth*, edited by John Webster, 92–110. Cambridge: Cambridge University Press, 2000.

McGrath, Alister. *Reformation Thought: An Introduction*. 2nd ed. Cambridge: Blackwell, 1993.

McPartlan, Paul. *The Eucharist Makes the Church: Henri de Lubac and John Zizioulas in Dialogue*. Edinburgh: T. & T. Clark, 1993.

Migliore, Daniel. "Reforming the Theology and Practice of Baptism: The Challenge of Karl Barth." In *Toward the Future of Reformed Theology: Tasks, Topics, Traditions*, edited by David Willis and Michael Welker, 494–511. Grand Rapids: Eerdmans, 1999.

———. "Karl Barth's First Lectures in Dogmatics: *Instruction in the Christian Religion*." In *The Göttingen Dogmatics*, by Karl Barth, edited by Hannelotte Reiffen, XV–LXII. Translated by Geoffrey W. Bromiley. Grand Rapids: Eerdmans, 1991.

Milbank, John. *The Suspended Middle: Henri de Lubac and the Debate concerning the Supernatural*. Grand Rapids: Eerdmans, 2005.

———. *Theology and Social Theory: Beyond Secular Reason*. Cambridge, MA: Blackwell, 1990.

———. *The Word Made Strange: Theology, Language, Culture*. Cambridge, MA: Blackwell, 1997.

Molnar, Paul. *Divine Freedom and the Doctrine of the Immanent Trinity: In Dialogue with Karl Barth and Contemporary Theology*. Edinburgh: T. & T. Clark, 2002.

———. *Karl Barth and the Theology of the Lord's Supper: A Systematic Investigation*. Issues in Systematic Theology 1. New York: Lang, 1996.

Moltmann, Jürgen. *The Church in the Power of the Spirit*. Translated by Margaret Kohl. Minneapolis: Fortress, 1993.

———. *The Trinity and the Kingdom*. Translated by Margaret Kohl. New York: Harper Collins, 1981.

Mullins, E. Y. *The Christian Religion in Its Doctrinal Expression*. Philadelphia: Judson, 1917.

O'Donovan, Oliver. "Karl Barth and Ramsey's 'Uses of Power.'" *Journal of Religious Ethics* 19 (1991) 1–30.

O'Grady, Colm. *The Church in the Theology of Karl Barth*. Washington, DC: Corpus, 1968.

Okholm, Dennis. "Defending the Cause of the Christian Church: Karl Barth's Justification of War." *Christian Scholar's Review* 16 (1987) 144–62.

Osborne, Robert. "A 'Personalistic' Appraisal of Barth's Political Ethics." *Studies in Religion* 12 (1983) 313–24.

Pannenberg, Wolfhart. *Systematic Theology*. Vol. 3. Translated by Geoffrey W. Bromiley. Grand Rapids: Eerdmans, 1998.

Parker, T. H. L. *Calvin: An Introduction to His Thought*. Louisville: Westminster John Knox, 1995.

Pipkin, H. Wayne. "The Baptismal Theology of Balthasar Hubmaier." In *Essays in Anabaptist Theology*, edited by H. Wayne Pipkin, 87–109. Elkhart, IN: Institute of Mennonite Studies, 1994.

Reimer, A. James. "The Adequacy of a Voluntaristic Theology for a Voluntaristic Age." In *The Believer's Church: A Voluntary Church*, edited by William Brackney, 135–48. Kitchener, ON: Pandora co-published with Herald, 1998.

Richardson, Kurt Anders. *Reading Karl Barth: New Directions for North American Theology*. Grand Rapids: Baker, 2004.

Robinson, H. Wheeler. *The Life and Faith of the Baptists*. Rev. ed. London: Kingsgate, 1946.

Rogers, Eugene F., Jr. "The Eclipse of the Spirit in Karl Barth." In *Conversing with Barth*, edited by John C. McDowell and Mike Higton, 173–90. Burlington, VT: Ashgate, 2004.

———. "The Mystery of the Spirit in the Three Traditions: Calvin, Rahner, and Florensky or, You *Keep* Wondering Where the Spirit Went." *Modern Theology* 19 (2003) 243–60.

Rosato, Philip, SJ. "Karl Barth as Spokesman and Practitioner of the Christian Concept of Peace." *Studia Missionalia* 38 (1989) 112–32.

Schleiermacher, F. D. E. *The Christian Faith*. Edited by H. R. Mackintosh and J. S. Stewart. Edinburgh: T. & T. Clark, 1989.

Schlüter, Richard. *Karl Barths Tauflehre*. Paderborn: Bonifacius, 1973.

Schwenckfeld, Caspar. "An Answer to Luther's Malediction." In *Spiritual and Anabaptist Writers*, edited by George H. Williams and Angel M. Mergal, 163–81. Philadelphia: Westminster, 1957.

Simons, Menno. "On the Ban: Questions and Answers." In *Spiritual and Anabaptist Writers*, edited by George H. Williams and Angel M. Mergal, 263–71. Philadelphia: Westminster, 1957.

Snyder, C. Arnold. *Anabaptist History and Theology: An Introduction*. Kitchener, ON: Pandora, 1995.

Sonderegger, Katherine. *That Jesus Christ Was Born a Jew: Karl Barth's 'Doctrine of Israel.'* University Park: Pennsylvania University Press, 1992.

Sorge, Sheldon. "Karl Barth's Reception in North America: Ecclesiology as a Case Study." PhD diss., Duke University, 1987.

Spinks, Brian. "Karl Barth's Teaching on Baptism: Its Development, Antecedents and the 'Liturgical Factor.'" *Ecclesia Orans* 14 (1997) 261–88.

Spross, Daniel. "The Doctrine of Sanctification in the Theology of Karl Barth." *Wesleyan Theological Journal* 20 (1985) 54–76.

Sykes, Stephen. "Authority and Openness in the Church." In *Karl Barth: Centenary Essays*, edited by S.W. Sykes, 69–86. Cambridge: Cambridge University Press, 1989.

Tanner, Kathryn. *God and Creation in Christian Theology*. New York: Blackwell, 1988.

Thompson, John. *The Holy Spirit in the Theology of Karl Barth*. Princeton Theological Monograph Series 23. Allison Park, PA: Pickwick, 1991.

Thompson, Philip E. "Sacraments and Religious Liberty." In *Baptist Sacramentalism*, edited by Anthony Cross and Philip E. Thompson, 36–54. Carlisle, Cumbria: Paternoster, 2003.

Torrance, T. F. *Theology in Reconciliation: Essays towards Evangelical Catholic Unity in East and West*. Grand Rapids: Eerdmans, 1975.

Troeltsch, Ernst. *The Social Teaching of the Christian Church*. Vol. 2. Translated by Olive Wyon. Louisville: Westminster John Knox, 1992.

Vaughn, J. Barry. "Benjamin Keach." In *Baptist Theologians*, edited by Timothy George and David S. Dockery, 49–76. Nashville: Broadman & Holman, 1999.

Volf, Miroslav. *After Our Likeness: The Church in the Image of the Trinity*. Grand Rapids: Eerdmans, 1998.

Webster, John. *Barth's Ethics of Reconciliation*. New York: Cambridge University Press, 1995.

———. *Barth's Moral Theology: Human Action in Barth's Thought*. Grand Rapids: Eerdmans, 1998.

———. "Translator's Introduction." In *God's Being is in Becoming: The Trinitarian Being of God in the Theology of Karl Barth*, by Eberhard Jüngel. Translated by John Webster. Grand Rapids: Eerdmans, 2001.

Wendel, François. *Calvin: Origins and Development of His Religion Thought*. Translated by Philip Mairet. Grand Rapids: Baker, 1963.

Werpehowski, William. "Karl Barth and Politics." In *The Cambridge Companion to Karl Barth*, edited by John Webster, 228–42. New York: Cambridge University Press, 2000.

———. "Narrative and Ethics in Barth." *Theology Today* 43 (1986) 334–53.

White, R. E. O. *The Biblical Doctrine of Initiation*. Grand Rapids: Eerdmans, 1960.

Wiley, David N. "The Church as the Elect in the Theology of Calvin." In *John Calvin and the Church: A Prism of Reform*, edited by Timothy George, 96–117. Louisville: Westminster John Knox, 1990.

Williams, D. H. *Retrieving the Tradition and Renewing Evangelicalism*. Grand Rapids: Eerdmans, 1999.

Williams, Rowan. "Barth, War, & the State." In *Reckoning With Barth: Essays in Commemoration of the Centenary of Karl Barth's Birth*, edited by Nigel Biggar, 170–90. London: Mowbray, 1988.

Wood, Ralph C. *The Comedy of Redemption: Christian Faith and Comic Vision in Four American Novelists*. Notre Dame, IN: University of Notre Dame Press, 1988.

Yocum, John. *Ecclesial Mediation in Karl Barth*. Burlington, VT: Ashgate, 2004.

Yoder, John H. "Adjusting to the Changing Shape of the Debate on Infant Baptism." In *Oekumennisme*, edited by A. Lambo, 201–14. Amsterdam: Algemene Doopsgezinde Sociëteit, 1989.

———. "The Basis of Barth's Social Ethics." Unpublished Paper delivered to Midwestern Section of the Karl Barth Society, September 29–30, 1978.

———. *Body Politics: Five Practices of the Christian Community Before the Watching World*. Scottdale, PA: Herald, 2001.

———. *For the Nations: Essays Public and Evangelical*. Grand Rapids: Eerdmans, 1999.

———. *The Fulness of Christ: Paul's Revolutionary Vision of Universal Ministry*. Elgin, IL: Brethren, 1987.

———. *Karl Barth and the Problem of War*. Studies in Christian Ethics Series. Nashville: Abingdon, 1970.

———. "Karl Barth: How His Mind Kept Changing." In *How Karl Barth Changed My Mind*, edited by Donald K. McKim, 166–71. Grand Rapids: Eerdmans, 1986.

———. "Karl Barth, Post-Christendom Theologian." Unpublished Paper delivered to the Karl Barth Society, June 8, 1995.

———. "On Not Being Ashamed of the Gospel: Particularity, Pluralism, and Validation." *Faith and Philosophy* 9.3 (1992) 285–300.

———. *The Politics of Jesus: Behold the Man! Our Victorious Lamb!* 2nd ed. Grand Rapids: Eerdmans, 1994.

———. *The Royal Priesthood: Essays Ecclesiological and Ecumenical*. Edited by Michael G. Cartwright. Grand Rapids: Eerdmans, 1994.

———. "Review of *Karl Barth and Radical Politics*." *The Journal of Church and State* 20 (1978) 338–39.

Yoder, John Howard, editor. *The Legacy of Michael Sattler*. Translated by John Howard Yoder. Scottdale, PA: Herald, 1973.

Zizioulas, John. *Being as Communion: Studies in Personhood and the Church*. Crestwood, NY: St. Vladimir's Seminary Press, 1985.

Zwingli, Ulrich. "On Baptism." In *Zwingli and Bullinger*, edited by Geoffrey W. Bromiley, 129–75. Philadelphia: Westminster, 1953.

www.ingramcontent.com/pod-product-compliance
Lightning Source LLC
Chambersburg PA
CBHW051738230426
43670CB00012B/2077